crochet
FOR TODAY

A LEISURE ARTS PUBLICATION
PRESENTED BY OXMOOR HOUSE

EDITORIAL STAFF

Vice President and Editor-in-Chief:
   Anne Van Wagner Childs
Executive Director: Sandra Graham Case
Editorial Director: Susan Frantz Wiles
Publications Director: Carla Bentley
Creative Art Director: Gloria Bearden
Production Art Director: Melinda Stout

PRODUCTION
Managing Editor: Susan White Sullivan
Senior Technical Editor: Cathy Hardy
Instructional Editors: Sarah J. Green and
   Jackie Botnik Stanfill

EDITORIAL
Managing Editor: Linda L. Trimble
Associate Editor: Tammi Williamson Bradley
Assistant Editors: Terri Leming Davidson,
   Robyn Sheffield-Edwards, and Darla Burdette Kelsay
Copy Editor: Laura Lee Weland

ART
Book/Magazine Art Director: Diane M. Hugo
Senior Production Artist: M. Katherine Yancey
Assistant Production Artist: Dana Vaughn
Photography Stylists: Sondra Daniel, Karen Hall,
   Aurora Huston, Christina Tiano Myers, Zaneta Senger,
   and Alaina Sokora

BUSINESS STAFF

Publisher: Bruce Akin
Vice President, Finance: Tom Siebenmorgen
Vice President, Retail Sales: Thomas L. Carlisle
Retail Sales Director: Richard Tignor
Vice President, Retail Marketing: Pam Stebbins
Retail Marketing Director: Margaret Sweetin
Retail Customer Services Manager: Carolyn Pruss
General Merchandise Manager: Russ Barnett
Distribution Director: Ed M. Strackbein
Vice President, Marketing: Guy A. Crossley
Marketing Manager: Byron L. Taylor
Print Production Manager: Laura Lockhart
Print Production Coordinator: Nancy Reddick Baker

CROCHET COLLECTION SERIES

Library of Congress Catalog Number: 95-81882
Hardcover ISBN 0-8487-4095-5
Softcover ISBN 1-57486-022-4

crochet
FOR TODAY

Do you love crochet that's beautiful yet practical, and rich with detail yet fun to do? Then Crochet for Today *is the book for you! This volume features a marvelous mixture of traditional and modern designs for today's crocheter. You'll discover projects to suit every style, from classic elegance to whimsical trendsetters. And for those of you who like to see quick results, we've clearly marked lots of items that work up fast — and look fabulous!*

There are few things as inviting as a handmade afghan, and we've included a wide selection of patterns — from sophisticated to nostalgic — in Wrapped Up in Afghans. All Through the House is filled with wonderful decorating ideas for the living and dining rooms, the kitchen, and the bedroom. You'll find a remembrance for everyone in Gifts for All, and Just for Fun features a variety of notions, both practical and fanciful. Our Rock-A-Bye Collection includes charming projects for welcoming a new arrival, from baby afghans to accents for the nursery. You can round out the family's wardrobes with the stylish wearables in our Fashion Corner, and Hooked on Holidays will help you celebrate special days all through the year.

Whether you're an experienced crocheter or a beginner, our easy-to-follow instructions, diagrams, and helpful hints make it a breeze to achieve beautiful results. So choose a pattern, grab your supplies, and get hooked on crochet today!

Anne Childs

LEISURE ARTS, INC.
LITTLE ROCK, ARKANSAS

table of contents

rock-a-bye collection 76

fashion corner 90

hooked on holidays 106

wrapped up in afghans

In today's fast-paced world, the satisfaction of stitching — and then wrapping up in — a cozy afghan is a welcome relaxation. The appeal of these snuggly covers goes far beyond their luxurious warmth, however. Soft and soothing, a favorite afghan can be as comforting as a long-treasured teddy bear and as lovely an accent as a vase of roses. In this diverse collection, you'll find nine charming designs to fill your every afghan need and keep your fingers busy with hours of crocheting fun.

Quick ALLURING MILE-A-MINUTE

Lacy shells give our ever-popular mile-a-minute design feminine allure. The afghan is worked in serene green and ecru for a soothing addition to the bedroom.

Finished Size: Approximately 52" x 66"

MATERIALS

Worsted Weight Yarn, approximately:
Color A (Ecru) - 25 ounces, (710 grams, 1,715 yards)
Color B (Green) - 18 ounces, (510 grams, 1,235 yards)
Crochet hook, size I (5.50 mm) **or** size needed for gauge
Yarn needle

GAUGE: Center = 2³/₄" wide and 4 rows = 4"
One Strip = 5³/₄" wide x 66" long

STRIP (Make 9)
CENTER
With Color A, ch 10.

Note: To work **Shell**, tr in st or sp indicated, (ch 1, tr) 5 times in same st or sp.

Row 1 (Right side): Work Shell in seventh ch from hook, skip next 2 chs, tr in last ch.

Note: Loop a short piece of yarn around any stitch to mark last row as **right** side and bottom edge.

Rows 2-62: Ch 4, turn; work Shell in center ch-1 sp, tr in top of beginning ch.

Row 63: Ch 6, turn; sc in center ch-1 sp, ch 2, tr in top of beginning ch; finish off.

EDGING

Rnd 1: With **right** side facing, join Color B with slip st in center sc at top; ch 3 **(counts as first dc, now and throughout)**, (4 dc, ch 2, 3 dc) in first sp, 3 dc in end of each row across to last row, (3 dc, ch 2, 4 dc) in last row, dc in free loop of same ch as first Shell *(Fig. 28b, page 138)*, (4 dc, ch 2, 3 dc) in first row, 3 dc in end of each row across to last row, (3 dc, ch 2, 4 dc) in last row; join with slip st to first dc, finish off.

Note: To work **V-St**, (dc, ch 1, dc) in st or sp indicated.

Rnd 2: With **right** side facing, join Color A with slip st in first dc; ch 4, dc in same st, skip next 2 dc, work V-St in next dc, † skip next dc, work (V-St, ch 1, V-St) in next corner ch-2 sp, work V-St in center dc of each 3-dc group across to next corner ch-2 sp, work (V-St, ch 1, V-St) in corner ch-2 sp, skip next dc, work V-St in next dc †, (skip next 2 dc, work V-St in next dc) twice, repeat from † to † once; join with slip st to third ch of beginning ch-4, finish off.

Rnd 3: With **right** side facing, join Color B with slip st in first V-St (ch-1 sp); ch 3, 2 dc in same sp, 3 dc in each V-St around working (2 dc, ch 3, 2 dc) in each corner ch-1 sp; join with slip st to first dc, finish off.

ASSEMBLY

With **wrong** sides together and Color B, and working through **inside** loops only, whipstitch Strips together, placing bottom edges at the same end *(Fig. 35b, page 140)*.

Quick SNOWGLORIES

As lovely as a snowy patch of early flowers, this delightful cover-up will chase away winter's chill. Brushed acrylic yarn is used to create the exquisite throw, which is fashioned in strips with cluster stitches using a join-as-you-go method. A scalloped edging is added to the finished afghan.

Finished Size: Approximately 45" x 66"

MATERIALS

Worsted Weight Brushed Acrylic Yarn, approximately:
    29 ounces, (820 grams, 2,235 yards)
Crochet hook, size H (5.00 mm) **or** size needed for gauge

GAUGE: (ch 5, work 2-tr Cluster in fifth ch from hook) 3
    times = 3"
    One Strip = 3" wide and 63" long

PATTERN STITCHES

2-TR CLUSTER

★ YO twice, insert hook in st indicated, YO and pull up a loop, (YO and draw through 2 loops on hook) twice; repeat from ★ once **more**, YO and draw through all 3 loops on hook *(Figs. 13a & b, page 134)*.

3-TR CLUSTER

★ YO twice, insert hook in st indicated, YO and pull up a loop, (YO and draw through 2 loops on hook) twice; repeat from ★ 2 times **more**, YO and draw through all 4 loops on hook.

SHELL

(Dc, ch 1) 7 times in sp or loop indicated.

FIRST STRIP

Foundation Row (Right side): (Ch 5, work 2-tr Cluster in fifth ch from hook) 50 times: 50 Clusters.

Note: Loop a short piece of yarn around any stitch to mark last row as **right** side.

Rnd 1: Ch 1, sc in top of first Cluster, ch 4, (work 3-tr Cluster, ch 4) twice in ch at base of first 2-tr Cluster, ★ sc in ch at base of next 2-tr Cluster, ch 4, (work 3-tr Cluster, ch 4) twice in ch at base of next 2-tr Cluster; repeat from ★ around working in same chs along second side; join with slip st to first sc: 25 flowers.

Rnd 2: Slip st in first ch-4 sp, ch 1, (sc, ch 5) twice in same sp, † (sc, ch 3, sc) in next ch-4 sp, ch 5, ★ sc in next 2 ch-4 sps, ch 5, (sc, ch 3, sc) in next ch-4 sp, ch 5; repeat from ★ 23 times **more** †, place marker around last ch-5 worked for joining and edging placement, (sc, ch 5) twice in each of next 2 ch-4 sps, repeat from † to † once, (sc, ch 5) twice in last ch-4 sp; join with slip st to first sc, finish off.

REMAINING 13 STRIPS

Work same as First Strip through Rnd 1.

Rnd 2 (Joining rnd): Slip st in first ch-4 sp, ch 1, (sc, ch 5) twice in same sp, (sc, ch 3, sc) in next ch-4 sp, ch 5, [sc in next 2 ch-4 sps, ch 5, (sc, ch 3, sc) in next ch-4 sp, ch 5] 24 times, place marker around last ch-5 worked for joining and edging placement, (sc, ch 5) twice in next ch-4 sp, (sc, ch 5, sc) in next ch-4 sp, ch 2, with **wrong** sides together, sc in marked loop on **previous Strip** *(Fig. 32, page 138)*, ch 2, sc in next ch-4 sp on **new Strip**, ch 1, sc in next ch-3 sp on **previous Strip**, ch 1, sc in same sp on **new Strip**, ch 2, sc in next loop on **previous Strip**, ch 2, ★ sc in next 2 ch-4 sps on **new Strip**, ch 2, sc in next loop on **previous Strip**, ch 2, sc in next ch-4 sp on **new Strip**, ch 1, sc in next ch-3 sp on **previous Strip**, ch 1, sc in same sp on **new Strip**, ch 2, sc in next loop on **previous Strip**, ch 2; repeat from ★ 23 times **more**, (sc, ch 5) twice in last ch-4 sp on **new Strip**; join with slip st to first sc, finish off.

EDGING

Rnd 1: With **right** side facing, join yarn with slip st in marked loop on last Strip worked; ch 1, sc in same loop and in next loop, ch 1, work Shell in next loop, † sc in next loop, ch 3, sc in next joining, ch 3, sc in next loop, ch 1, work Shell in next loop †; repeat from † to † 12 times **more**, sc in next 2 loops, (ch 1, work Shell in next ch-3 sp, sc in next 2 loops) 25 times, ch 1, work Shell in next loop, repeat from † to † 13 times, (sc in next 2 loops, ch 1, work Shell in next ch-3 sp) across; join with slip st to first sc.

Rnd 2: Slip st in next sc, ch 1, sc in same st, † ch 3, skip next ch-1 sp, (sc in next ch-1 sp, ch 3) 6 times, ★ skip next ch-1 sp, (sc in next ch-3 sp, ch 3) twice, skip next ch-1 sp, (sc in next ch-1 sp, ch 3) 6 times; repeat from ★ 12 times **more**, skip next ch-1 sp and next sc, sc in next sc, ch 3, skip next ch-1 sp, sc in next ch-1 sp, (ch 3, sc in next ch-1 sp) 5 times, [skip next 2 ch-1 sps, sc in next ch-1 sp, (ch 3, sc in next ch-1 sp) 5 times] 24 times, ch 3, skip next ch-1 sp and next sc †, sc in next sc, repeat from † to † once; join with slip st to first sc, finish off.

KINGLY COVER-UP

Abundantly fringed, this handsome afghan is crafted in white and shades of blue for a wrap worthy of royalty — or the king of your heart! The richly textured afghan is worked using a combination of simple stitches that give a complex look.

Finished Size: Approximately 53" x 64"

MATERIALS

Worsted Weight Yarn, approximately:
Color A (White) - 11 ounces, (310 grams, 815 yards)
Color B (Light Blue) - 7 ounces, (200 grams, 520 yards)
Color C (Medium Blue) - 15 ounces, (430 grams, 1,115 yards)
Color D (Dark Blue) - 9 ounces, (260 grams, 670 yards)
Crochet hook, size J (6.00 mm) **or** size needed for gauge

Note: Each row is worked across length of afghan.

GAUGE: In pattern, 13 sts = 4" and 16 rows = 9"

With Color C, ch 210 **loosely**.

Row 1 (Right side)**:** Sc in second ch from hook and in each ch across changing to Color A in last sc *(Fig. 31a, page 138)*: 209 sc.

Note: Loop a short piece of yarn around any stitch to mark last row as **right** side.

Row 2: Ch 3 **(counts as first dc, now and throughout)**, turn; skip next sc, 3 dc in next sc, (skip next 2 sc, 3 dc in next sc) across to last 2 sc, skip next sc, dc in last sc: 69 3-dc groups.

Note: To work **Cluster** (uses next 3 dc), ★ YO, insert hook in **next** st, YO and pull up a loop, YO and draw through 2 loops on hook; repeat from ★ 2 times **more**, YO and draw through all 4 loops on hook *(Figs. 14a & b, page 134)*.

Row 3: Ch 4 **(counts as first dc plus ch 1)**, turn; working in Back Loops Only *(Fig. 27, page 138)*, work Cluster, (ch 2, work Cluster) across to last dc, ch 1, dc in last dc changing to Color C: 70 sps.

Row 4: Ch 1, turn; working in both loops, 2 sc in first ch-1 sp, (sc in next Cluster, 2 sc in next sp) across changing to Color B in last sc: 209 sc.

Row 5: Ch 3, turn; skip next sc, 3 dc in next sc, (skip next 2 sc, 3 dc in next sc) across to last 2 sc, skip next sc, dc in last sc changing to Color C: 69 3-dc groups.

Row 6: Ch 1, turn; sc in Back Loop Only of each dc across changing to Color D in last sc: 209 sc.

Row 7: Ch 4 **(counts as first tr)**, turn; tr in Back Loop Only of next sc and in each sc across.

Row 8: Ch 4, turn; tr in both loops of next tr and in each st across.

Row 9: Ch 4, turn; tr in next tr and in each st across changing to Color C in last tr.

Row 10: Ch 1, turn; sc in Back Loop Only of each st across changing to Color B in last sc.

Row 11: Ch 4, turn; working in Back Loops Only, work Cluster, (ch 2, work Cluster) across to last sc, ch 1, dc in last sc changing to Color C: 70 sps.

Row 12: Ch 1, turn; working in both loops, 2 sc in first ch-1 sp, (sc in next Cluster, 2 sc in next sp) across changing to Color A in last sc: 209 sc.

Row 13: Ch 3, turn; skip next sc, 3 dc in next sc, (skip next 2 sc, 3 dc in next sc) across to last 2 sc, skip next sc, dc in last sc: 69 3-dc groups.

Row 14: Ch 4, turn; working in Front Loops Only, work Cluster, (ch 2, work Cluster) across to last dc, ch 1, dc in last dc changing to Color C: 70 sps.

Row 15: Ch 1, turn; working in both loops, 2 sc in first ch-1 sp, (sc in next Cluster, 2 sc in next sp) across changing to Color B in last sc: 209 sc.

Row 16: Ch 4, turn; tr in Front Loop Only of next sc and in each sc across changing to Color C in last tr.

Row 17: Ch 1, turn; sc in both loops of each st across changing to Color A in last sc.

Rows 18-95: Repeat Rows 2-17, 4 times, then repeat Rows 2-15 once **more**; at end of Row 95, do **not** change colors, finish off.

Add fringe using 6 strands of Color C, each 16" long *(Figs. 37a & b, page 141)*; spacing evenly, attach across end of rows on each end of afghan.

11

POPCORN RIPPLE

Worked in a harmony of gentle hues, this cozy pleaser uses puffy popcorn stitches to enhance the familiar ripple pattern. Drape the afghan across the foot of a bed as a silent invitation to stay and rest awhile.

Finished Size: Approximately 49" x 66"

MATERIALS

Worsted Weight Yarn, approximately:

Color A (Taupe) - 20 ounces, (570 grams, 1,315 yards)
Color B (Light Rose) - 15 ounces, (430 grams, 985 yards)
Color C (Rose) - 15 ounces, (430 grams, 985 yards)
Crochet hook, size I (5.50 mm) **or** size needed for gauge

GAUGE: 14 dc = 4"

In pattern, 1 repeat = 3¼" and 6 rows = 4"

Gauge Swatch: (6½" x 5")
Ch 31 **loosely**.
Rows 1-6: Work same as afghan; at end of Row 6, do **not** change colors, finish off.

PATTERN STITCHES

POPCORN

Work 4 dc in st indicated, drop loop from hook, insert hook in first dc of 4-dc group, hook dropped loop and draw through *(Fig. 15a, page 134)*.

DECREASE (uses next 2 dc)

★ YO, insert hook in **next** dc, YO and pull up a loop, YO and draw through 2 loops on hook; repeat from ★ once **more**, YO and draw through all 3 loops on hook.

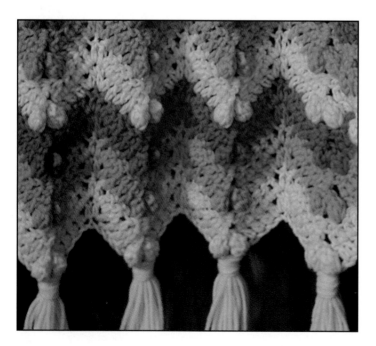

COLOR SEQUENCE
2 Rows each Color A *(Fig. 31a, page 138)*, ★ Color B, Color C, Color A; repeat from ★ throughout.

With Color A, ch 213 **loosely**.

Row 1 (Right side)**:** 2 Dc in fourth ch from hook, dc in next 3 chs, skip next ch, work Popcorn in next ch, skip next 2 chs, work Popcorn in next ch, skip next ch, dc in next 3 chs, ★ (dc, ch 1, dc) in each of next 2 chs, dc in next 3 chs, skip next ch, work Popcorn in next ch, skip next 2 chs, work Popcorn in next ch, skip next ch, dc in next 3 chs; repeat from ★ across to last ch, 3 dc in last ch: 30 Popcorns.

Row 2: Ch 3 **(counts as first dc, now and throughout)**, turn; 2 dc in same st, dc in next 3 dc, decrease, skip next 2 Popcorns, decrease, ★ dc in next 2 dc and in next ch-1 sp, (dc, ch 1, dc) in each of next 2 dc, dc in next ch-1 sp and in next 2 dc, decrease, skip next 2 Popcorns, decrease; repeat from ★ across to last 4 sts, dc in next 3 dc, 3 dc in last st changing colors in last dc worked.

Row 3: Ch 3, turn; 2 dc in same st, dc in next 3 dc, skip next dc, work Popcorn in next dc, skip next 2 decreases, work Popcorn in next dc, ★ skip next dc, dc in next 2 dc and in next ch-1 sp, (dc, ch 1, dc) in each of next 2 dc, dc in next ch-1 sp and in next 2 dc, skip next dc, work Popcorn in next dc, skip next 2 decreases, work Popcorn in next dc; repeat from ★ across to last 5 sts, skip next dc, dc in next 3 dc, 3 dc in last dc.

Repeat Rows 2 and 3 for pattern, until afghan measures approximately 66", ending by working Row 2 with Color A; do **not** change colors, finish off.

Add fringe using 12 strands of Color A, each 17" long *(Figs. 37a & b, page 141)*; attach in each point across each end of afghan.

Quick DANDY DIAMONDS

A pleasing accent for any decor, this double-strand dandy features a distinctive diamond pattern that's formed with post stitches. Cables created with chain loops add interest to the afghan.

Finished Size: Approximately 48" x 64"

MATERIALS
Worsted Weight Yarn, approximately:
70 ounces, (1,990 grams, 4,085 yards)
Crochet hook, size N (9.00 mm) **or** size needed for gauge

Note: Entire afghan is worked holding 2 strands of yarn together.

GAUGE: In pattern, 9 dc and 5 rows = 4"

PATTERN STITCHES
BACK POST DOUBLE CROCHET *(abbreviated BPdc)*
★ YO, insert hook from **back** to **front** around post of dc indicated *(Fig. 17, page 135)*, YO and pull up a loop **even** with loop on hook, (YO and draw through 2 loops on hook) twice. Skip dc in front of BPdc.
FRONT POST DOUBLE CROCHET *(abbreviated FPdc)*
★ YO, insert hook from **front** to **back** around post of dc indicated, YO and pull up a loop **even** with loop on hook, (YO and draw through 2 loops on hook) twice. Skip dc behind FPdc.

BODY
Ch 148 **loosely**.
Row 1 (Right side): Dc in fourth ch from hook and in next 11 chs **(3 skipped chs count as first dc)**, (ch 8, skip next 6 chs, dc in next 13 chs) across: 7 loops.
Row 2: Ch 3 **(counts as first dc, now and throughout)**, turn; work BPdc around next dc, working in Front Loops Only *(Fig. 27, page 138)*, dc in next 9 sts, work BPdc around next dc, dc in next dc, ★ ch 8, dc in next dc, work BPdc around next dc, dc in next 9 sts, work BPdc around next dc, dc in next dc; repeat from ★ across: 16 BPdc.
Row 3: Ch 3, turn; working in Back Loops Only, dc in next st, work FPdc around next dc, dc in next 7 sts, work FPdc around next dc, dc in next 2 sts, ★ ch 8, dc in next 2 sts, work FPdc around next dc, dc in next 7 sts, work FPdc around next dc, dc in next 2 sts; repeat from ★ across.
Row 4: Ch 3, turn; working in Front Loops Only, dc in next 2 sts, work BPdc around next dc, dc in next 5 sts, work BPdc around next dc, dc in next 3 sts, ★ ch 8, dc in next 3 sts, work BPdc around next dc, dc in next 5 sts, work BPdc around next dc, dc in next 3 sts; repeat from ★ across.

Row 5: Ch 3, turn; working in Back Loops Only, (dc in next 3 sts, work FPdc around next dc) twice, dc in next 4 sts, ★ ch 8, dc in next 4 sts, work FPdc around next dc, dc in next 3 sts, work FPdc around next dc, dc in next 4 sts; repeat from ★ across.
Row 6: Ch 3, turn; working in Front Loops Only, dc in next 4 sts, work BPdc around next dc, dc in next st, work BPdc around next dc, dc in next 5 sts, ★ ch 8, dc in next 5 sts, work BPdc around next dc, dc in next st, work BPdc around next dc, dc in next 5 sts; repeat from ★ across.
Row 7: Ch 3, turn; working in Back Loops Only, dc in next 5 sts, work FPdc around next dc, dc in next 6 sts, ★ ch 8, dc in next 6 sts, work FPdc around next dc, dc in next 6 sts; repeat from ★ across.
Row 8: Repeat Row 6.
Row 9: Repeat Row 5.
Row 10: Repeat Row 4.
Row 11: Repeat Row 3.
Repeat Rows 2-11 for pattern until afghan measures approximately 69", ending by working Row 11; do **not** finish off.
Note: Afghan must measure approximately 69" before weaving chains in order to obtain 64" in length after the chains have been woven.

Chains: With **right** side facing, pull ch-8 on Row 2 behind skipped ch-6 on Row 1 *(Fig. 1a)*, and bring it up in front of ch-6, ★ pull ch-8 on next row from **back** to **front** through previous loop *(Fig. 1b)*; repeat from ★ to top of afghan. Repeat for each set of ch-8 sps.

Fig. 1a

Fig. 1b

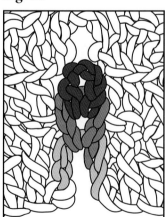

Next Row: Ch 3, turn; work BPdc around next dc, working in Front Loops Only, dc in next 9 sts, work BPdc around next dc, dc in next dc, ★ working in front of next loop, dc in next dc, work BPdc around next dc, dc in next 9 sts, work BPdc around next dc, dc in next dc; repeat from ★ across: 16 BPdc.

Last Row: Ch 1, turn; working in both loops, sc in first 12 sts, holding loop in front of next dc, sc in both loop and in dc, ★ sc in next 12 sts, holding loop in front of next dc, sc in both loop and in dc; repeat from ★ across to last 13 sts, sc in last 13 sts; finish off.

BOTTOM EDGING

With **right** side facing and working in free loops of beginning ch *(Fig. 28b, page 138)*, join yarn with slip st in first ch; ch 1, sc in each ch across skipping loops; finish off.

GRANNY'S GRANNY

The tri-tone granny squares in this vibrant afghan are bordered with dramatic black to intensify the cover's overall appeal. A handy joining method and a placement diagram add to the fun of creating this visual delight.

Finished Size: Approximately 53" x 63"

Note: We used 6 colors (rose, peach, yellow, green, blue, and purple) in light, medium, and dark shades to make our afghan.

MATERIALS

Worsted Weight Yarn, approximately:

Black - 21 ounces, (600 grams, 1,380 yards)

6 Light Shades - 2 ounces, (60 grams, 130 yards) **each**

6 Medium Shades - 1½ ounces, (40 grams, 100 yards) **each**

6 Dark Shades - 2½ ounces, (70 grams, 165 yards) **each**

Crochet hook, size K (6.50 mm) **or** size needed for gauge

GAUGE: One Square = 5"

FIRST SQUARE

Note: Work First Square in shades of first color as indicated in either top corner square on Placement Diagram.

With dark shade, ch 4; join with slip st to form a ring.

Rnd 1 (Right side): Ch 3 **(counts as first dc, now and throughout)**, 2 dc in ring, ch 2, (3 dc in ring, ch 2) 3 times; join with slip st to first dc, finish off: 4 ch-2 sps.

Note: Loop a short piece of yarn around any stitch to mark last round as **right** side.

Rnd 2: With **right** side facing, join medium shade with slip st in any ch-2 sp; ch 3, (2 dc, ch 2, 3 dc) in same sp, ch 1, ★ (3 dc, ch 2, 3 dc) in next ch-2 sp, ch 1; repeat from ★ around; join with slip st to first dc, finish off: 8 sps.

Rnd 3: With **right** side facing, join light shade with slip st in any corner ch-2 sp; ch 3, (2 dc, ch 2, 3 dc) in same sp, ch 1, 3 dc in next ch-1 sp, ch 1, ★ (3 dc, ch 2, 3 dc) in next corner ch-2 sp, ch 1, 3 dc in next ch-1 sp, ch 1; repeat from ★ around; join with slip st to first dc, finish off: 12 sps.

Rnd 4: With **right** side facing, join Black with slip st in any corner ch-2 sp; ch 3, (2 dc, ch 2, 3 dc) in same sp, ch 1, (3 dc in next ch-1 sp, ch 1) twice, ★ (3 dc, ch 2, 3 dc) in next corner ch-2 sp, ch 1, (3 dc in next ch-1 sp, ch 1) twice; repeat from ★ around; join with slip st to first dc, finish off: 16 sps.

REMAINING SQUARES

Work same as First Square through Rnd 3, working in shades of next color indicated on Placement Diagram; then work One-Sided or Two-Sided Joining.

ONE-SIDED JOINING

Rnd 4: With **right** side facing, join Black with slip st in ch-1 sp to **left** of any corner ch-2 sp; ch 3, 2 dc in same sp, ch 1, 3 dc in next ch-1 sp, ch 1, ★ (3 dc, ch 2, 3 dc) in next corner ch-2 sp, ch 1, (3 dc in next ch-1 sp, ch 1) twice; repeat from ★ once **more**, 3 dc in next corner ch-2 sp, ch 1, with **wrong** sides together, sc in corner ch-2 sp on **previous Square** *(Fig. 32, page 138)*, ch 1, 3 dc in same sp on **new Square**, (sc in next ch-1 sp on **previous Square**, 3 dc in next sp on **new Square**) 3 times, ch 1, sc in next corner ch-2 sp on **previous Square**, ch 1, 3 dc in same sp on **new Square**, ch 1; join with slip st to first dc, finish off.

TWO-SIDED JOINING

Rnd 4: With **right** side facing, join Black with slip st in ch-1 sp to **left** of any corner ch-2 sp; ch 3, 2 dc in same sp, ch 1, 3 dc in next ch-1 sp, ch 1, (3 dc, ch 2, 3 dc) in next corner ch-2 sp, ch 1, (3 dc in next sp, ch 1) 3 times, with **wrong** sides together, sc in corner ch-2 sp on **previous Square**, ch 1, 3 dc in same sp on **new Square**, (sc in next ch-1 sp on **previous Square**, 3 dc in next sp on **new Square**) 3 times, ch 1, sc in next corner ch-2 sp on **previous Square** and on **adjacent Square**, ch 1, 3 dc in same sp on **new Square**, (sc in next ch-1 sp on **previous Square**, 3 dc in next sp on **new Square**) 3 times, ch 1, sc in next corner ch-2 sp on **previous Square**, ch 1, 3 dc in same sp on **new Square**, ch 1; join with slip st to first dc, finish off.

PLACEMENT DIAGRAM

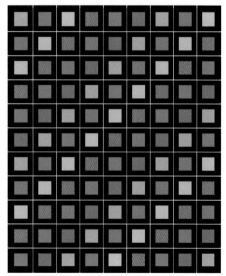

EDGING

Rnd 1: With **right** side facing, join Black with slip st in any corner ch-2 sp; ch 3, (2 dc, ch 2, 3 dc) in same sp, ch 1, (3 dc in next ch-1 sp, ch 1) 3 times, † dc in next corner sp, dc in next joining sc, dc in corner sp on next Square, ch 1, (3 dc in next ch-1 sp, ch 1) 3 times †, repeat from † to † across to next corner ch-2 sp, ★ (3 dc, ch 2, 3 dc) in corner ch-2 sp, ch 1, (3 dc in next ch-1 sp, ch 1) 3 times, repeat from † to † across to next corner ch-2 sp; repeat from ★ around; join with slip st to first dc, finish off.

Rnd 2: With **right** side facing, join any medium shade with slip st in any corner ch-2 sp; ch 3, (2 dc, ch 2, 3 dc) in same sp, ch 1, (3 dc in next ch-1 sp, ch 1) across to next corner ch-2 sp, ★ (3 dc, ch 2, 3 dc) in corner ch-2 sp, ch 1, (3 dc in next ch-1 sp, ch 1) across to next corner ch-2 sp; repeat from ★ around; join with slip st to first dc, finish off.

Rnds 3-7: Repeat Rnd 2, working in the following Color Sequence: 1 Rnd each of Black, (any medium shade, Black) twice; do **not** finish off at end of Rnd 7.

Rnd 8: Slip st in next 2 dc and in next corner ch-2 sp, ch 1, sc in same sp, ★ † ch 2, sc in next dc, ch 2, skip next dc, sc in next dc, ch 2, (skip next ch-1 sp, sc in next dc, ch 2, skip next dc, sc in next dc, ch 2) across to next corner ch-2 sp †, sc in corner ch-2 sp; repeat from ★ 2 times **more**, then repeat from † to † once; join with slip st to first sc, finish off.

DIAMONDS FOR HIM

This warming wrap, designed with the gentleman in mind, will be a welcome cold-weather companion. Featuring an impressive diamond motif, the masculine afghan is worked in panels of black and grey worsted weight yarns and finished with generous fringe.

Finished Size: Approximately 50" x 72"

MATERIALS
Worsted Weight Yarn, approximately:
    Color A (Black) - 31 ounces, (880 grams, 1,905 yards)
    Color B (Grey) - 22 ounces, (620 grams, 1,350 yards)
Crochet hook, size J (6.00 mm) **or** size needed for gauge
Yarn needle

GAUGE: 7 dc and 3 rows = 1³/₄"
    One Diamond = 3¹/₄" wide x 4" high
    One Panel = 5¹/₂" wide x 72" long

PANEL (Make 9)
DIAMONDS
With Color A, ch 14 **loosely**.
Row 1 (Right side)**:** Dc in sixth ch from hook, (ch 1, skip next ch, dc in next ch) across: 5 sps.
Note: Loop a short piece of yarn around any stitch to mark last row as **right** side and bottom edge.
Row 2: Ch 4 **(counts as first dc plus ch 1, now and throughout Diamonds)**, turn; dc in next dc, (dc in next ch-1 sp, dc in next dc) 3 times, ch 1, skip next ch, dc in next ch.

Rows 3 and 4: Ch 4, turn; dc in next 7 dc, ch 1, dc in last dc.
Row 5: Ch 4, turn; dc in next dc, (ch 1, skip next dc, dc in next dc) 3 times, ch 1, dc in last dc.
Row 6: Turn; slip st **loosely** in each dc and in each ch-1 sp across.
Row 7: Ch 14 **loosely**; dc in sixth ch from hook, (ch 1, skip next ch, dc in next ch) across: 5 sps.
Repeat Rows 2-7 until 18 Diamonds are complete, ending by working Row 5; finish off.

SIDE

Note: To **decrease**, ★ YO twice, insert hook in **next** st or sp, YO and pull up a loop, (YO and draw through 2 loops on hook) twice; repeat from ★ once **more**, YO and draw through all 3 loops on hook **(counts as one tr)**.

Row 1: With **wrong** side facing and working across one side of all Diamonds, join Color B with slip st in sp at either point; ch 4 **(counts as first tr, now and throughout)**, 2 tr in next sp, 2 dc in next sp, 2 hdc in next sp, 2 sc in next sp, 2 hdc in next sp, ★ 2 dc in each of next 2 sps, decrease working in next 2 sps, 2 dc in each of next 2 sps, 2 hdc in next sp, 2 sc in next sp, 2 hdc in next sp; repeat from ★ across to last 3 sps, 2 dc in next sp, 2 tr in next sp, tr in last sp: 271 sts.
Row 2: Ch 4, turn; decrease, tr in next dc, dc in next 2 sts, hdc in next hdc, sc in next 2 sc, hdc in next hdc, ★ dc in next 3 sts, decrease, tr in next st, decrease, dc in next 3 sts, hdc in next hdc, sc in next 2 sc, hdc in next hdc; repeat from ★ across to last 6 sts, dc in next 2 sts, tr in next dc, decrease, tr in last tr; finish off: 235 sts.
Row 3: With **right** side facing, join Color A with slip st in first st; ch 3, dc in next st and in each st across; finish off.
Repeat for second side.

ASSEMBLY

With **wrong** sides together and Color A, and working through **both** loops, whipstitch Panels together, placing bottom edges at the same end **(Fig. 35a, page 140)**.

Add fringe using 5 strands of Color A, each 16" long **(Figs. 37a & b, page 141)**; spacing evenly, attach across end of rows on each end of afghan.

IMPRESSIVE POPPIES

Our vibrant poppy afghan features three-dimensional flowers stitched on a field of creamy squares bordered with lush green. The corner chains in the squares create a crisscross pattern across the completed cover.

Finished Size: Approximately 45" x 63"

MATERIALS

Worsted Weight Yarn, approximately:
  MC (Ecru) - 26 ounces, (740 grams, 1,635 yards)
  Color A (Green) - 10 ounces, (280 grams, 630 yards)
  Color B (Red) - 7 ounces, (200 grams, 440 yards)
  Color C (Black) - 2 ounces, (60 grams, 125 yards)
Crochet hook, size J (6.00 mm) **or** size needed for gauge
Yarn needle

GAUGE: 13 dc = 4"
        Rnds 1-4 of Solid Square = 5"
        One Square = 9"

SOLID SQUARE (Make 17)

With MC, ch 4; join with slip st to form a ring.

Rnd 1 (Right side): Ch 3 **(counts as first dc, now and throughout)**, dc in ring, ch 3, (2 dc in ring, ch 3) 3 times; join with slip st to first dc: 8 dc.

Note: Loop a short piece of yarn around any stitch to mark last round as **right** side.

Rnd 2: Ch 3, dc in next dc, (2 dc, ch 3, 2 dc) in next ch-3 sp, ★ dc in next 2 dc, (2 dc, ch 3, 2 dc) in next ch-3 sp; repeat from ★ around; join with slip st to first dc: 24 dc.

Rnds 3-7: Ch 3, ★ dc in next dc and in each dc across to next corner ch-3 sp, (2 dc, ch 3, 2 dc) in corner ch-3 sp; repeat from ★ 3 times **more**, dc in each dc across; join with slip st to first dc; at end of Rnd 7, finish off: 104 dc.

Rnd 8: With **right** side facing, join Color A with slip st in any corner ch-3 sp; ch 1, ★ (2 sc, ch 3, 2 sc) in corner ch-3 sp, sc in each dc across to next corner ch-3 sp; repeat from ★ around; join with slip st to first sc, finish off: 120 sc.

FLOWER SQUARE (Make 18)

Rnd 1 (Right side): With Color C, ch 2, 6 sc in second ch from hook; do **not** join.

Rnd 2: Working in Back Loops Only **(Fig. 27, page 138)**, (3 sc in next sc, 2 sc in next sc) 3 times: 15 sc.

Rnd 3: Ch 1, working in free loops of Rnd 1 **(Fig. 28a, page 138)**, (slip st, ch 6, slip st) in next sc, (ch 6, slip st) twice in each sc around; finish off: 11 loops.

Rnd 4: With **right** side facing, join Color B with slip st in any sc on Rnd 2; ch 1, sc in same st, ch 3, skip next 2 sc, (sc in next sc, ch 3, skip next 2 sc) around; join with slip st to first sc: 5 ch-3 sps.

Rnd 5: (Slip st, ch 4, 12 dtr, ch 4, slip st) in each ch-3 sp around; join with slip st to first slip st: 5 petals.

Rnd 6: Ch 8, working **behind** petals, (slip st in first slip st of next petal, ch 8) around; join with slip st to same st as joining, finish off: 5 loops.

Rnd 7: With **right** side facing, join Color A with slip st in any loop; ch 3, 11 dc in same loop and in each loop around; join with slip st to first dc: 56 dc.

Note: To work **Cluster**, ★ YO, insert hook in dc indicated, YO and pull up a loop, YO and draw through 2 loops on hook; repeat from ★ 2 times **more**, YO and draw through all 4 loops on hook **(Figs. 13a & b, page 134)**.

Rnd 8: Ch 1, sc in same st, ch 3, (skip next dc, sc in next dc, ch 3) 5 times, skip next dc, work (Cluster, ch 3, Cluster) in next dc, ch 3, skip next dc, ★ (sc in next dc, ch 3, skip next dc) 6 times, work (Cluster, ch 3, Cluster) in next dc, ch 3, skip next dc; repeat from ★ around; join with slip st to first sc, finish off: 32 ch-3 sps.

Rnd 9: With **right** side facing, join MC with slip st in any corner ch-3 sp (between Clusters), ch 3, dc in same sp, 2 dc in each of next 7 ch-3 sps, ★ (2 dc, ch 3, 2 dc) in next corner ch-3 sp, 2 dc in each of next 7 ch-3 sps; repeat from ★ around, 2 dc in same sp as first dc, ch 1, hdc in first dc to form last sp: 72 dc.

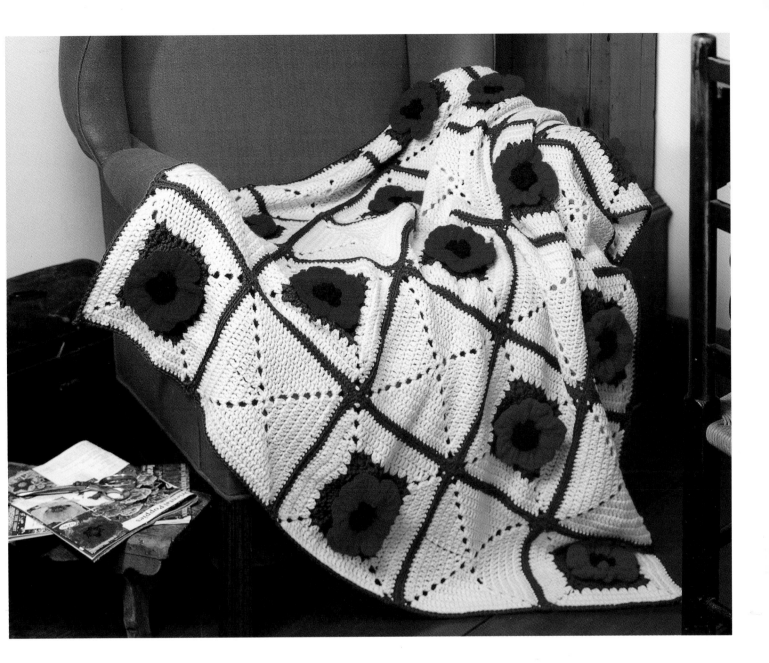

Rnds 10 and 11: Ch 3, dc in same sp, dc in each dc across to next corner ch-3 sp, ★ (2 dc, ch 3, 2 dc) in corner ch-3 sp, dc in each dc across to next corner ch-3 sp; repeat from ★ around, 2 dc in same sp as first dc, ch 1, hdc in first dc to form last sp; at end of Rnd 11, finish off: 104 dc.

Rnd 12: With **right** side facing, join Color A with slip st in first corner sp; ch 1, (2 sc, ch 3, 2 sc) in same sp, sc in each dc across to next corner ch-3 sp, ★ (2 sc, ch 3, 2 sc) in corner ch-3 sp, sc in each dc across to next corner ch-3 sp; repeat from ★ around; join with slip st to first sc, finish off: 120 sc.

ASSEMBLY

With **wrong** sides together and Color A, and working through **inside** loops only, whipstitch Squares together *(Fig. 35b, page 140)*. Form 5 vertical strips of 7 Squares each following Placement Diagram. Whipstitch strips together, securing seam at each joining.

PLACEMENT DIAGRAM

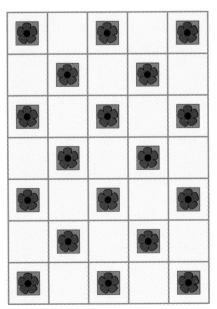

RADIANT MOSAIC

A mosaic of radiantly colored motifs distinguishes this unusual afghan, which features several cluster stitch variations to please — and challenge — the advanced stitcher. Diagrams and close-up photos are helpful guides.

Finished Size: Approximately 44" x 60"

MATERIALS
Worsted Weight Yarn, approximately:
    Color A (Aqua) - 6 ounces, (170 grams, 340 yards)
    Color B (Fuchsia) - 10 ounces, (280 grams, 565 yards)
    Color C (Purple) - 20 ounces, (570 grams, 1,130 yards)
    Color D (Black) - 16 ounces, (450 grams, 905 yards)
Crochet hook, size I (5.50 mm) **or** size needed for gauge

GAUGE: Rnds 1 and 2 = 3^1/$_2$"
       One Motif = 6" (from straight edge to straight edge)
       One Strip = 8^3/$_4$" wide x 60" long

PATTERN STITCHES
2-DC CLUSTER
★ YO, insert hook in sp indicated, YO and pull up a loop, YO and draw through 2 loops on hook; repeat from ★ once **more**, YO and draw through all 3 loops on hook *(Figs. 13a & b, page 134)*.

4-DC CLUSTER (uses next 4 sts)
★ YO, insert hook in **next** st, YO and pull up a loop, YO and draw through 2 loops on hook; repeat from ★ 3 times **more**, YO and draw through all 5 loops on hook.

5-DC CLUSTER (uses next 5 sts)
★ YO, insert hook in **next** st, YO and pull up a loop, YO and draw through 2 loops on hook; repeat from ★ 4 times **more**, YO and draw through all 6 loops on hook *(Figs. 14a & b, page 134)*.

DECREASE
Pull up a loop in next 2 sc, YO and draw through all 3 loops on hook **(counts as one sc)**.

FRONT POST TREBLE CROCHET *(abbreviated FPtr)*
YO twice, insert hook from **front** to **back** around post of st indicated *(Fig. 22, page 135)*, YO and pull up a loop, (YO and draw through 2 loops on hook) 3 times.

FRONT POST TREBLE CLUSTER *(abbreviated FPtr Cluster)*
YO twice, insert hook from **front** to **back** around first post of next 5-dc Cluster *(Fig. 1a)*, YO and pull up a loop, (YO and draw through 2 loops on hook) twice, YO, insert hook in top of same Cluster *(Fig. 1b)*, YO and pull up a loop, YO and draw through 2 loops on hook, YO twice, skip next 3 posts on same Cluster, insert hook from **front** to **back** around next post *(Fig. 1c)*, YO and pull up a loop, (YO and draw through 2 loops on hook) twice, YO and draw through all 4 loops on hook.

Fig. 1a

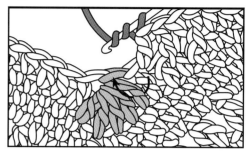

Fig. 1b

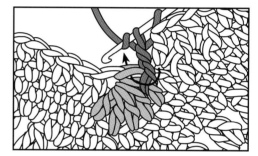

Fig. 1c

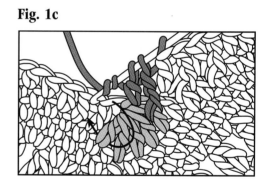

BACK POST DOUBLE CROCHET *(abbreviated BPdc)*
YO, insert hook from **back** to **front** around post of st indicated *(Fig. 21, page 135)*, YO and pull up a loop, (YO and draw through 2 loops on hook) twice.

FRONT POST DOUBLE TREBLE CLUSTER *(abbreviated FPdtr Cluster)*
Working from **front** to **back** around posts of 6-post st group on Rnd 3, YO 3 times, insert hook around post of first FPtr, YO and pull up a loop, (YO and draw through 2 loops on hook) 3 times, ★ YO 3 times, insert hook around **next** post, YO and pull up a loop, (YO and draw through 2 loops on hook) 3 times; repeat from ★ 4 times **more**, YO and draw through all 7 loops on hook.

MOTIF (Make 45)

With Color A, ch 5; join with slip st to form a ring.

Rnd 1 (Right side)**:** Ch 2, dc in ring, ch 2, (work 2-dc Cluster in ring, ch 2) 7 times; skip beginning ch-2 and join with slip st to first dc, finish off: 8 ch-2 sps.

Note: Loop a short piece of yarn around any stitch to mark last round as **right** side.

Rnd 2: With **right** side facing, join Color B with slip st in any ch-2 sp; ch 2, (dc, ch 2, work 2-dc Cluster) in same sp, ch 2, (work 2-dc Cluster, ch 2) twice in next ch-2 sp and in each ch-2 sp around; skip beginning ch-2 and join with slip st to first dc, finish off: 16 ch-2 sps.

Rnd 3: With **right** side facing, join Color C with slip st in first ch-2 sp; ch 2, (dc, ch 2, work 2-dc Cluster) in same sp, ch 2, work 2-dc Cluster in next ch-2 sp, ch 2, ★ (work 2-dc Cluster, ch 2) twice in next ch-2 sp, work 2-dc Cluster in next ch-2 sp, ch 2; repeat from ★ around; skip beginning ch-2 and join with slip st to first dc, finish off: 24 ch-2 sps.

Rnd 4: With **right** side facing, join Color D with slip st in first ch-2 sp; ch 1, 3 sc in same sp, 2 sc in each of next 2 ch-2 sps, (3 sc in next ch-2 sp, 2 sc in each of next 2 ch-2 sps) around; join with slip st to first sc: 56 sc.

Rnd 5: Ch 1, sc in same st, (sc, hdc, sc) in next sc, ★ sc in next 6 sc, (sc, hdc, sc) in next sc; repeat from ★ 6 times **more**, sc in last 5 sc; join with slip st to first sc, finish off: 72 sts.

JOINING

Join Motifs into 5 vertical strips of 9 Motifs each as follows: With **right** sides together and working through **outside** loops only, join Color D with slip st in any corner hdc; slip st in each st across to next corner hdc; finish off.

Do **not** join strips.

BORDER

Rnd 1: With **right** side of any strip facing, join Color A with slip st in corner hdc at Point A on Placement Diagram; ch 1, 2 sc in same st, † skip next sc, sc in next 6 sc, skip next sc, 2 sc in next hdc, skip next sc, sc in next 6 sc, skip next sc, sc in next joining, skip next sc, sc in next 6 sc, skip next sc, 2 sc in next hdc †; repeat from † to † 7 times **more**, (skip next sc, sc in next 6 sc, skip next sc, 2 sc in next hdc) 4 times, repeat from † to † 8 times, skip next sc, sc in next 6 sc, (skip next sc, 2 sc in next hdc, skip next sc, sc in next 6 sc) 3 times, skip last sc; join with slip st to first sc changing to Color B *(Fig. 31b, page 138)*: 432 sc.

PLACEMENT DIAGRAM

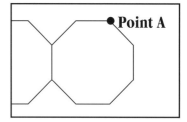

Point A

Rnd 2: Ch 1, sc in same st, † 2 sc in next sc, sc in next 6 sc, ★ 2 sc in next sc, hdc in next 2 sc, dc in next 3 sc, work 5-dc Cluster, dc in next 3 sc, hdc in next 2 sc, 2 sc in next sc, sc in next 6 sc; repeat from ★ 7 times **more**, 2 sc in next sc, sc in next 8 sc, (sc, hdc) in next sc, (hdc, dc) in next sc, (dc, tr) in next sc, tr in next sc, dtr in next sc, tr in next sc, (tr, dc) in next sc, (dc, hdc) in next sc, (hdc, sc) in next sc †, sc in next 7 sc, repeat from † to † once, sc in last 6 sc; join with slip st to first sc changing to Color C: 416 sts.

Rnd 3: Ch 1, sc in same st and in next sc, † 2 sc in next sc, sc in next 7 sc, hdc in next 2 sts, (work FPtr around next st, dc in next dc) twice, work FPtr Cluster, (dc in next dc, work FPtr around next st) twice, hdc in next 2 sts, ★ sc in next 8 sc, hdc in next 2 sts, (work FPtr around next st, dc in next dc) twice, work FPtr Cluster, (dc in next dc, work FPtr around next st) twice, hdc in next 2 sts; repeat from ★ 6 times **more**, sc in next 7 sc, 2 sc in next sc, sc in next 4 sc, decrease, sc in next 4 sc, 2 sc in next hdc, sc in next 5 sts, (sc, hdc, sc) in next dtr, sc in next 5 sts, 2 sc in next hdc, sc in next 4 sc, decrease †, sc in next 3 sc, repeat from † to † once, sc in last sc; join with slip st to first sc changing to Color D: 424 sts.

Rnd 4: Ch 1, sc in same st and in next 2 sc, † 2 sc in next sc, sc in next 9 sts, (hdc in next FPtr, work BPdc around next dc) twice, work BPdc around center post of next FPtr Cluster *(Fig. 2)*, (work BPdc around next dc, hdc in next FPtr) twice, ★ sc in next 12 sts, (hdc in next FPtr, work BPdc around next dc) twice, work BPdc around center post of next FPtr Cluster, (work BPdc around next dc, hdc in next FPtr) twice; repeat from ★ 6 times **more**, sc in next 10 sts, 2 sc in next sc, sc in next 17 sc, (sc, hdc, sc) in next hdc †, sc in next 17 sc, repeat from † to † once, sc in last 14 sc; join with slip st to first sc: 432 sts.

Fig. 2

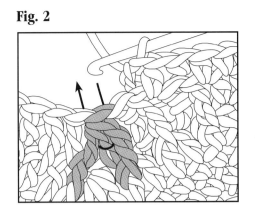

Rnd 5: Ch 1, sc in same st and in next 3 sc, † 2 sc in next sc, sc in next 9 sc, work 4-dc Cluster, dc in next BPdc, work 4-dc Cluster, ★ sc in next 12 sc, work 4-dc Cluster, dc in next BPdc, work 4-dc Cluster; repeat from ★ 6 times **more**, sc in next 11 sc, 2 sc in next sc, sc in next 18 sc, (sc, hdc, sc) in next hdc †, sc in next 19 sc, repeat from † to † once **more**, sc in last 15 sc; join with slip st to first sc changing to Color C: 344 sts.

Rnd 6: Ch 1, sc in same st and in next 4 sc, † 2 sc in next sc, sc in next 11 sts, (work FPdtr Cluster, skip next 4-dc Cluster, sc in next 14 sts) 7 times, work FPdtr Cluster, skip next 4-dc Cluster, sc in next 12 sts, 2 sc in next sc, sc in next 19 sc, (sc, hdc, sc) in next hdc †, sc in next 21 sc, repeat from † to † once, sc in last 16 sc; join with slip st to first sc, finish off.

Repeat for remaining strips.

ASSEMBLY

Join strips as follows: With **right** sides together, matching sts and working through **outside** loops only, join Color C with slip st in corner sc; slip st in each st across to next corner sc; finish off.

Add tassels using Color C, each 7" long *(Figs. 38a & b, page 142)*; attach to hdc at each point.

all through the house

While accessories for today's interiors embrace a wide range of decorating styles, it's most important that home accents reflect your personal tastes. This diverse collection of household designs showcases Victorian elegance, contemporary flair, and country charm to beautify even the simplest of spaces. You'll discover that a touch of crochet is often all it takes to awaken your decor!

IN THE LIVING ROOM

Inspired by Morocco's beautiful mosaics, these pretty accessories will warm a favorite spot in your home. (Below) Graceful touches for teatime, our quick-to-stitch coasters are made with bedspread weight cotton thread. (Opposite) The colorful afghan is worked in squares, which are joined into a full-size throw. A coordinating pillow, stitched with double strands of yarn, completes the ensemble.

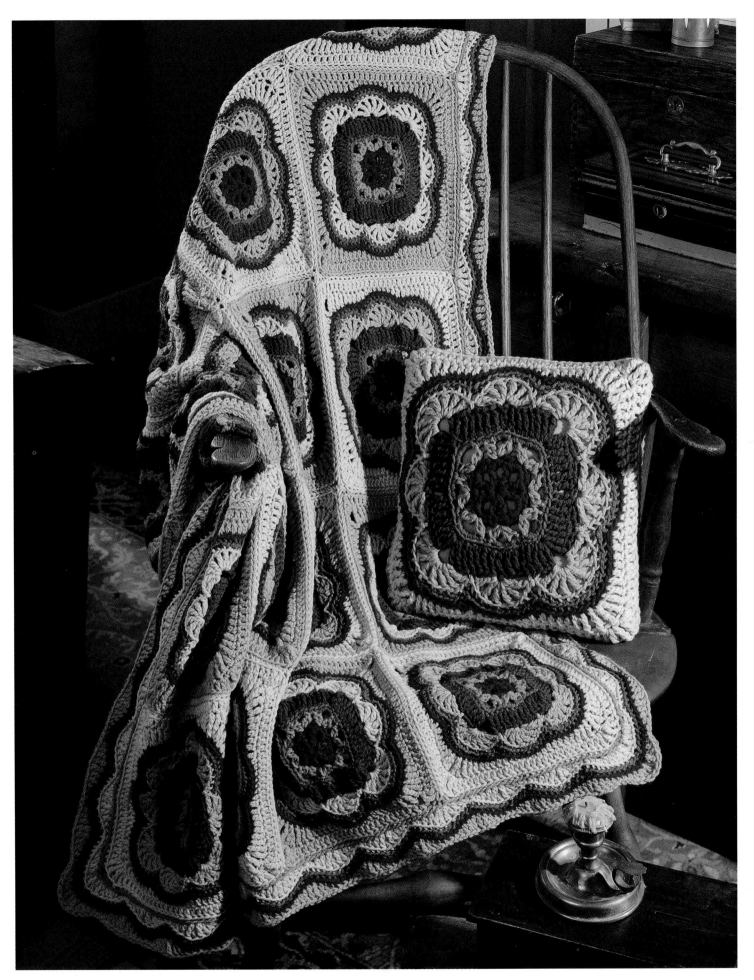

MOROCCAN TILE AFGHAN

Finished Size: Approximately 50" x 69"

MATERIALS
Worsted Weight Yarn, approximately:
Color A (Maroon) - 6 ounces, (170 grams, 410 yards)
Color B (Light Blue) - 3 ounces, (90 grams, 205 yards)
Color C (Blue) - 7 ounces, (200 grams, 480 yards)
Color D (Dark Blue) - 6 ounces, (170 grams, 410 yards)
Color E (Ecru) - 13 ounces, (370 grams, 890 yards)
Color F (Tan) - 12 ounces, (340 grams, 825 yards)
Crochet hook, size J (6.00 mm) **or** size needed for gauge
Yarn needle

GAUGE: Rnds 1-5 = 5"
One Square = 9¼"

SQUARE #1 (Make 18)
With Color A, ch 4; join with slip st to form a ring.
Rnd 1 (Right side)**:** Ch 4, dc in ring, ch 2, (dc in ring, ch 1, dc in ring, ch 2) 3 times; join with slip st to third ch of beginning ch-4: 8 sps.
Note: Loop a short piece of yarn around any stitch to mark last round as **right** side.
Rnd 2: Slip st in first ch-1 sp, ch 1, 3 sc in same sp, 5 sc in next ch-2 sp, (3 sc in next ch-1 sp, 5 sc in next ch-2 sp) around; join with slip st to first sc, finish off: 32 sc.
Note: To work **Cluster**, ★ YO, insert hook in st indicated, YO and pull up a loop, YO and draw through 2 loops on hook; repeat from ★ once **more**, YO and draw through all 3 loops on hook (*Figs. 13a & b, page 134*).
Rnd 3: With **right** side facing, join Color B with slip st in center sc of any 3-sc group; ch 2, dc in same st, skip next 3 sc, work (Cluster, ch 4, Cluster) in next sc, ★ skip next 3 sc, work (Cluster, ch 3, Cluster) in next sc, skip next 3 sc, work (Cluster, ch 4, Cluster) in next sc; repeat from ★ 2 times **more**, skip last 3 sc, work Cluster in same st as beginning ch-2, ch 3, skip beginning ch-2 and join with slip st to first dc, finish off: 16 Clusters.
Rnd 4: With **right** side facing, join Color C with slip st in first st; ch 1, sc in same st and in next Cluster, 5 sc in next ch-4 sp, sc in next 2 Clusters, 3 sc in next ch-3 sp, ★ sc in next 2 Clusters, 5 sc in next ch-4 sp, sc in next 2 Clusters, 3 sc in next ch-3 sp; repeat from ★ around; join with slip st to first sc, finish off: 48 sc.
Rnd 5: With **right** side facing and working in Back Loops Only (*Fig. 27, page 138*), join Color D with slip st in center sc of any 5-sc group; ch 4 **(counts as first tr)**, (tr, ch 2, 2 tr) in same st, tr in next 11 sc, ★ (2 tr, ch 2, 2 tr) in next sc, tr in next 11 sc; repeat from ★ around; join with slip st to first tr, finish off: 60 tr.

Rnd 6: With **right** side facing and working in both loops, join Color F with slip st in fourth tr to **right** of any corner ch-2 sp; ★ skip next 3 tr, tr in corner ch-2 sp, (ch 1, tr) 7 times in same sp, skip next 3 tr, slip st in next tr, skip next 3 tr, tr in next tr, (ch 1, tr) 5 times in same st, skip next 3 tr, slip st in next tr; repeat from ★ around working last slip st in first slip st, finish off: 56 tr.
Note: Work next 3 rounds in Back Loops Only.
Rnd 7: With **right** side facing, join Color C with slip st in center ch of any corner; ch 1, 2 sc in same st, sc in next tr, (2 sc in next ch, sc in next tr) twice, ★ † sc in next ch, skip next 2 tr, sc in next ch and in next tr, (2 sc in next ch, sc in next tr) 3 times, sc in next ch, skip next 2 tr, sc in next ch and in next tr †, (2 sc in next ch, sc in next tr) 5 times; repeat from ★ 2 times **more**, then repeat from † to † once, (2 sc in next ch, sc in next tr) twice; join with slip st to first sc, finish off: 120 sc.
Rnd 8: With **right** side facing, join Color A with slip st in first sc; ch 1, sc in same st and in next 8 sc, ★ † skip next 2 sc, sc in next 10 sc, skip next 2 sc †, sc in next 16 sc; repeat from ★ 2 times **more**, then repeat from † to † once, sc in last 7 sc; join with slip st to first sc, finish off: 104 sc.
Rnd 9: With **right** side facing, join Color E with slip st in first sc; ch 5, dtr in same st and in next sc, ★ † tr in next 2 sc, dc in next 4 sc, skip next sc, dc in next sc, hdc in next sc, sc in next 5 sc, hdc in next sc, dc in next sc, skip next sc, dc in next 4 sc, tr in next 2 sc, dtr in next sc †, 2 dtr in next sc, dtr in next sc; repeat from ★ 2 times **more**, then repeat from † to † once; join with slip st to top of beginning ch-5: 100 sts.
Rnd 10: Working in both loops, ch 3, (tr, dtr) in same st, (dtr, tr, dc) in next st, dc in next 23 sts, ★ (dc, tr, dtr) in next st, (dtr, tr, dc) in next st, dc in next 23 sts; repeat from ★ around; join with slip st to top of beginning ch-3, finish off: 116 sts.

SQUARE #2 (Make 17)
Work same as Square #1 working Rnd 6 with Color E and Rnds 9 and 10 with Color F.

ASSEMBLY
With **wrong** sides together and Color E, and working through **inside** loops only, whipstitch Squares together, forming 5 vertical strips of 7 Squares each, alternating Square #1 with Square #2, and beginning in first dtr and ending in last dtr on each side (*Fig. 35b, page 140*); then whipstitch strips together, securing seam at each joining.

Continued on page 45.

MOROCCAN TILE COASTER

Finished Size: Approximately 4" x 4"

MATERIALS

Bedspread Weight Cotton Thread (size 10), approximately:
  Color A (Maroon) - 7 yards **each**
  Color B (Ecru) - 15 yards **each**
  Color C (Tan) - 14 yards **each**
Steel crochet hook, size 6 (1.80 mm) **or** size needed for gauge

GAUGE: Rnds 1-5 = 2¼"

COASTER

With Color A, ch 4; join with slip st to form a ring.

Rnd 1 (Right side)**:** Ch 4, dc in ring, ch 2, (dc in ring, ch 1, dc in ring, ch 2) 3 times; join with slip st to third ch of beginning ch-4: 8 sps.

Note: Loop a short piece of thread around any stitch to mark last round as **right** side.

Rnd 2: Slip st in first ch-1 sp, ch 1, 3 sc in same sp, 5 sc in next ch-2 sp, (3 sc in next ch-1 sp, 5 sc in next ch-2 sp) around; join with slip st to first sc, finish off: 32 sc.

Note: To work **Cluster,** ★ YO, insert hook in st indicated, YO and pull up a loop, YO and draw through 2 loops on hook; repeat from ★ once **more,** YO and draw through all 3 loops on hook *(Figs. 13a & b, page 134)*.

Rnd 3: With **right** side facing, join Color B with slip st in center sc of any 3-sc group; ch 2, dc in same st, skip next 3 sc, work (Cluster, ch 4, Cluster) in next sc, ★ skip next 3 sc, work (Cluster, ch 3, Cluster) in next sc, skip next 3 sc, work (Cluster, ch 4, Cluster) in next sc; repeat from ★ 2 times **more,** skip last 3 sc, work Cluster in same st as beginning ch-2, ch 3, skip beginning ch-2 and join with slip st to first dc: 16 Clusters.

Rnd 4: Ch 1, sc in same st and in next Cluster, 5 sc in next ch-4 sp, sc in next 2 Clusters, 3 sc in next ch-3 sp, ★ sc in next 2 Clusters, 5 sc in next ch-4 sp, sc in next 2 Clusters, 3 sc in next ch-3 sp; repeat from ★ around; join with slip st to Back Loop Only of first sc *(Fig. 27, page 138)*: 48 sc.

Rnd 5: Ch 4 **(counts as first tr),** working in Back Loops Only, tr in next 3 sc, (2 tr, ch 2, 2 tr) in next sc, ★ tr in next 11 sc, (2 tr, ch 2, 2 tr) in next sc; repeat from ★ around to last 7 sc, tr in last 7 sc; join with slip st to first tr: 60 tr.

Rnd 6: Working in both loops, slip st in next 2 tr, ★ † skip next 3 tr, tr in corner ch-2 sp, (ch 1, tr) 7 times in same sp, skip next 3 tr, slip st in next tr, skip next 3 tr, tr in next tr, (ch 1, tr) 5 times in same st †, skip next 3 tr, slip st in next tr; repeat from ★ 2 times **more,** then repeat from † to † once, skip next tr and next 2 slip sts; join with slip st to next slip st, finish off: 56 tr.

Note: Work next 3 rounds in Back Loops Only.

Rnd 7: With **right** side facing, join Color A with slip st in center ch of any corner; ch 1, 2 sc in same st, sc in next tr, (2 sc in next

ch, sc in next tr) twice, ★ † sc in next ch, skip next 2 tr, sc in next ch and in next tr, (2 sc in next ch, sc in next tr) 3 times, sc in next ch, skip next 2 tr, sc in next ch and in next tr †, (2 sc in next ch, sc in next tr) 5 times; repeat from ★ 2 times **more,** then repeat from † to † once, (2 sc in next ch, sc in next tr) twice; join with slip st to first sc: 120 sc.

Rnd 8: Ch 1, sc in same st and in next 8 sc, ★ † skip next 2 sc, sc in next 10 sc, skip next 2 sc †, sc in next 16 sc; repeat from ★ 2 times **more,** then repeat from † to † once, sc in last 7 sc; join with slip st to first sc, finish off: 104 sc.

Rnd 9: With **right** side facing, join Color C with slip st in first sc; ch 5, dtr in same st and in next sc, ★ † tr in next 2 sc, dc in next 4 sc, skip next sc, dc in next sc, hdc in next sc, sc in next 5 sc, hdc in next sc, dc in next sc, skip next sc, dc in next 4 sc, tr in next 2 sc, dtr in next sc †, 2 dtr in next sc, dtr in next sc; repeat from ★ 2 times **more,** then repeat from † to † once; join with slip st to top of beginning ch-5: 100 sts.

Rnd 10: Working in both loops, ch 3, (tr, dtr) in same st, (dtr, tr, dc) in next st, dc in next 23 sts, ★ (dc, tr, dtr) in next st, (dtr, tr, dc) in next st, dc in next 23 sts; repeat from ★ around; join with slip st to top of beginning ch-3, finish off: 116 sts. See Washing and Blocking, page 140.

MOROCCAN TILE PILLOW

Finished Size: Approximately 12" square

MATERIALS

Worsted Weight Yarn, approximately:
  Color A (Maroon) - 1 ounce, (30 grams, 70 yards)
  Color B (Light Blue) - ½ ounce, (15 grams, 35 yards)
  Color C (Blue) - 1 ounce, (30 grams, 70 yards)
  Color D (Dark Blue) - ¾ ounce, (20 grams, 50 yards)
  Color E (Ecru) - 1½ ounces, (40 grams, 105 yards)
  Color F (Tan) - 1 ounce, (30 grams, 70 yards)
Crochet hook, size K (6.50 mm) **or** size needed for gauge
Yarn needle
12" purchased pillow form **or** ½ yard 44/45" wide fabric and polyester fiberfill

Note: Entire Pillow is worked holding 2 strands of yarn together.

GAUGE: Rnds 1-3 = 4½"

SQUARE (Make 2)

Work same as Moroccan Tile Afghan Square #1.

FINISHING

Make pillow form if desired, page 140.

JOINING

With **wrong** sides together and Color E, and working through **inside** loops only, whipstitch Squares together, inserting pillow form before closing *(Fig. 35b, page 140)*.

FOR THE DINING ROOM

Charming accents for a china cabinet or a shelf of collectibles, these dainty edgings are typical of Victorian accents that were used to beautify everyday furnishings. The patterns, featuring fans, points, and scallops, are worked in fine size 20 cotton thread and embellished with satin ribbon.

CHINA CABINET EDGINGS

Finished Size: Edging #1 - approximately 3½" wide
Edging #2 - approximately 3½" wide
Edging #3 - approximately 3" wide

Note: These Edgings are worked across the width and can easily be made any length.

MATERIALS
Crochet Cotton Thread (size 20), approximately:
Edging #1 - 6 yards per inch
Edging #2 - 7¾ yards per inch
Edging #3 - 6½ yards per inch
Steel crochet hook, size 10 (1.30 mm) **or** size needed for gauge
Satin ribbon:
Edging #1 - desired length of ⅛" wide ribbon
Edging #2 - desired length of ¼" wide ribbon
Edging #3 - desired length of ⅜" wide ribbon
Tapestry needle
Sewing needle and thread

GAUGE: 13 dc and 6 rows = 1"

EDGING #1
Ch 10.
Row 1: 2 Dc in fourth ch from hook, ch 2, 3 dc in next ch, skip next 4 chs, (3 dc, ch 2, 3 dc) in last ch.
Row 2 (Right side): Ch 5, turn; (3 dc, ch 2, 3 dc) in first ch-2 sp, ch 1, (3 dc, ch 2, 3 dc) in next ch-2 sp, ch 2, skip next 2 dc, dc in top of beginning ch.
Note: Loop a short piece of thread around any stitch to mark last row as **right** side.
Row 3: Ch 5, turn; skip first ch-2 sp, dc in next dc, ch 2, (3 dc, ch 2, 3 dc) in next ch-2 sp, ch 1, (3 dc, ch 2, 3 dc) in next ch-2 sp.
Row 4: Ch 5, turn; (3 dc, ch 2, 3 dc) in first ch-2 sp, ch 1, (3 dc, ch 2, 3 dc) in next ch-2 sp, ch 2, skip next 2 dc, (dc in next dc, ch 2) twice, skip next 2 chs, dc in next ch.
Row 5: Ch 5, turn; skip first ch-2 sp, dc in next dc, ch 2, dc in next dc, 2 dc in next ch-2 sp, dc in next dc, ch 2, skip next 2 dc, (3 dc, ch 2, 3 dc) in next ch-2 sp, ch 1, (3 dc, ch 2, 3 dc) in next ch-2 sp.

Row 6: Ch 5, turn; (3 dc, ch 2, 3 dc) in first ch-2 sp, ch 1, (3 dc, ch 2, 3 dc) in next ch-2 sp, ch 2, skip next 2 dc, dc in next dc, 2 dc in next ch-2 sp, dc in next 4 dc, 2 dc in next ch-2 sp, dc in next dc, ch 2, skip next 2 chs, dc in next ch.
Row 7: Ch 5, turn; skip first ch-2 sp, dc in next dc, ch 2, skip next 2 dc, dc in next 4 dc, ch 2, skip next 2 dc, (dc in next dc, ch 2) twice, skip next 2 dc, (3 dc, ch 2, 3 dc) in next ch-2 sp, ch 1, (3 dc, ch 2, 3 dc) in next ch-2 sp.
Row 8: Ch 5, turn; (3 dc, ch 2, 3 dc) in first ch-2 sp, ch 1, (3 dc, ch 2, 3 dc) in next ch-2 sp, ch 2, skip next 2 dc, (dc in next dc, ch 2) 4 times, skip next 2 dc, (dc in next dc, ch 2) twice, skip next 2 chs, dc in next ch.
Row 9: Ch 5, turn; skip first ch-2 sp, dc in next dc, (ch 2, dc in next dc) twice, (2 dc in next ch-2 sp, dc in next dc) 4 times, ch 2, skip next 2 dc, (3 dc, ch 2, 3 dc) in next ch-2 sp, ch 1, (3 dc, ch 2, 3 dc) in next ch-2 sp.
Row 10: Ch 5, turn; (3 dc, ch 2, 3 dc) in first ch-2 sp, ch 1, (3 dc, ch 2, 3 dc) in next ch-2 sp, ch 2, skip next 2 dc, dc in next dc, ch 2, dc in next 4 dc, ch 3, skip next 2 dc, slip st in next dc, ch 3, skip next 2 dc, dc in next 4 dc, ch 2, (dc in next dc, ch 2) twice, skip next 2 chs, dc in next ch.
Row 11: Ch 5, turn; skip first ch-2 sp, (dc in next dc, 2 dc in next ch-2 sp) twice, dc in next 4 dc, ch 5, dc in next 4 dc, (2 dc in next ch-2 sp, dc in next dc) twice, ch 2, skip next 2 dc, (3 dc, ch 2, 3 dc) in next ch-2 sp, ch 1, (3 dc, ch 2, 3 dc) in next ch-2 sp.
Row 12: Ch 5, turn; (3 dc, ch 2, 3 dc) in first ch-2 sp, ch 1, (3 dc, ch 2, 3 dc) in next ch-2 sp, ch 2, skip next 2 dc, dc in next dc, ch 2, dc in next 4 dc, ch 3, skip next 2 dc, slip st in next dc, ch 3, skip next 2 dc, dc in next dc, ch 3, slip st in next ch-5 sp, ch 3, dc in next dc, ch 3, skip next 2 dc, slip st in next dc, ch 3, skip next 2 dc, dc in next 4 dc, ch 2, skip next 2 chs, dc in next ch.
Row 13: Ch 5, turn; skip first ch-2 sp, dc in next 4 dc, ch 5, (dc in next dc, ch 5) twice, dc in next 4 dc, ch 2, (dc in next dc, ch 2) twice, skip next 2 dc, (3 dc, ch 2, 3 dc) in next ch-2 sp, ch 1, (3 dc, ch 2, 3 dc) in next ch-2 sp.
Row 14: Ch 5, turn; (3 dc, ch 2, 3 dc) in first ch-2 sp, ch 1, (3 dc, ch 2, 3 dc) in next ch-2 sp, ch 2, skip next 2 dc, dc in next dc, 2 dc in next ch-2 sp, (dc in next dc, ch 2) twice, dc in next 4 dc, 5 dc in next ch-5 sp, dc in next dc, ch 3, slip st in next ch-5 sp, ch 3, dc in next dc, 5 dc in next ch-5 sp, dc in next 4 dc, ch 2, skip next 2 chs, dc in next ch.

#2

#1

#3

Row 15: Ch 5, turn; skip first ch-2 sp, dc in next dc, ch 2, skip next 2 dc, dc in next dc, ch 2, skip next 2 dc, dc in next 4 dc, ch 5, dc in next 4 dc, ch 2, (skip next 2 dc, dc in next dc, ch 2) twice, dc in next dc, 2 dc in next ch-2 sp, dc in next 4 dc, 2 dc in next ch-2 sp, dc in next dc, ch 2, skip next 2 dc, (3 dc, ch 2, 3 dc) in next ch-2 sp, ch 1, (3 dc, ch 2, 3 dc) in next ch-2 sp.

Row 16: Ch 5, turn; (3 dc, ch 2, 3 dc) in first ch-2 sp, ch 1, (3 dc, ch 2, 3 dc) in next ch-2 sp, ch 2, skip next 2 dc, (dc in next dc, ch 2) twice, skip next 2 dc, dc in next 4 dc, ch 2, skip next 2 dc, (dc in next dc, ch 2) 3 times, dc in next 4 dc, 5 dc in next ch-5 sp, dc in next 4 dc, ch 2, (dc in next dc, ch 2) twice, skip next 2 chs, dc in next ch.

Row 17: Ch 5, turn; skip first ch-2 sp, (dc in next dc, ch 2) 3 times, (skip next 2 dc, dc in next dc, ch 2) 4 times, (dc in next dc, ch 2) 4 times, skip next 2 dc, (dc in next dc, ch 2) 4 times, skip next 2 dc, (3 dc, ch 2, 3 dc) in next ch-2 sp, ch 1, (3 dc, ch 2, 3 dc) in next ch-2 sp.

Row 18: Ch 5, turn; (3 dc, ch 2, 3 dc) in first ch-2 sp, ch 1, (3 dc, ch 2, 3 dc) in next ch-2 sp, ch 2, skip next 2 dc, dc in next dc, leave remaining sts unworked.
Repeat Rows 3-18 for pattern, ending by working Row 17.

Note: To work **Cluster**, ★ YO, insert hook in st or sp indicated, YO and pull up a loop, YO and draw through 2 loops on hook; repeat from ★ once **more**, YO and draw through all 3 loops on hook *(Figs. 13a & b, page 134)*.

Edging: Turn; slip st in first 3 dc and in next ch-2 sp, ch 1, (sc, ch 3, work Cluster) in same sp, ch 2, skip next 2 dc, (sc, ch 3, work Cluster) in next dc, ch 2, (sc, ch 3, work Cluster) in next ch-2 sp, ch 2, skip next 2 dc, (sc, ch 3, work Cluster) in next dc, ★ † ch 2, [(sc, ch 3, work Cluster) in next dc, ch 2] across to last sp, skip next 2 chs, (sc, ch 3, work Cluster) in next ch, ch 2, [(sc, ch 3, work Cluster) in top of next row, ch 2] across †, (sc, ch 3, work Cluster) in dc at corner; repeat from ★ across to last point, then repeat from † to † once; working in free loops of beginning ch *(Fig. 28b, page 138)*, skip next 3 chs, (sc, ch 3, work Cluster) in next ch, ch 2, skip next 4 chs, (sc, ch 3, work Cluster) in next ch, ch 2, slip st in end of row; finish off.

FINISHING
See Washing and Blocking, page 140.
Weave ribbon through sps along top of Edging.
Turn ends of ribbon under ½" to wrong side and sew in place.

EDGING #2
Note: To work **Shell**, (2 dc, ch 2, 2 dc) in st or sp indicated.
Ch 16.
Row 1: (Dc, ch 2, 2 dc) in fourth ch from hook, ch 3, dc in top of dc just worked, skip next 4 chs, work Shell in next ch, ch 6, skip next 6 chs, sc in last ch, ch 8, slip st in top of sc just worked.

Row 2 (Right side): Ch 3 **(counts as first dc, now and throughout)**, turn; 9 dc in first loop, ch 5, skip next loop, work Shell in next Shell (ch-2 sp), ch 3, dc in top of dc just worked, work Shell in last ch-2 sp.

Note: Loop a short piece of thread around any stitch to mark last row as **right** side.

Row 3: Ch 5, turn; slip st in fourth ch from hook, ch 2, work Shell in first Shell, ch 3, dc in top of dc just worked, work Shell in next Shell, ch 3, sc **around** loops of previous 2 rows, ch 3, dc in next dc, (ch 3, skip next 2 dc, dc in next dc) 3 times.

Row 4: Ch 3, turn; (4 dc in next ch-3 sp, dc in next dc) 3 times, ch 6, skip next 2 ch-3 sps, work Shell in next Shell, ch 3, dc in top of dc just worked, work Shell in last Shell.

Row 5: Ch 5, turn; slip st in fourth ch from hook, ch 2, work Shell in first Shell, ch 3, dc in top of dc just worked, work Shell in next Shell, ch 5, skip next loop, dc in next dc, (ch 6, skip next 4 dc, dc in next dc) 3 times.

Row 6: Ch 3, turn; (7 dc in next loop, dc in next dc) 3 times, ch 3, sc **around** loops of previous 2 rows, ch 3, work Shell in next Shell, ch 3, dc in top of dc just worked, work Shell in last Shell.

Row 7: Ch 5, turn; slip st in fourth ch from hook, ch 2, work Shell in first Shell, ch 3, dc in top of dc just worked, work Shell in next Shell, ch 6, skip next 2 ch-3 sps, dc in each dc across.

Row 8: Ch 3, turn; (dc, ch 2, 2 dc) in first dc, (skip next 3 dc, work Shell in next dc) 6 times, ch 5, skip next loop, work Shell in next Shell, ch 3, dc in top of dc just worked, work Shell in last Shell.

Row 9: Ch 5, turn; slip st in fourth ch from hook, ch 2, work Shell in first Shell, ch 3, dc in top of dc just worked, work Shell in next Shell, ch 3, sc **around** loops of previous 2 rows, ch 3, work Shell in each Shell across.

Row 10: Turn; slip st in first 2 dc and in next ch-2 sp, ch 3, (dc, ch 2, 2 dc) in same sp, (ch 1, work Shell in next Shell) 6 times, ch 6, skip next 2 ch-3 sps, work Shell in next Shell, ch 3, dc in top of dc just worked, work Shell in last Shell.

Row 11: Ch 5, turn; slip st in fourth ch from hook, ch 2, work Shell in first Shell, ch 3, dc in top of dc just worked, work Shell in next Shell, ch 5, skip next loop, (2 dc, ch 3, 2 dc) in next Shell, [ch 1, (2 dc, ch 3, 2 dc) in next Shell] across.

Row 12: Turn; slip st in first 2 dc and in next ch-3 sp, ch 3, (3 dc, ch 1, 4 dc) in same sp, (4 dc, ch 1, 4 dc) in next 6 ch-3 sps, ch 3, sc **around** loops of previous 2 rows, ch 3, work Shell in next Shell, ch 3, dc in top of dc just worked, work Shell in last Shell.

Row 13: Ch 5, turn; slip st in fourth ch from hook, ch 2, work Shell in first Shell, ch 3, dc in top of dc just worked, work Shell in next Shell, ch 6, skip next 2 ch-3 sps, sc in next ch-1 sp, ch 8, slip st in top of sc just worked, leave remaining sts unworked.

Row 14: Ch 3, turn; 12 dc in first loop, ch 5, skip next loop, work Shell in next Shell, ch 3, dc in top of dc just worked, work Shell in last Shell.

Row 15: Ch 5, turn; slip st in fourth ch from hook, ch 2, work Shell in first Shell, ch 3, dc in top of dc just worked, work Shell in next Shell, ch 3, sc **around** loops of previous 2 rows, ch 3, dc in next dc, (ch 3, skip next 2 dc, dc in next dc) 4 times, skip next 3 dc on last row of previous scallop (Row 12), dc in next dc.

Row 16: Ch 3, turn; (4 dc in next ch-3 sp, dc in next dc) 4 times, ch 6, skip next 2 ch-3 sps, work Shell in next Shell, ch 3, dc in top of dc just worked, work Shell in last Shell.

Row 17: Ch 5, turn; slip st in fourth ch from hook, ch 2, work Shell in first Shell, ch 3, dc in top of dc just worked, work Shell in next Shell, ch 5, skip next loop, dc in next dc, (ch 6, skip next 4 dc, dc in next dc) 4 times, sc in next ch-1 sp on previous scallop.

Row 18: Ch 3, turn; (7 dc in next loop, dc in next dc) 4 times, ch 3, sc **around** loops of previous 2 rows, ch 3, work Shell in next Shell, ch 3, dc in top of dc just worked, work Shell in last Shell.

Row 19: Ch 5, turn; slip st in fourth ch from hook, ch 2, work Shell in first Shell, ch 3, dc in top of dc just worked, work Shell in next Shell, ch 6, skip next 2 ch-3 sps, dc in each dc across, skip next 3 dc on previous scallop, dc in next dc.

Row 20: Ch 3, turn; (dc, ch 2, 2 dc) in next dc, (skip next 3 dc, work Shell in next dc) 8 times, ch 5, skip next loop, work Shell in next Shell, ch 3, dc in top of dc just worked, work Shell in last Shell.

Row 21: Ch 5, turn; slip st in fourth ch from hook, ch 2, work Shell in first Shell, ch 3, dc in top of dc just worked, work Shell in next Shell, ch 3, sc **around** loops of previous 2 rows, ch 3, work Shell in each Shell across, sc in next ch-1 sp on previous scallop.

Row 22: Turn; slip st in first 2 dc and in next ch-2 sp, ch 3, (dc, ch 2, 2 dc) in same sp, (ch 1, work Shell in next Shell) 8 times, ch 6, skip next 2 ch-3 sps, work Shell in next Shell, ch 3, dc in top of dc just worked, work Shell in last Shell.

Row 23: Ch 5, turn; slip st in fourth ch from hook, ch 2, work Shell in first Shell, ch 3, dc in top of dc just worked, work Shell in next Shell, ch 5, skip next loop, (2 dc, ch 3, 2 dc) in next Shell, [ch 1, (2 dc, ch 3, 2 dc) in next Shell] across, skip next 3 dc on previous scallop, dc in next dc, ch 3, sc in next ch-1 sp.

Row 24: Ch 1, turn; (4 dc, ch 1, 4 dc) in next 9 ch-3 sps, ch 3, sc **around** loops of previous 2 rows, ch 3, work Shell in next Shell, ch 3, dc in top of dc just worked, work Shell in last Shell.
Repeat Rows 13-24 for pattern, ending by working Row 24; finish off.

FINISHING
See Washing and Blocking, page 140.
Weave ribbon through sps along top of Edging.
Turn ends of ribbon under ½" to wrong side and sew in place.

EDGING #3
Ch 14.
Note: To work **Shell**, (2 dc, ch 2, 2 dc) in st or sp indicated.
Row 1: Work Shell in seventh ch from hook, ch 6, skip next 6 chs, work Shell in last ch.
Row 2 (Right side): Ch 3 **(counts as first dc, now and throughout)**, turn; dc in next dc, work Shell in next ch-2 sp, ch 3, sc in next loop, ch 3, work Shell in last ch-2 sp.
Note: Loop a short piece of thread around any stitch to mark last row as **right** side.
Row 3: Ch 5, turn; work Shell in first ch-2 sp, ch 6, skip next 2 ch-3 sps, work Shell in next ch-2 sp, dc in last 4 dc.
Row 4: Ch 3, turn; dc in next 5 dc, work Shell in next ch-2 sp, ch 3, sc in next loop, ch 3, work Shell in last ch-2 sp.
Row 5: Ch 5, turn; work Shell in first ch-2 sp, ch 6, skip next 2 ch-3 sps, work Shell in next ch-2 sp, dc in last 8 dc.
Row 6: Ch 3, turn; dc in next 9 dc, work Shell in next ch-2 sp, ch 3, sc in next loop, ch 3, work Shell in last ch-2 sp.
Row 7: Ch 5, turn; work Shell in first ch-2 sp, ch 6, skip next 2 ch-3 sps, work Shell in next ch-2 sp, dc in last 12 dc.
Row 8: Ch 3, turn; dc in next 13 dc, work Shell in next ch-2 sp, ch 3, sc in next loop, ch 3, work Shell in last ch-2 sp.
Row 9: Ch 5, turn; work Shell in first ch-2 sp, ch 6, skip next 2 ch-3 sps, work Shell in next ch-2 sp, dc in last 16 dc.
Row 10: Ch 3, turn; dc in next 17 dc, work Shell in next ch-2 sp, ch 3, sc in next loop, ch 3, work Shell in last ch-2 sp.
Row 11: Ch 5, turn; work Shell in first ch-2 sp, ch 6, skip next 2 ch-3 sps, work Shell in next ch-2 sp, leave remaining sts unworked.
Row 12: Ch 3, turn; work Shell in first ch-2 sp, ch 3, sc in next loop, ch 3, work Shell in last ch-2 sp.
Row 13: Ch 5, turn; work Shell in first ch-2 sp, ch 6, skip next 2 ch-3 sps, work Shell in next ch-2 sp, ch 3, work Shell in sp formed by beginning ch-3, ch 3, skip next 2 dc on previous point, sc in next dc.
Row 14: Ch 3, turn; (work Shell, ch 2, 2 dc) in first ch-2 sp, ch 3, skip next ch-3 sp, dc in next 2 dc, work Shell in next ch-2 sp, ch 3, sc in next loop, ch 3, work Shell in last ch-2 sp.
Row 15: Ch 5, turn; work Shell in first ch-2 sp, ch 6, skip next 2 ch-3 sps, work Shell in next ch-2 sp, dc in next 4 dc, ch 3, skip next ch-3 sp, work Shell in next ch-2 sp, ch 2, work Shell in next ch-2 sp, ch 3, skip next 4 dc on previous point, sc in next dc.

Continued on page 45.

IN THE KITCHEN

Bring country-fresh cheer to your kitchen with this appealing collection! (Below) Crocheted with fabric strips, the apple-shaped coasters and basket are charming table accents. A removable lid makes the basket ideal for holding packets of sugar or sweetener. (Opposite) Whimsically designed with a loop "stem" that serves as a napkin ring, a coordinating place mat continues the theme.

*I*t's a snap to brighten your kitchen with these simple projects! (Right) *A quick-to-stitch apple motif is crocheted with bedspread weight cotton thread and appliquéd onto a purchased towel.* (Below) *Our handy pot holders, worked with double strands of thread, feature a pleasing checkerboard pattern and a sweet apple shape.* (Opposite) *Worked with a jumbo hook and wide fabric strips, a checkerboard rug unifies this homey collection.*

APPLE BASKET

Finished Size: Approximately 4" tall x 4½" in diameter

MATERIALS
100% Cotton Fabric, 44/45" wide, approximately:
Red - 1 yard
Brown - small amount
Green - small amount
Crochet hook, size K (6.50 mm) **or** size needed for gauge
Yarn needle

Prepare fabric and tear into 1" wide strips *(see Preparing Fabric Strips and Joining Fabric Strips, page 139)*.

GAUGE: Rnds 1-3 = 3"

BASKET
Rnd 1 (Right side): With Red, ch 2 **loosely**, 6 sc in second ch from hook; do **not** join, place fabric marker *(see Markers, page 137)*.
Note: Work in Back Loops Only throughout *(Fig. 27, page 138)*.
Rnd 2: 2 Sc in each sc around: 12 sc.
Rnd 3: (Sc in next sc, 2 sc in next sc) around: 18 sc.
Rnd 4: (Sc in next 2 sc, 2 sc in next sc) around: 24 sc.
Rnd 5: (Sc in next 7 sc, 2 sc in next sc) around: 27 sc.
Rnds 6-8: Sc in each sc around.
Note: To **decrease**, pull up a loop in next 2 sc, YO and draw through all 3 loops on hook **(counts as one sc)**.
Rnd 9: (Sc in next 7 sc, decrease) around: 24 sc.
Rnd 10: (Sc in next 6 sc, decrease) around; slip st in next sc, finish off: 21 sc.

LID
Work same as Rnds 1-3 of Basket; at end of Rnd 3, slip st in next sc, finish off.

STEM
With Brown and leaving a long end, ch 5 **loosely**; sc in second ch from hook and in each ch across; finish off leaving a long end.

LEAF
With Green and leaving a long end, ch 3 **loosely**; sc in second ch from hook, (sc, ch 3, sc) in last ch; working in free loops of beginning ch *(Fig. 28b, page 138)*, sc in next ch, slip st in next ch; finish off leaving a long end.

Pull long ends of Leaf and Stem through center of Lid to **wrong** side; weave ends through sts to secure.

APPLE COASTER

Finished Size: Approximately 5" x 4½"

MATERIALS
100% Cotton Fabric, 44/45" wide, approximately:
Red - ⅓ yard **each**
Green - small amount
Brown - small amount
Crochet hook, size K (6.50 mm) **or** size needed for gauge
Yarn needle

Prepare fabric and tear into 1" wide strips *(see Preparing Fabric Strips and Joining Fabric Strips, page 139)*.

GAUGE: Rnd 1 = 2¼"

APPLE
Rnd 1 (Right side): With Red, ch 4, 11 dc in fourth ch from hook; join with slip st to top of beginning ch-4: 12 sts.
Note: Loop a scrap piece of fabric around any stitch to mark last round as **right** side.
Rnd 2: Ch 1, (sc, hdc, dc) in same st, 2 htr in next dc *(Figs. 9a & b, page 132)*, 2 dc in each of next 3 sts, (2 htr, dc, slip st) in next dc, (slip st, dc, 2 htr) in next dc, 2 dc in each of next 3 sts, 2 htr in next dc, (dc, hdc, sc) in last dc; join with slip st to first sc, finish off.

STEM
With **right** side facing, join Brown with slip st in sp **before** first sc *(Fig. 29, page 138)*; ch 3, dc in same sp; finish off.

LEAF
With Green, ch 5 **loosely**; sc in third ch from hook and in next ch, (sc, slip st) in last ch; finish off leaving a long end for sewing.

With **right** side facing, sew Leaf around sc to **left** of Stem.

APPLE PLACE MAT & NAPKIN

Quick

Finished Size: Approximately 12" x 11½"

MATERIALS

100% Cotton Fabric, 44/45" wide, approximately:
Red - 2½ yards
Brown - small amount
Green - 14" square
Crochet hook, size K (6.50 mm) **or** size needed for gauge
Yarn needle

Prepare fabric and tear into 1½" wide strips *(see Preparing Fabric Strips and Joining Fabric Strips, page 139)*.

GAUGE: 4 sc and 4 rows = 2"

APPLE

With Red, ch 24 **loosely**.

Row 1: 2 Sc in second ch from hook, † (skip next ch, pull up a loop in next ch) 3 times, YO and draw through all 4 loops on hook, skip next ch †, sc in next 7 chs, repeat from † to † once, 2 sc in last ch: 13 sts.

Row 2 (Right side): Ch 1, turn; 2 sc in first sc, sc in next sc, hdc in next 9 sts, sc in next sc, 2 sc in last sc: 15 sts.

Note: Loop a scrap piece of fabric around any stitch to mark last row as **right** side.

Rows 3 and 4: Ch 1, turn; 2 sc in first sc, sc in each st across to last sc, 2 sc in last sc: 19 sc.

Rows 5-14: Ch 1, turn; sc in each sc across.

Note: To **decrease**, pull up a loop in next 2 sc, YO and draw through all 3 loops on hook **(counts as one sc)**.

Rows 15 and 16: Ch 1, turn; decrease, sc in each sc across to last 2 sc, decrease; at end of Row 16, do **not** finish off: 15 sc.

EDGING

Rnd 1: Ch 1, sc in end of each row across; working in free loops of beginning ch *(Fig. 28b, page 138)*, sc in first ch, skip next 5 chs, 2 sc in next ch, skip next ch, sc in next 3 chs, slip st in next ch, sc in next 3 chs, skip next ch, 2 sc in next ch, skip next 5 chs, sc in last ch; sc in end of each row across; 2 sc in first sc, hdc in next sc, (dc, tr) in next sc, tr in next sc, (tr, dc) in next sc, hdc in next sc, sc in next sc, slip st in next sc, sc in next sc, hdc in next sc, (dc, tr) in next sc, tr in next sc, (tr, dc) in next sc, hdc in next sc, 2 sc in last sc; join with slip st to Back Loop Only of first sc *(Fig. 27, page 138)*.

Rnd 2: Slip st in in Back Loop Only of each st around; join with slip st to first st, finish off.

STEM

With Brown, ch 10 **loosely**; sc in second ch from hook and in each ch across; finish off leaving a long end for sewing.

With **right** side facing, sew one end of Stem to center top of Apple; fold Stem in half to form a loop and sew first sc to **wrong** side of Apple.

NAPKIN (LEAF)

Make a ¼" hem on all sides of green fabric.
Using photo as a guide for placement, insert fabric through Stem.

CHECKERED FABRIC RUG

Finished Size: Approximately 23" x 30"

MATERIALS

100% Cotton Fabric, 44/45" wide, approximately:
Color A (Red) - 10 yards
Color B (Off-white) - 8 yards
Crochet hook, size Q (15.00 mm) **or** size needed for gauge

Prepare fabric and tear into 3" wide strips *(see Preparing Fabric Strips and Joining Fabric Strips, page 139)*.

GAUGE: 5 dc = 4" and 2 rows = 3½"

With Color A, ch 37 **loosely**.

Row 1 (Right side): Dc in fourth ch from hook and in next 5 chs changing to Color B in last dc worked, (dc in next 7 chs changing colors in last dc worked) 3 times, dc in last 7 chs: 35 sts.

Rows 2 and 3: Ch 3 **(counts as first dc, now and throughout)**, turn; dc in next 6 dc changing colors in last dc worked, (dc in next 7 dc changing colors in last dc worked) 3 times, dc in last 7 sts.

Row 4: Ch 3, turn; dc in next 6 dc changing colors in last dc worked, (dc in next 7 dc changing colors in last dc worked) 4 times.

Rows 5-7: Repeat Row 2, 3 times.

Row 8: Ch 3, turn; dc in next 6 dc changing colors in last dc worked, (dc in next 7 dc changing colors in last dc worked) 4 times.

Rows 9-12: Repeat Row 2, 4 times.

Edging: Ch 1, turn; sc evenly around working 3 sc in each corner; join with slip st to first sc, finish off.

Quick CHECKERED POT HOLDER

Finished Size: Approximately 6" x 5½"

MATERIALS
Bedspread Weight Cotton Thread (size 10), approximately:
Color A (Red) - 80 yards
Color B (Natural) - 60 yards
Steel crochet hook, size 1 (2.75 mm) **or** size needed for gauge

Note: Pot holder is worked holding 2 strands of thread together.

GAUGE: 13 sc and 13 rows = 2"

With Color A, ch 37 **loosely**.
Row 1 (Right side): Sc in second ch from hook and in next 3 chs changing to Color B in last sc worked *(Fig. 31a, page 138)*, (sc in next 4 chs changing colors in last sc worked) 7 times, sc in last 4 chs: 36 sc.
Note: Loop a short piece of thread around any stitch to mark last row as **right** *side.*
Row 2: Ch 1, turn; sc in first 4 sc changing colors in last sc worked, (sc in next 4 sc changing colors in last sc worked) 7 times, sc in last 4 sc.
Row 3: Ch 1, turn; sc in first 4 sc changing colors in last sc worked, (sc in next 4 sc changing colors in last sc worked) across.
Rows 4 and 5: Ch 1, turn; sc in first 4 sc changing colors in last sc worked, (sc in next 4 sc changing colors in last sc worked) 7 times, sc in last 4 sc.
Rows 6-30: Repeat Rows 3-5, 8 times, then repeat Row 3 once **more**.
Rows 31-33: Repeat Row 4, 3 times.
Edging: Ch 2, hdc evenly across end of rows; working in free loops of beginning ch *(Fig. 28b, page 138)*, (2 hdc, ch 3, 2 hdc) in first ch, hdc in each ch across to last ch, (2 hdc, ch 3, 2 hdc) in last ch; hdc evenly across end of rows; 2 hdc in first sc, ch 15 **loosely** (loop), being careful not to twist ch, join with slip st to first ch, sc in each ch around, 2 hdc in same st as last hdc worked, hdc in each sc across to last sc, (2 hdc, ch 3, 2 hdc) in last sc; join with slip st to top of beginning ch-2, finish off.

Quick APPLE POT HOLDER

Finished Size: Approximately 7" x 6"

MATERIALS
Bedspread Weight Cotton Thread (size 10), approximately:
Red - 115 yards
Green - 15 yards
Brown - 4 yards
Steel crochet hook, size 0 (3.25 mm) **or** size needed for gauge
Tapestry needle

Note: Pot holder is worked holding 2 strands of thread together.

GAUGE: 13 sc and 13 rows = 2¼"

APPLE
With Red, ch 19 **loosely**.
Row 1 (Right side): Sc in second ch from hook and in each ch across: 18 sc.
Note: Loop a short piece of thread around any stitch to mark last row as **right** *side.*
Row 2: Ch 1, turn; sc in each sc across.
Row 3: Ch 1, turn; 2 sc in first sc, sc in each sc across to last sc, 2 sc in last sc: 20 sc.
Rows 4-7: Repeat Rows 2 and 3, twice: 24 sc.
Row 8: Ch 1, turn; sc in each sc across.
Row 9: Ch 1, turn; 2 sc in first sc, sc in each sc across: 25 sc.
Rows 10 and 11: Repeat Rows 2 and 3: 27 sc.
Row 12: Ch 1, turn; sc in each sc across.
Row 13: Ch 1, turn; sc in each sc across to last sc, 2 sc in last sc: 28 sc.
Rows 14 and 15: Repeat Rows 8 and 9: 29 sc.
Rows 16 and 17: Repeat Rows 12 and 13: 30 sc.
Rows 18 and 19: Repeat Rows 2 and 3: 32 sc.
Rows 20-24: Ch 1, turn; sc in each sc across.
Note: To **decrease**, *pull up a loop in next 2 sc, YO and draw through all 3 loops on hook* **(counts as one sc)**.
Row 25: Decrease, sc in each sc across to last 2 sc, decrease: 30 sc.
Rows 26-28: Ch 1, turn; sc in each sc across.
Row 29: Repeat Row 25: 28 sc.
Rows 30 and 31: Ch 1, turn; sc in each sc across; do **not** finish off.

LEFT TOP
Row 1: Ch 1, turn; decrease, sc in next 12 sc, leave remaining 14 sc unworked: 13 sc.
Rows 2 and 3: Ch 1, turn; sc in each sc across.
Rows 4 and 5: Decrease, sc in each sc across to last 2 sc, decrease: 9 sc.
Finish off.

RIGHT TOP

Row 1: With **wrong** side facing, join Red with slip st in first unworked sc on Row 31; ch 1, sc in same st and in each sc across to last 2 sc, decrease: 13 sc.

Rows 2-5: Work same as Left Top; at end of Row 5, do **not** finish off.

EDGING

Ch 1, turn; 2 sc in first sc, sc in next 7 sc, 2 sc in next sc; sc in end of next 10 rows; 2 sc in next sc, sc in next 7 sc, 2 sc in next sc; sc in end of each row across; working in free loops of beginning ch *(Fig. 28b, page 138)*, sc in first ch, † hdc in next ch, dc in next 2 chs, 2 dc in next ch, dc in next 2 chs, hdc in next ch †, sc in next 2 chs, repeat from † to † once, sc in last ch; sc in end of each row across; join with slip st to first sc, finish off.

LEAF (Make 2)

With Green, ch 18 **loosely**.

Rnd 1: Slip st in third ch from hook, sc in next ch, † hdc in next ch, dc in next ch, htr in next ch *(Figs. 9a & b, page 132)*, tr in next 3 chs, 2 tr in next ch, tr in next 3 chs, htr in next ch, dc in next ch, hdc in next ch †, (sc, ch 2, sc) in last ch; working in free loops of beginning ch, repeat from † to † once, sc in next ch, slip st in next ch; finish off leaving a long end for sewing.

LOOP

With **right** side facing, join Brown with slip st to center top of Apple; ch 15 **loosely**; sc in second ch from hook and in each ch across, fold Loop in half, slip st in same st as joining **and** in first sc; finish off.

Using photo as a guide for placement, sew Leaves to Apple.

Quick THREAD APPLE APPLIQUÉ

Finished Size: Approximately 2¹/₂" tall x 2¹/₄" wide

MATERIALS

Bedspread Weight Cotton Thread (size 10), approximately:
    Red - 12 yards
    Green - small amount
    Brown - small amount
Crochet hook, size 7 (1.65 mm) **or** size needed for gauge
Tapestry needle
Purchased kitchen towel
Sewing needle and thread

GAUGE: 9 sc and 9 rows = 1"

APPLE

With Red, ch 16 **loosely**.

Row 1 (Right side): 2 Sc in second ch from hook, † (skip next ch, pull up a loop in next ch) twice, YO and draw through all 3 loops on hook, skip next ch †, sc in next 3 chs, repeat from † to † once, 2 sc in last ch: 9 sts.

Note: Loop a short piece of thread around any stitch to mark last row as **right** side.

Rows 2-4: Ch 1, turn; 2 sc in first sc, sc in each st across to last sc, 2 sc in last sc: 15 sc.

Rows 5-8: Ch 1, turn; sc in each sc across.

Row 9: Ch 1, turn; 2 sc in first sc, sc in each sc across to last sc, 2 sc in last sc: 17 sc.

Row 10: Ch 1, turn; sc in each sc across.

Row 11: Repeat Row 9: 19 sc.

Rows 12-18: Ch 1, turn; sc in each sc across.

Note: To **decrease**, pull up a loop in next 2 sc, YO and draw through all 3 loops on hook **(counts as one sc)**.

Row 19: Ch 1, turn; decrease, sc in each sc across to last 2 sc, decrease: 17 sc.

Row 20: Ch 1, turn; sc in each sc across.

Rows 21 and 22: Repeat Rows 19 and 20: 15 sc.

Row 23: Ch 1, turn; sc in first 3 sc, hdc in next sc, dc in next 3 sc, slip st in next sc, dc in next 3 sc, hdc in next sc, sc in last 3 sc.

Row 24: Ch 1, turn; decrease, sc in next 2 sts, hdc in next dc, sc in next dc, slip st in next 3 sts, sc in next dc, hdc in next dc, sc in next 2 sts, decrease; finish off.

LEAF

With Green, ch 14 **loosely**; sc in second ch from hook and in next ch, hdc in next 2 chs, dc in next 2 chs, 2 tr in next ch, dc in next 2 chs, hdc in next 2 chs, sc in next ch, (sc, ch 1, sc) in last ch; working in free loops of beginning ch *(Fig. 28b, page 138)*, sc in next ch, hdc in next 2 chs, dc in next 2 chs, 2 tr in next ch, dc in next 2 chs, hdc in next 2 chs, sc in next 2 chs, ch 1; join with slip st to first sc, finish off leaving a long end for sewing.

STEM

With Brown, ch 7 **loosely**; slip st in second ch from hook and in each ch across; finish off leaving a long end for sewing.

FINISHING

Sew Leaf and Stem to top of Apple.
See Washing and Blocking, page 140.
Sew Apple to kitchen towel.

FOR THE BEDROOM

This exquisite coverlet will transform your bedroom into a haven for dreams and slumber. Lavishly textured with popcorn stitches, the bedspread has a repeated geometric motif and is worked in size 10 cotton thread. Our instructions let you re-create this antique beauty for any size bed.

THREAD COVERLET

Finished Size: Twin Size - approximately 58" x 86"
Full Size - approximately 73" x 86"
Queen Size - approximately 81" x 90"
King Size - approximately 95" x 90"

MATERIALS

Bedspread Weight Cotton Thread (size 10), approximately:
Twin Size - 11,675 yards
Full Size - 14,785 yards
Queen Size - 17, 220 yards
King Size - 20,495 yards
Steel crochet hook, size 7 (1.65 mm) **or** size needed for gauge
Tapestry needle

GAUGE: 9 dc and 4 rows = 1"
One Motif = 4¹/₂" (from straight edge to straight edge)

MOTIF

(Make 278 for Twin Size, 352 for Full Size, 410 for Queen Size, and 488 for King Size)
Ch 6, join with slip st to form a ring.

Rnd 1 (Right side)**:** Ch 3 **(counts as first dc, now and throughout)**, 17 dc in ring; join with slip st to first dc: 18 dc.
Note: Work in Back Loops Only throughout (Fig. 27, page 138).

Rnd 2: Ch 3, dc in same st and in next dc, (2 dc in each of next 2 dc, dc in next dc) around to last dc, 2 dc in last dc; join with slip st to first dc: 30 dc.

Rnd 3: Ch 3, dc in same st and in next 3 dc, (2 dc in each of next 2 dc, dc in next 3 dc) around to last dc, 2 dc in last dc; join with slip st to first dc: 42 dc.

*Note: To work **Popcorn**, 5 dc in next dc, drop loop from hook, insert hook in first dc of 5-dc group, hook dropped loop and draw through (Fig. 15b, page 134), ch 1 to close.*

Rnd 4: Ch 3, dc in same st and in next 2 dc, work Popcorn in next dc, dc in next 2 dc, 2 dc in next dc, ch 2, ★ 2 dc in next dc, dc in next 2 dc, work Popcorn in next dc, dc in next 2 dc, 2 dc in next dc, ch 2; repeat from ★ around; join with slip st to first dc: 6 Popcorns.

Rnd 5: Ch 3, dc in same st and in next 7 sts, 2 dc in next dc, ch 2, ★ 2 dc in next dc, dc in next 7 sts, 2 dc in next dc, ch 2; repeat from ★ around; join with slip st to first dc: 66 dc.

Rnd 6: Ch 3, dc in same st and in next 2 dc, work Popcorn in next dc, dc in next 3 dc, work Popcorn in next dc, dc in next 2 dc, 2 dc in next dc, ch 3, ★ 2 dc in next dc, dc in next 2 dc, work Popcorn in next dc, dc in next 3 dc, work Popcorn in next dc, dc in next 2 dc, 2 dc in next dc, ch 3; repeat from ★ around; join with slip st to first dc: 12 Popcorns.

Rnd 7: Ch 3, dc in same st and in next 11 sts, 2 dc in next dc, ch 3, ★ 2 dc in next dc, dc in next 11 sts, 2 dc in next dc, ch 3; repeat from ★ around; join with slip st to first dc: 90 dc.

Rnd 8: Ch 3, dc in same st and in next 2 dc, work Popcorn in next dc, (dc in next 3 dc, work Popcorn in next dc) twice, dc in next 2 dc, 2 dc in next dc, ch 3, ★ 2 dc in next dc, dc in next 2 dc, work Popcorn in next dc, (dc in next 3 dc, work Popcorn in next dc) twice, dc in next 2 dc, 2 dc in next dc, ch 3; repeat from ★ around; join with slip st to first dc: 18 Popcorns.

Rnd 9: Ch 3, dc in same st and in next 15 sts, 2 dc in next dc, ch 3, ★ 2 dc in next dc, dc in next 15 sts, 2 dc in next dc, ch 3; repeat from ★ around; join with slip st to first dc, finish off: 114 dc.

ASSEMBLY

With **wrong** sides together and working through **inside** loops only, whipstitch Motifs together, following Placement Diagram, page 44 *(Fig. 35b, page 140)*.

See Washing and Blocking, page 140.

THREAD COVERLET
PLACEMENT DIAGRAMS

Twin Size

King Size

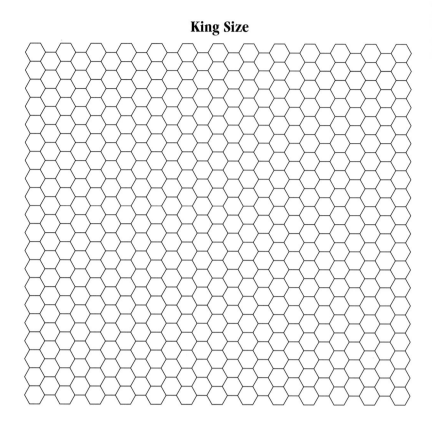

Full Size

Queen Size

MOROCCAN TILE AFGHAN

Continued from page 28.

EDGING

Note: Work in Back Loops Only throughout.

Rnd 1: With **right** side facing, skip 2 dtr on any corner and join Color B with slip st in next tr; ch 1, 2 sc in same st, ★ † (sc in each st across to next joining, dc in joining) across to last Square, sc in next 28 sts, (sc, hdc, dc) in next dtr, (dc, hdc, sc) in next dtr †, 2 sc in next tr; repeat from ★ 2 times **more**, then repeat from † to † once; join with slip st to first sc changing to Color E *(Fig. 31b, page 138)*: 736 sts.

Note: To **decrease**, pull up a loop in next 2 sc, YO and draw through all 3 loops on hook **(counts as one sc)**.

Rnd 2: Ch 3, hdc in same st, ★ † (hdc, sc) in next sc, sc in next sc, decrease, sc in next st, (hdc in next st, dc in next st, 2 tr in each of next 2 sts, dc in next st, hdc in next st, sc in next st, decrease, sc in next sc) across to within 3 sts of next hdc at corner, (sc, hdc) in next sc, (hdc, dc) in next sc, dc in next sc, (dc, tr) in next hdc, tr in next 2 dc, (tr, dc) in next hdc, dc in next sc †, (dc, hdc) in next sc; repeat from ★ 2 times **more**, then repeat from † to † once; join with slip st to top of beginning ch-3 changing to Color C: 824 sts.

Rnd 3: Ch 1, sc in same st and in next 4 sts, ★ † (skip next sc, sc in next 4 sts, 2 sc in each of next 2 tr, sc in next 4 sts) across to within 8 sts of next tr at corner, skip next sc, sc in next 8 sts, 2 sc in each of next 2 tr †, sc in next 8 sts; repeat from ★ 2 times **more**, then repeat from † to † once, sc in last 3 sts; join with slip st to first sc changing to Color A: 896 sc.

Rnd 4: Ch 1, sc in same st and in next 3 sc, ★ † (skip next 2 sc, sc in next 4 sc, 2 sc in each of next 2 sc, sc in next 4 sc) across to within 9 sts of next 2-sc group at corner, skip next 2 sc, sc in next 8 sc, 2 sc in each of next 2 sc †, sc in next 8 sc; repeat from ★ 2 times **more**, then repeat from † to † once, sc in last 4 sc; join with slip st to first sc changing to Color F.

Rnd 5: Ch 2, ★ † dc in next 2 sc, tr in next 2 sc, dc in next 2 sc, hdc in next sc, (sc in next sc, decrease, sc in next sc, hdc in next sc, dc in next 2 sc, tr in next 2 sc, dc in next 2 sc, hdc in next sc) across to within 4 sts of next 2-sc group at corner, sc in next 2 sc, hdc in next sc, dc in next sc, (dc, tr) in next sc, tr in next 2 sc, (tr, dc) in next sc, dc in next sc, hdc in next sc, sc in next 2 sc †, hdc in next sc; repeat from ★ 2 times **more**, then repeat from † to † once; join with slip st to top of beginning ch-2, finish off.

CHINA CABINET EDGINGS

Continued from page 33.

Row 16: Ch 3, turn; work Shell in next ch-2 sp, (ch 2, work Shell in next ch-2 sp) twice, ch 3, skip next ch-3 sp, dc in next 6 dc, work Shell in next ch-2 sp, ch 3, sc in next loop, ch 3, work Shell in last ch-2 sp.

Row 17: Ch 5, turn; work Shell in first ch-2 sp, ch 6, skip next 2 ch-3 sps, work Shell in next ch-2 sp, dc in next 8 dc, ch 3, skip next ch-3 sp, work Shell in next ch-2 sp, ch 3, skip next ch-2 sp, (work Shell, ch 2, 2 dc) in next ch-2 sp, ch 3, skip next ch-2 sp, work Shell in next ch-2 sp, ch 3, skip next 3 dc on previous point, sc in next dc.

Row 18: Ch 3, turn; work Shell in first ch-2 sp, ch 3, skip next ch-3 sp, (work Shell in next ch-2 sp, ch 3) twice, skip next ch-3 sp, work Shell in next ch-2 sp, ch 3, skip next ch-3 sp, dc in next 10 dc, work Shell in next ch-2 sp, ch 3, sc in next loop, ch 3, work Shell in last ch-2 sp.

Row 19: Ch 5, turn; work Shell in first ch-2 sp, ch 6, skip next 2 ch-3 sps, work Shell in next ch-2 sp, dc in next 12 dc, ch 3, skip next ch-3 sp, work Shell in next ch-2 sp, ch 3, skip next ch-3 sp, (work Shell in next sp, ch 3) 3 times, skip next ch-3 sp, work Shell in next ch-2 sp, ch 3, skip next 3 dc on previous point, sc in next dc.

Row 20: Ch 3, turn; work Shell in first ch-2 sp, ch 3, (skip next ch-3 sp, work Shell in next ch-2 sp, ch 3) 4 times, skip next ch-3 sp, dc in next 14 dc, work Shell in next ch-2 sp, ch 3, sc in next loop, ch 3, work Shell in last ch-2 sp.

Row 21: Ch 5, turn; work Shell in first ch-2 sp, ch 6, skip next 2 ch-3 sps, work Shell in next ch-2 sp, dc in next 16 dc, ch 3, (skip next ch-3 sp, work Shell in next ch-2 sp, ch 3) 5 times, skip next 3 dc on previous point, sc in next dc.

Row 22: Ch 3, turn; ★ (2 dc, ch 3, slip st in third ch from hook, 2 dc) in next ch-2 sp, ch 4, skip next ch-3 sp; repeat from ★ 4 times **more**, dc in next 18 dc, work Shell in next ch-2 sp, ch 3, sc in next loop, ch 3, work Shell in last ch-2 sp. Repeat Rows 11-22 for pattern, ending by working Row 22; finish off.

FINISHING

See Washing and Blocking, page 140.
Weave ribbon through sps along top of Edging.
Turn ends of ribbon under 1/2" to wrong side and sew in place.

gifts for all

Special people deserve gifts with a personal touch, and what could be more appropriate than a handcrafted surprise! When developing this assortment of gifts, we thought of some of our favorite people, including Mom and Dad, and fun gift-giving occasions such as a birthday or a housewarming. But you don't have to wait to share these presents, since the nicest reason is often "just because!"

Quick SWEET SEWING NOTIONS

Here's a sweet surprise for a seamstress! Featuring a medallion motif, our coordinating sewing notions are crocheted with cotton thread. The needle case is lined with fabric and has a felt circle to safely secure needles. Satin ribbon is woven through the eyelet rounds of the larger pincushion, and the beribboned chatelaine features a smaller pincushion, a thimble holder, and a loop to hold scissors.

Finished Size: Needle Case - 4" in diameter
Pincushion - 4" in diameter
Chatelaine - 2½" in diameter and 30" long

MATERIALS
Bedspread Weight Cotton Thread (size 10), approximately:
Needle Case - 55 yards
Pincushion - 54 yards
Chatelaine - 75 yards
Steel crochet hook, size 7 (1.65 mm) **or** size needed for gauge
Fabric - 15" square
Felt - 4" square
Polyester fiberfill
2 yards of ¼" wide ribbon
Tapestry needle
Sewing needle and thread
Small scissors
Thimble

GAUGE: 9 sts = 1"
Rnds 1-3 of Needle Case = 1½"

NEEDLE CASE
Ch 5; join with slip st to form a ring.
Rnd 1 (Right side): Ch 3 **(counts as first dc, now and throughout)**, 13 dc in ring; join with slip st to first dc: 14 dc.

Note: Loop a short piece of thread around any stitch to mark last round as **right** side.
Rnd 2: Ch 1, sc in same st, (ch 3, sc in next dc) around, ch 1, hdc in first sc to form last sp: 14 sps.
Rnd 3: Ch 5, dc in next ch-3 sp, (ch 2, dc in next ch-3 sp) around, ch 1, sc in third ch of beginning ch-5 to form last sp.
Rnd 4: Ch 3, dc in same sp, (2 dc, ch 2, 2 dc) in next ch-2 sp and in each ch-2 sp around, 2 dc in same sp as first dc, ch 1, sc in first dc to form last sp.
Rnd 5: Ch 3, (hdc, sc) in same sp, (sc, hdc, 2 dc, hdc, sc) in next ch-2 sp and in each ch-2 sp around, (sc, hdc, dc) in same sp as first dc; join with slip st to first dc: 14 scallops.
Rnd 6: Ch 1, sc in same st, ch 6, (sc in second dc of next scallop, ch 6) around; join with slip st to first sc: 14 loops.
Rnd 7: Slip st in first loop, ch 3, 7 dc in same loop, 8 dc in next loop and in each loop around; join with slip st to first dc.
Rnd 8: Ch 8, skip next 7 dc, sc in sp **before** next dc *(Fig. 29, page 138)*, (ch 8, skip next 8 dc, sc in sp **before** next dc) around; join with slip st to first ch.
Rnd 9: Ch 1, (sc, hdc, 5 dc, hdc, sc) in each loop around; join with slip st to first sc, finish off.

Repeat for second side; do **not** finish off.

Joining: With **wrong** sides together and working through **inside** loops of **both** pieces, slip st in first 23 sts, ch 15, **turn**; slip st in top of next scallop, **turn**; 30 sc in loop, slip st in same st as ch and in next 13 sts; finish off.

LINING

Using crocheted piece through Rnd 7 for pattern and adding ¼" seam allowance, cut 4 circles from fabric.

With **right** sides together and leaving an opening for turning, sew 2 fabric circles together using ¼" seam allowance.

Clip curve; turn right side out.

Sew opening closed.

Repeat for remaining 2 fabric circles.

Press fabric circles.

FINISHING

Cut a circle from felt slightly smaller than Lining.

Sew one Lining to wrong side of each crocheted piece along top of Rnd 7.

Place felt circle between both Linings and sew all 3 pieces together along edge of 2 8-dc groups at center of joining.

LARGE PINCUSHION

FRONT AND BACK

Make 2 pieces same as Needle Case through Rnd 9; finish off.

CUSHION

Using crocheted piece through Rnd 7 for pattern and adding ¼" seam allowance, cut 2 circles from fabric.

With **right** sides together and leaving an opening for turning, sew fabric circles together using ¼" seam allowance.

Clip curve; turn right side out.

Stuff Cushion with polyester fiberfill.

Sew opening closed.

Joining: With **wrong** sides of crocheted pieces together, weave 1 yard of ribbon through loops on Rnd 8, inserting Cushion before closing; tie ribbon in a bow.

CHATELAINE

SMALL PINCUSHION

BACK

Work same as Needle Case through Rnd 4; finish off.

CUSHION

Using crocheted piece for pattern and adding ¼" seam allowance, cut 2 circles from fabric.

With **right** sides together and leaving an opening for turning, sew fabric circles together using ¼" seam allowance.

Clip curve; turn right side out.

Stuff Cushion firmly with polyester fiberfill. Sew opening closed.

FRONT

Work same as Needle Case through Rnd 4; do **not** finish off.

Joining Rnd: Ch 3, with **wrong** sides together and working in ch-2 sps of **both** pieces, (hdc, sc) in same sp, (sc, hdc, 2 dc, hdc, sc) in next ch-2 sp and in each ch-2 sp around inserting Cushion before closing, (sc, hdc, dc) in same sp as first dc; join with slip st to first dc, do **not** finish off: 14 scallops.

STRAP

Row 1 (Right side): Ch 1, sc in same st, ch 1, sc in second dc of next scallop.

Row 2: Ch 5, turn; skip next ch, tr in last sc.

Row 3: Ch 5, turn; skip next ch, tr in next ch.

Repeat Row 3 until piece measures approximately 30" or to desired length, ending by working a **right** side row.

Edging: Ch 1, do **not** turn; (sc, hdc, 2 dc, hdc, sc) in each sp around working in ch-1 sp on Row 1, (sc, hdc, 2 dc, hdc) twice in same sp as first group; join with slip st to first sc, finish off.

THIMBLE HOLDER

Rnd 1 (Right side): Ch 4, 11 dc in fourth ch from hook; join with slip st to top of beginning ch: 12 sts.

Note: Mark last round as **right** side.

Rnd 2: Ch 3, dc in next 2 dc, 2 dc in next dc, (dc in next 3 dc, 2 dc in next dc) twice; join with slip st to first dc: 15 dc.

Rnd 3: Ch 3, dc in next 3 dc, 2 dc in next dc, (dc in next 4 dc, 2 dc in next dc) twice; join with slip st to first dc: 18 dc.

Rnd 4: Ch 7, skip next 2 dc, (dc in next dc, ch 4, skip next 2 dc) around; join with slip st to third ch of beginning ch-7: 6 sps.

Rnd 5: Slip st in first ch-4 sp, ch 1, (sc, hdc, 2 dc, hdc, sc) in same sp and in each ch-4 sp around; join with slip st to first sc, finish off.

FINISHING

Weave 1 yard of ribbon through sps of Strap. Sew end of ribbon to wrong side of Strap near Pincushion. Insert second end of ribbon through scissors and sew ribbon in place. Sew Thimble Holder to Strap above Pincushion.

Insert thimble in Holder.

Quick FANCY FINGERTIP TOWEL

An elegant housewarming gift, our linen fingertip towel is fashioned by attaching a dainty edging to a piece of linen. Tiny picots are formed along the edge as the beautiful trim is worked in size 20 cotton thread.

Finished Size: Edging - approximately 1¼" x 13"
Towel - approximately 13" x 17"

MATERIALS

Cotton Crochet Thread (size 20), approximately 35 yards
Steel crochet hook, size 9 (1.40 mm) **or** size needed for gauge
Linen - 14" x 18"
Pins
Sewing needle and thread

GAUGE: 20 dc = 2"

EDGING

Ch 135 **loosely**.

Row 1 (Right side): Dc in fourth ch from hook and in each ch across: 133 sts.

Note: Loop a short piece of thread around any stitch to mark last row as **right** side.

Row 2: Ch 1, turn; sc in first dc, ★ ch 3, skip next 5 dc, dc in next dc, (ch 1, dc) 4 times in same dc, ch 3, skip next 5 dc, sc in next st; repeat from ★ across: 11 dc groups.

Note: To work **Shell**, (2 dc, ch 1, 2 dc) in st or sp indicated.

Row 3: Ch 3, turn; (dc, ch 1, 2 dc) in first sc, ★ ch 1, skip next ch-3 sp, sc in next ch-1 sp, (ch 3, sc in next ch-1 sp) 3 times, ch 1, work Shell in next sc; repeat from ★ across: 12 Shells.

Row 4: Turn; slip st in first 2 dc and in next ch-1 sp, ch 3, (dc, ch 1, 2 dc) in same sp, ★ ch 2, skip next ch-1 sp, sc in next ch-3 sp, (ch 3, sc in next ch-3 sp) twice, ch 2, work Shell in next Shell (ch-1 sp); repeat from ★ across.

Row 5: Turn; slip st in first 2 dc and in next ch-1 sp, ch 3, (dc, ch 1, 2 dc) in same sp, ★ ch 3, skip next ch-2 sp, (sc in next ch-3 sp, ch 3) twice, work Shell in next Shell; repeat from ★ across.

Row 6: Turn; slip st in first 2 dc and in next ch-1 sp, ch 3, (dc, ch 4, slip st in fourth ch from hook, 2 dc) in same sp, ★ ch 4, skip next ch-3 sp, sc in next ch-3 sp, ch 4, (2 dc, ch 4, slip st in fourth ch from hook, 2 dc) in next Shell; repeat from ★ across; finish off.

FINISHING

See Washing and Blocking, page 140.

For towel, press edges of linen ¼" to wrong side; press ¼" to wrong side again and hem. Pin Edging along hemline on right side of linen and sew in place.

DELIGHTFUL DOILY SET

These airy doilies make wonderful "thank-you" gifts for a friend who enjoys old-fashioned beauty. Stitched with bedspread weight cotton thread, our large doily features a lacy center surrounded by rounds of pretty shells. For a delightful match, we created a smaller doily using portions of the large pattern.

Finished Size: Large Doily - approximately 14" in diameter
Small Doily - approximately 8½" in diameter

MATERIALS

Bedspread Weight Cotton Thread (size 10), approximately:
Large - 200 yards
Small - 70 yards
Steel crochet hook, size 7 (1.65 mm) **or** size needed for gauge

GAUGE: Rnds 1-3 = 1½"

LARGE DOILY

Ch 6; join with slip st to form a ring.
Rnd 1 (Right side)**:** Ch 1, 12 sc in ring; join with slip st to first sc.
Rnd 2: Ch 1, sc in same st, (ch 5, skip next sc, sc in next sc) 5 times, ch 2, skip last sc, dc in first sc to form last loop: 6 loops.
Rnd 3: Ch 6, (3 dc, hdc, sc) in same loop, (sc, hdc, 3 dc, ch 3, 3 dc, hdc, sc) in next loop and in each loop around, (sc, hdc, 2 dc) in same loop as beginning ch-6; join with slip st to third ch of beginning ch-6 **(now and throughout, unless otherwise specified).**
Rnd 4: Slip st in first ch-3 sp, ch 6, dc in same sp, ch 9, ★ (dc, ch 3, dc) in next ch-3 sp, ch 9; repeat from ★ around; join.
Rnd 5: Slip st in first ch-3 sp, ch 6, dc in same sp, ch 5, (sc, ch 5) twice in next loop, ★ (dc, ch 3, dc) in next ch-3 sp, ch 5, (sc, ch 5) twice in next loop; repeat from ★ around; join.
Rnd 6: Slip st in first ch-3 sp, ch 6, dc in same sp, ch 5, sc in next loop, ch 5, (dc, ch 3, dc) in next loop, ch 5, sc in next loop, ch 5, ★ (dc, ch 3, dc) in next ch-3 sp, ch 5, sc in next loop, ch 5, (dc, ch 3, dc) in next loop, ch 5, sc in next loop, ch 5; repeat from ★ around; join.
Rnd 7: Slip st in first ch-3 sp, ch 6, dc in same sp, ch 9, skip next 2 loops, ★ (dc, ch 3, dc) in next ch-3 sp, ch 9, skip next 2 loops; repeat from ★ around; join.
Rnd 8: Slip st in first ch-3 sp, ch 6, dc in same sp, ch 5, (sc, ch 5) twice in next loop, ★ (dc, ch 3, dc) in next ch-3 sp, ch 5, (sc, ch 5) twice in next loop; repeat from ★ around; join.
Rnd 9: Slip st in first ch-3 sp, ch 6, dc in same sp, ch 7, skip next loop, sc in next loop, ch 7, skip next loop, ★ (dc, ch 3, dc) in next ch-3 sp, ch 7, skip next loop, sc in next loop, ch 7, skip next loop; repeat from ★ around; join.

Rnd 10: Slip st in first ch-3 sp, ch 6, dc in same sp, ch 13, skip next 2 loops, ★ (dc, ch 3, dc) in next ch-3 sp, ch 13, skip next 2 loops; repeat from ★ around; join.
Rnd 11: Slip st in first ch-3 sp, ch 6, dc in same sp, ch 7, (sc, ch 7) twice in next loop, ★ (dc, ch 3, dc) in next ch-3 sp, ch 7, (sc, ch 7) twice in next loop; repeat from ★ around; join.
Rnd 12: Slip st in first ch-3 sp, ch 6, dc in same sp, ch 7, sc in next loop, ch 7, (dc, ch 3, dc) in next loop, ch 7, sc in next loop, ch 7, ★ (dc, ch 3, dc) in next ch-3 sp, ch 7, sc in next loop, ch 7, (dc, ch 3, dc) in next loop, ch 7, sc in next loop, ch 7; repeat from ★ around; join.
Rnds 13-16: Repeat Rnds 7-10.
Rnd 17: Slip st in first ch-3 sp, ch 6, dc in same sp, ch 5, (sc, ch 5) twice in next loop, ★ (dc, ch 3, dc) in next ch-3 sp, ch 5, (sc, ch 5) twice in next loop; repeat from ★ around; join.
Rnd 18: Slip st in first ch-3 sp, ch 6, dc in same sp, ch 1, skip next loop, (6 dc, ch 3, 6 dc) in next loop, ch 1, skip next loop, ★ (dc, ch 3, dc) in next ch-3 sp, ch 1, skip next loop, (6 dc, ch 3, 6 dc) in next loop, ch 1, skip next loop; repeat from ★ around; join.
Rnd 19: Slip st in first ch-3 sp, ch 6, dc in same sp, ch 7, sc in next ch-3 sp, ch 7, ★ (dc, ch 3, dc) in next ch-3 sp, ch 7, sc in next ch-3 sp, ch 7; repeat from ★ around; join.
Rnd 20: Slip st in first ch-3 sp, ch 1, (sc, ch 5, sc) in same sp, ch 5, (sc in next loop, ch 5) twice, ★ (sc, ch 5, sc) in next ch-3 sp, ch 5, (sc in next loop, ch 5) twice; repeat from ★ around; join with slip st to first sc.
Rnd 21: Slip st in first loop, ch 3, (5 dc, ch 3, 6 dc) in same loop, skip next loop, ★ (6 dc, ch 3, 6 dc) in next loop, skip next loop; repeat from ★ around; join with slip st to top of beginning ch-3.
Rnd 22: Slip st in next 5 dc and in next ch-3 sp, ch 1, sc in same sp, ch 9, (sc in next ch-3 sp, ch 9) around; join with slip st to first sc: 48 loops.
Rnd 23: Ch 8, dc in same st, ch 7, ★ (dc, ch 5, dc) in next sc, ch 7; repeat from ★ around; join with slip st to third ch of beginning ch-8.
Rnd 24: Slip st in first loop, ch 3, (5 dc, ch 3, 6 dc) in same loop, ch 1, sc **around** loops in previous 2 rnds, ch 1, ★ (6 dc, ch 3, 6 dc) in next loop, ch 1, sc **around** loops in previous 2 rnds, ch 1; repeat from ★ around; join with slip st to top of beginning ch-3, finish off.

See Washing and Blocking, page 140.

SMALL DOILY

Work same as Large Doily through Rnd 10.

Rnd 11: Slip st in first ch-3 sp, ch 6, dc in same sp, ch 5, (sc, ch 5) twice in next loop, ★ (dc, ch 3, dc) in next ch-3 sp, ch 5, (sc, ch 5) twice in next loop; repeat from ★ around; join.

Rnd 12: Slip st in first ch-3 sp, ch 6, dc in same sp, ch 3, skip next loop, (6 dc, ch 3, 6 dc) in next loop, ch 3, skip next loop, ★ (dc, ch 3, dc) in next ch-3 sp, ch 3, skip next loop, (6 dc, ch 3, 6 dc) in next loop, ch 3, skip next loop; repeat from ★ around; join.

Rnd 13: Slip st in first ch-3 sp, ch 6, dc in same sp, ch 9, skip next ch-3 sp, sc in next ch-3 sp, ch 9, skip next ch-3 sp, ★ (dc, ch 3, dc) in next ch-3 sp, ch 9, skip next ch-3 sp, sc in next ch-3 sp, ch 9, skip next ch-3 sp; repeat from ★ around; join.

Rnd 14: Slip st in first ch-3 sp, ch 1, (sc, ch 5, sc) in same sp, ch 7, sc in next loop, ch 5, sc in next loop, ch 7, ★ (sc, ch 5, sc) in next ch-3 sp, ch 7, sc in next loop, ch 5, sc in next loop, ch 7; repeat from ★ around; join with slip st to first sc.

Rnd 15: Slip st in first loop, ch 3, (5 dc, ch 3, 6 dc) in same loop, ch 1, sc **around** loops in previous 2 rnds, ch 1, ★ (6 dc, ch 3, 6 dc) in next loop, ch 1, sc **around** loops in previous 2 rnds, ch 1; repeat from ★ around; join with slip st to top of beginning ch-3, finish off.

See Washing and Blocking, page 140.

Quick ITTY-BITTY AFGHAN

This doll-size delight will charm a little girl or a collector of miniatures. The tiny afghan is stitched with cotton thread and features floral motifs worked in variegated pastels. Each "flower" is surrounded by black fill-in motifs.

Finished Size: Approximately 7" x 9"

MATERIALS
Bedspread Weight Cotton Thread (size 10), approximately:
  MC (Black) - 80 yards
  CC (Variegated) - 40 yards
Steel crochet hook, size 7 (1.65 mm) **or** size needed for gauge

GAUGE: One Motif = 2¼" (point to point)

PATTERN STITCHES
HDC CLUSTER
★ YO, insert hook in sp indicated, YO and pull up a loop; repeat from ★ once **more**, YO and draw through all 5 loops on hook *(Figs. 13a & b, page 134)*.
TR CLUSTER
★ YO twice, insert hook in st or sp indicated, YO and pull up a loop, (YO and draw through 2 loops on hook) twice; repeat from ★ once **more**, YO and draw through all 3 loops on hook.

FIRST MOTIF
With CC, ch 6; join with slip st to form a ring.
Rnd 1 (Right side)**:** Ch 2, hdc in ring, (ch 3, work hdc Cluster in ring) 7 times, ch 1, skip beginning ch-2 and work hdc in first hdc to form last sp: 8 sps.
Note: Loop a short piece of thread around any stitch to mark last round as **right** side.
Rnd 2: Ch 1, sc in same sp, ch 5, (sc in next ch-3 sp, ch 5) around; join with slip st to first sc: 8 loops.
Rnd 3: Ch 1, 5 sc in each loop around; join with slip st to first sc, finish off: 40 sc.
Rnd 4: With **right** side facing, join MC with slip st in center sc of any 5-sc group; ch 1, sc in same st, ch 7, (sc in center sc of next 5-sc group, ch 7) around; join with slip st to first sc: 8 loops.
Rnd 5: Ch 1, (4 sc, ch 3, 4 sc) in each loop around; join with slip st to first sc, finish off.

ADDITIONAL MOTIFS
Work same as First Motif through Rnd 4.
Work One-Sided or Two-Sided Joining, forming 3 vertical strips of 4 Motifs each.

ONE-SIDED JOINING
Rnd 5: Ch 1, (4 sc, ch 3, 4 sc) in first 6 loops, 4 sc in next loop, ch 1, with **wrong** sides together, slip st in corresponding ch-3 sp on **previous Motif** *(Fig. 32, page 138)*, ch 1, 4 sc in same loop on **new Motif**, 4 sc in next loop, ch 1, slip st in next ch-3 sp on **previous Motif**, ch 1, 4 sc in same loop on **new Motif**; join with slip st to first sc, finish off.

TWO-SIDED JOINING
Rnd 5: Ch 1, (4 sc, ch 3, 4 sc) in first 4 loops, ★ 4 sc in next loop, ch 1, with **wrong** sides together, slip st in corresponding ch-3 sp on **previous Motif**, ch 1, 4 sc in same loop on **new Motif**, 4 sc in next loop, ch 1, slip st in next ch-3 sp on **previous Motif**, ch 1, 4 sc in same loop on **new Motif**; repeat from ★ once **more**; join with slip st to first sc, finish off.

FILL-IN MOTIF
With MC, ch 4; join with slip st to form a ring.
Rnd 1 (Right side)**:** Ch 1, (sc in ring, ch 7) 4 times; join with slip st to first sc: 4 loops.
Rnd 2: Ch 1, 4 sc in first loop, ch 1, with **wrong** sides of joined Motifs together and working in joining sp between Motifs, slip st in any joining, ch 1, 4 sc in same loop on **Fill-In Motif**, ★ 4 sc in next loop, ch 1, slip st in next joining, ch 1, 4 sc in same loop on **Fill-In Motif**; repeat from ★ around; join with slip st to first sc, finish off.
Repeat for remaining 5 openings between joined Motifs.

EDGING

Rnd 1: With **right** side facing, join MC with slip st in sp **between** corner 4-sc groups on top right corner *(Fig. 29, page 138)*; ch 3, work (tr, ch 7, tr Cluster) in same sp, † ch 3, sc in next ch-3 sp, ch 5, sc in next ch-3 sp, ch 3, ★ work (tr Cluster, ch 5, tr Cluster) in next joining, ch 3, sc in next ch-3 sp, ch 5, sc in next ch-3 sp, ch 3; repeat from ★ once **more**, skip next 4 sc, work (tr Cluster, ch 7, tr Cluster) in sp **before** next sc, ch 3, sc in next ch-3 sp, ch 5, sc in next ch-3 sp, ch 3, [work (tr Cluster, ch 5, tr Cluster) in next joining, ch 3, sc in next ch-3 sp, ch 5, sc in next ch-3 sp, ch 3] 3 times, skip next 4 sc †, work (tr Cluster, ch 7, tr Cluster) in sp **before** next sc, repeat from † to † once; skip beginning ch-3 and join with slip st to first tr.

Rnd 2: (Slip st, ch 1, 4 sc, ch 3, 4 sc) in first corner loop, 4 sc in next ch-3 sp, ★ (4 sc, ch 3, 4 sc) in next loop, 4 sc in next ch-3 sp; repeat from ★ around; join with slip st to first sc, finish off.

See Washing and Blocking, page 140.

Quick BASKET OF CHEER

*Crafted with size 5 cotton thread, our lovely striped basket is ideal
for delivering sweet treats, get-well wishes, or birthday surprises.
Add a ribbon-tied spray of flowers for a cheery finishing touch.*

Finished Size: Approximately 6" in diameter

MATERIALS
Cotton Crochet Thread (size 5), approximately:
  MC (White) - 88 yards
  CC (Blue) - 48 yards
Steel crochet hook, size 0 (3.25 mm) **or** size needed for gauge
Tapestry needle
Starching materials: Commercial fabric stiffener, blocking board, plastic wrap, resealable plastic bag, terry towel, paper towels, cardboard, and stainless steel pins

GAUGE: Rnds 1 and 2 of Bottom = 1¹/₂"

BOTTOM

With MC, ch 5; join with slip st to form a ring.
Rnd 1 (Right side)**:** Ch 3 **(counts as first dc, now and throughout)**, 11 dc in ring; join with slip st to first dc: 12 dc.
Note #1: Loop a short piece of thread around any stitch to mark last round as **right** side.
Note #2: To work **Front Post double crochet (abbreviated FPdc)**, YO, insert hook from **front** to **back** around post of st indicated, YO and pull up a loop **even** with loop on hook, (YO and draw through 2 loops on hook) twice.
Rnd 2: Slip st from **front** to **back** around first dc *(Fig. 17, page 135)*, ch 4, (work FPdc around next dc, ch 1) around; join with slip st to third ch of beginning ch-4: 12 ch-1 sps.
Rnd 3: Slip st from **front** to **back** around first dc, ch 6, (work FPdc around next FPdc, ch 3) around; join with slip st to third ch of beginning ch-6.
Rnd 4: Slip st from **front** to **back** around first dc, ch 4, dc in next ch-3 sp, ch 1, (work FPdc around next FPdc, ch 1, dc in next ch-3 sp, ch 1) around; join with slip st to third ch of beginning ch-4: 24 ch-1 sps.
Rnds 5 and 6: Slip st from **front** to **back** around first dc, ch 5, (work FPdc around next st, ch 2) around; join with slip st to third ch of beginning ch-5.
Rnd 7: Slip st from **front** to **back** around first dc, ch 6, (work FPdc around next FPdc, ch 3) around; join with slip st to third ch of beginning ch-6.
Rnd 8: Slip st from **front** to **back** around first dc, ch 4, dc in next ch-3 sp, ch 1, (work FPdc around next FPdc, ch 1, dc in next ch-3 sp, ch 1) around; join with slip st to third ch of beginning ch-4: 48 ch-1 sps.

Rnd 9: Ch 1, sc in first st, sc in each ch-1 sp and in each dc and each FPdc around; join with slip st to first sc, do **not** finish off: 96 sc.

SIDE

Ch 14 **loosely.**
Row 1: Dc in fourth ch from hook and in each ch across **(3 skipped chs count as first dc)**; drop MC, with **right** side facing, skip first 2 sc on Rnd 9 of Bottom, with CC, slip st in Back Loop Only of next sc *(Fig. 27, page 138)*: 12 dc.
Row 2: Ch 1, turn; sc in each dc across: 12 sc.
Row 3: Ch 3, turn; work FPdc around dc in row **below** next sc, skip sc behind FPdc **(now and throughout)**, (dc in next sc, work FPdc around dc in row **below** next sc) across; drop CC, skip next sc on Bottom, with MC, slip st in Back Loop Only of next sc.
Row 4: Ch 1, turn; sc in each FPdc and in each dc across.
Row 5: Ch 3, turn; dc in next sc, (work FPdc around dc in row **below** next sc, dc in next sc) across; drop MC, skip next sc on Bottom, with CC, slip st in Back Loop Only of next sc.
Row 6: Ch 1, turn; sc in each dc and in each FPdc across.
Rows 7-95: Repeat Rows 3-6, 22 times, then repeat Row 3 once **more.**
Joining: Turn; with **right** side of ends together and working through **both** loops of last row and in free loops of beginning ch *(Fig. 28b, page 138)*, slip st in each st across; do **not** finish off.

EDGING

Rnd 1: Ch 1, with **right** side facing, sc in joining and in end of each row around; join with slip st to Back Loop Only of first sc: 96 sc.
Rnd 2: Slip st in Back Loop Only of each sc around; join with slip st to first slip st, finish off.

HANDLE (Make 2)

With MC, ch 31 **loosely.**
Row 1 (Right side)**:** Sc in back ridge of second ch from hook and in each ch across *(Fig. 2a, page 131)*; finish off leaving a long end for sewing: 30 sc.

Spacing Handle ends 2 MC stripes apart, sew ends of Handle to Edging above MC stripe. Repeat to attach remaining Handle to opposite side of basket.
See Starching and Blocking, page 142.

Quick CHARMING CARNATIONS

Tipped with a blush of pink, our ruffly carnations look beautiful in a bud vase with dried florals and ribbon. What a charming remembrance for a special lady!

Finished Size: Approximately 2³/4" in diameter

MATERIALS

For **each** Carnation:

Bedspread Weight Cotton Thread (size 10), approximately:

MC (White) - 42 yards

CC (Pink) - 26 yards

Green - 4 yards

Steel crochet hook, size 7 (1.65 mm) **or** size needed for gauge

Tapestry needle

2 - 18" lengths of 18 gauge wire

Florist tape

Glue gun

GAUGE: 9 sts = 1"

BASE

Rnd 1 (Right side)**:** With Green, ch 5, 14 tr in fifth ch from hook; join with slip st to top of beginning ch: 15 sts.

Note: Loop a short piece of thread around any stitch to mark last round as **right** side.

Rnd 2: Ch 1, sc in Front Loop Only of same st and in each tr around *(Fig. 27, page 138)*; join with slip st to both loops of first sc.

Rnd 3: Ch 3 **loosely**, sc in second ch from hook, hdc in next ch, **turn**; working in both loops, slip st in next 3 sc, ★ ch 3 **loosely**, sc in second ch from hook, hdc in next ch, slip st in next 3 sc; repeat from ★ around, working last slip st in same sc as joining; finish off.

FLOWER

Rnd 1: With **right** side facing and working in free loops on Rnd 1 of Base **behind** Rnds 2 and 3 *(Fig. 28a, page 138)*, join MC with slip st in first st; ch 1, sc in same st and in next tr, 2 sc in next tr, (sc in next 2 tr, 2 sc in next tr) around; join with slip st to first sc: 20 sc.

Rnd 2: Ch 3 **(counts as first dc, now and throughout)**, dc in Back Loop Only of next sc and in each sc around; join with slip st to both loops of first dc.

Rnd 3: Ch 4 **(counts as first tr, now and throughout)**, tr in Back Loop Only of next dc and in each dc around; join with slip st to both loops of first tr.

Rnd 4: Ch 4, working in Back Loops Only, 2 tr in same st, 3 tr in next tr and in each tr around; join with slip st to both loops of first tr changing to CC *(Fig. 31b, page 138)*: 60 tr.

Rnd 5: Ch 1, working in Back Loops Only, sc in same st, ch 2, (sc, ch 2) twice in next tr, ★ sc in next tr, ch 2, (sc, ch 2) twice in next tr; repeat from ★ around; join with slip st to both loops of first sc, finish off.

Rnd 6: With **right** side facing and working in free loops on Rnd 3 of Flower, join MC with slip st in first tr; ch 1, sc in same st, ch 2, (sc in next tr, ch 2) around; join with slip st to first sc: 20 ch-2 sps.

Rnd 7: Slip st in first ch-2 sp, ch 4, tr in same sp, tr in next ch-2 sp, (2 tr in next ch-2 sp, tr in next ch-2 sp) around; join with slip st to first tr changing to CC: 30 tr.

Rnd 8: Repeat Rnd 5.

Rnd 9: With **right** side facing and working in free loops on Rnd 2 of Flower, join MC with slip st in first dc; ch 4, 2 tr in next dc, (tr in next dc, 2 tr in next dc) around; join with slip st to first tr: 30 tr.

Rnd 10: Ch 4, working in Back Loops Only, tr in same st, 2 tr in next tr and in each tr around; join with slip st to both loops of first tr changing to CC: 60 tr.

Rnd 11: Repeat Rnd 5.

Rnd 12: With **right** side facing and working in free loops on Rnd 9 of Flower, join MC with slip st in first tr; ch 1, sc in same st, ch 2, (sc in next tr, ch 2) around; join with slip st to first sc: 30 ch-2 sps.

Rnd 13: Repeat Rnd 7: 45 tr.

Rnd 14: Ch 1, working in Back Loops Only, sc in same st, ch 2, ★ (sc, ch 2) twice in next tr, sc in next tr, ch 2; repeat from ★ around; join with slip st to both loops of first sc, finish off.

Rnd 15: With **right** side facing and working in free loops on Rnd 1 of Flower, join MC with slip st in first sc; ch 1, 2 sc in same st, sc in next sc and in each sc around; join with slip st to first sc: 21 sc.

Rnd 16: Repeat Rnd 2.

Rnd 17: Ch 4, working in both loops, tr in same st, (tr in next dc, 2 tr in next dc) around; join with slip st to first tr: 32 tr.

Rnds 18 and 19: Repeat Rnds 4 and 5.

Rnd 20: With **right** side facing and working in free loops on Rnd 17 of Flower, join MC with slip st in first tr; ch 1, sc in same st, ch 2, (sc in next tr, ch 2) around; join with slip st to first sc: 32 ch-2 sps.

Rnd 21: Slip st in first ch-2 sp, ch 4, tr in same sp, 2 tr in next ch-2 sp and in each ch-2 sp around; join with slip st to first tr changing to CC: 64 tr.

Rnd 22: Repeat Rnd 5.

56

FINISHING

For stem, holding wire lengths together, insert through center of Base and bend end of wires 1/2" to secure.

Fill center of Base with glue, holding wires in position until glue hardens.

Wrap florist tape around bottom of Base and around wires.

These delicate lingerie hangers are wonderful gifts for the bride. Fashioned with shells or a pineapple motif, each accessory is worked in two pieces, slipped over a plastic clothes hanger, joined, and finished with ribbons and silk flowers.

MATERIALS
Worsted Weight Yarn, approximately:
    Pineapple Cover (White) - 1 ounce, (30 grams, 65 yards)
    Shells Cover (Rose) - 1¼ ounces, (35 grams, 80 yards)
Crochet hook, size G (4.00 mm) **or** size needed for gauge
Plastic clothes hanger
Yarn needle
Silk craft flowers
⅜" ribbon
Glue gun

GAUGE: 8 dc = 2"

PINEAPPLE COVER

Rnd 1 (Right side): Ch 4, 7 dc in fourth ch from hook; join with slip st to top of beginning ch: 8 sts.

Note #1: Loop a short piece of yarn around any stitch to mark last round as **right** side.

Note #2: To work **Shell**, (2 dc, ch 2, 2 dc) in st or sp indicated.

Rnd 2: Ch 3 **(counts as first dc, now and throughout)**, dc in same st, dc in next 3 dc, work Shell in next dc, dc in last 3 dc, 2 dc in same st as first dc, ch 1, sc in first dc to form last sp: 14 dc.

Rnd 3: Ch 3, dc in same sp, ch 1, skip next 3 dc, (dc, ch 3, dc) in next dc, ch 1, skip next 3 dc, work Shell in next ch-2 sp, ch 1, skip next 3 dc, (dc, ch 3, dc) in next dc, ch 1, skip last 3 dc, 2 dc in same sp as first dc, ch 1, sc in first dc to form last sp.

Rnd 4: Ch 3, dc in same sp, ch 1, skip next ch-1 sp, (dc, ch 3, dc) in center ch of next ch-3, ch 1, skip next ch-1 sp, work Shell in next Shell (ch-2 sp), ch 1, skip next ch-1 sp, (dc, ch 3, dc) in center ch of next ch-3, ch 1, skip last ch-1 sp, 2 dc in same sp as first dc, ch 1, sc in first dc to form last sp.

Rnd 5: Ch 3, dc in same sp, ch 2, skip next ch-1 sp, 4 dc in center ch of next ch-3, ch 2, skip next ch-1 sp, work Shell in next Shell, ch 2, skip next ch-1 sp, 4 dc in center ch of next ch-3, ch 2, skip last ch-1 sp, 2 dc in same sp as first dc, ch 1, sc in first dc to form last sp.

Rnd 6: Ch 3, dc in same sp, ch 2, skip next ch-2 sp, dc in next dc, (ch 1, dc in next dc) 3 times, ch 2, skip next ch-2 sp, work Shell in next Shell, ch 2, skip next ch-2 sp, dc in next dc, (ch 1, dc in next dc) 3 times, ch 2, skip last ch-2 sp, 2 dc in same sp as first dc, ch 1, sc in first dc to form last sp.

Rnd 7: Ch 3, dc in same sp, ch 3, skip next ch-2 sp, (sc in next ch-1 sp, ch 3) 3 times, skip next ch-2 sp, work Shell in next Shell, ch 3, skip next ch-2 sp, (sc in next ch-1 sp, ch 3) 3 times, skip last ch-2 sp, 2 dc in same sp as first dc, ch 1, sc in first dc to form last sp.

Rnd 8: Ch 3, dc in same sp, ch 4, skip next ch-3 sp, sc in next ch-3 sp, ch 3, sc in next ch-3 sp, ch 4, skip next ch-3 sp, work Shell in next Shell, ch 4, skip next ch-3 sp, sc in next ch-3 sp, ch 3, sc in next ch-3 sp, ch 4, skip last ch-3 sp, 2 dc in same sp as first dc, ch 1, sc in first dc to form last sp.

Rnd 9: Ch 3, dc in same sp, ch 5, skip next ch-4 sp, (sc, ch 3, sc) in next ch-3 sp, ch 5, skip next ch-4 sp, work Shell in next Shell, ch 5, skip next ch-4 sp, (sc, ch 3, sc) in next ch-3 sp, ch 5, skip last ch-4 sp, 2 dc in same sp as first dc, ch 1, sc in first dc to form last sp.

Rnd 10: Ch 3, dc in same sp, ch 4, skip next ch-5 sp, 6 dc in next ch-3 sp, ch 4, skip next ch-5 sp, work Shell in next Shell, ch 4, skip next ch-5 sp, 6 dc in next ch-3 sp, ch 4, skip last ch-5 sp, 2 dc in same sp as first dc, ch 1, sc in first dc to form last sp.

Rnd 11: Ch 3, dc in same sp, ch 3, skip next ch-4 sp, dc in next dc, (ch 1, dc in next dc) 5 times, ch 3, skip next ch-4 sp, work Shell in next Shell, ch 3, skip next ch-4 sp, dc in next dc, (ch 1, dc in next dc) 5 times, ch 3, skip last ch-4 sp, 2 dc in same sp as first dc, ch 1, sc in first dc to form last sp.

Rnd 12: Ch 3, dc in same sp, ch 4, skip next ch-3 sp, sc in next ch-1 sp, (ch 3, sc in next ch-1 sp) 4 times, ch 4, skip next ch-3 sp, work Shell in next Shell, ch 4, skip next ch-3 sp, sc in next ch-1 sp, (ch 3, sc in next ch-1 sp) 4 times, ch 4, skip last ch-3 sp, 2 dc in same sp as first dc, ch 1, sc in first dc to form last sp.

Rnd 13: Ch 3, dc in same sp, ch 5, skip next ch-4 sp, sc in next ch-3 sp, (ch 3, sc in next ch-3 sp) 3 times, ch 5, skip next ch-4 sp, work Shell in next Shell, ch 5, skip next ch-4 sp, sc in next ch-3 sp, (ch 3, sc in next ch-3 sp) 3 times, ch 5, skip last ch-4 sp, 2 dc in same sp as first dc, ch 1, sc in first dc to form last sp.

Rnd 14: Ch 3, dc in same sp, ch 6, skip next ch-5 sp, sc in next ch-3 sp, (ch 3, sc in next ch-3 sp) twice, ch 6, skip next ch-5 sp, work Shell in next Shell, ch 6, skip next ch-5 sp, sc in next ch-3 sp, (ch 3, sc in next ch-3 sp) twice, ch 6, skip last ch-5 sp, 2 dc in same sp as first dc, ch 1, sc in first dc to form last sp.

Rnd 15: Ch 3, dc in same sp, ch 7, skip next loop, sc in next ch-3 sp, ch 3, sc in next ch-3 sp, ch 7, skip next loop, work Shell in next Shell, ch 7, skip next loop, sc in next ch-3 sp, ch 3, sc in next ch-3 sp, ch 7, skip last loop, 2 dc in same sp as first dc, ch 1, sc in first dc to form last sp.

Rnd 16: Ch 3, dc in same sp, ch 8, skip next loop, sc in next ch-3 sp, (ch 7, slip st, ch 10, slip st, ch 7, slip st) in side of sc just worked *(Fig. 30, page 138)*, ch 8, skip next loop, work Shell in next Shell, ch 8, skip next loop, sc in next ch-3 sp, (ch 7, slip st, ch 10, slip st, ch 7, slip st) in side of sc just worked, ch 8, skip last loop, 2 dc in same sp as first dc, ch 1, sc in first dc to form last sp; finish off.

Repeat for second side; do **not** finish off.

FINISHING

Slip Covers onto hanger with pineapples to the center; matching top Shells, slip st through ch-2 sps of both Shells; finish off leaving a long end for wrapping hook of hanger.
Sew Shells together at bottom of hanger.
Wrap yarn around hook of hanger until hook is completely covered. Using yarn needle and holding yarn tight, weave yarn back and forth through several strands; cut yarn close to work. Glue yarn at end of hook to hold it in place.

Glue flowers to Cover as desired. Tie ribbon in a bow around hanger.

SHELLS COVER

Rnd 1 (Right side): Ch 4, 7 dc in fourth ch from hook; join with slip st to top of beginning ch: 8 sts.

Note #1: Loop a short piece of yarn around any stitch to mark last round as **right** side.

Note #2: To work **Shell,** (2 dc, ch 2, 2 dc) in st or sp indicated.

Rnd 2: Ch 3 **(counts as first dc, now and throughout)**, dc in same st, skip next dc, work Shell in next dc, ch 1, (skip next dc, work Shell in next dc) twice, ch 1, skip last dc, 2 dc in same st as first dc, ch 1, sc in first dc to form last sp: 4 Shells.

Rnd 3: Ch 3, dc in same sp, work Shell in next Shell (ch-2 sp), ch 2, work Shell in next 2 Shells, ch 2, 2 dc in same sp as beginning dc, ch 1, sc in first dc to form last sp.

Rnd 4: Ch 3, dc in same sp, work Shell in next Shell, ch 1, (long dc, ch 4, long dc) **around** sps in previous 2 rnds *(Fig. 6, page 131)*, ch 1, work Shell in next 2 Shells, ch 1, (long dc, ch 4, long dc) **around** sps in previous 2 rnds, ch 1, 2 dc in same sp as first dc, ch 1, sc in first dc to form last sp.

Rnd 5: Ch 3, dc in same sp, work Shell in next Shell, ch 3, skip next 3 sps, work Shell in next 2 Shells, ch 3, skip last 3 sps, 2 dc in same sp as first dc, ch 1, sc in first dc to form last sp.

Rnd 6: Ch 3, dc in same sp, work Shell in next Shell, ch 4, skip next ch-3 sp, work Shell in next 2 Shells, ch 4, skip last ch-3 sp, 2 dc in same sp as first dc, ch 1, sc in first dc to form last sp.

Rnd 7: Ch 3, dc in same sp, work Shell in next Shell, ch 2, (long dc, ch 6, long dc) **around** sps in previous 3 rnds, ch 2, work Shell in next 2 Shells, ch 2, (long dc, ch 6, long dc) **around** sps in previous 3 rnds, ch 2, 2 dc in same sp as first dc, ch 1, sc in first dc to form last sp.

Rnd 8: Ch 3, dc in same sp, work Shell in next Shell, ch 5, skip next 3 sps, work Shell in next 2 Shells, ch 5, skip last 3 sps, 2 dc in same sp as first dc, ch 1, sc in first dc to form last sp.

Rnd 9: Ch 3, dc in same sp, work Shell in next Shell, ch 6, skip next loop, work Shell in next 2 Shells, ch 6, skip last loop, 2 dc in same sp as first dc, ch 1, sc in first dc to form last sp.

Rnd 10: Ch 3, dc in same sp, work Shell in next Shell, ch 3, (long dc, ch 6, long dc) **around** sps in previous 3 rnds, ch 3, work Shell in next 2 Shells, ch 3, (long dc, ch 6, long dc) **around** sps in previous 3 rnds, ch 3, 2 dc in same sp as first dc, ch 1, sc in first dc to form last sp.

Rnd 11: Ch 3, dc in same sp, work Shell in next Shell, ch 7, skip next 3 sps, work Shell in next 2 Shells, ch 7, skip last 3 sps, 2 dc in same sp as beginning dc, ch 1, sc in first dc to form last sp.

Rnd 12: Ch 3, dc in same sp, work Shell in next Shell, ch 8, skip next loop, work Shell in next 2 Shells, ch 8, skip last loop, 2 dc in same sp as beginning dc, ch 1, sc in first dc to form last sp.

Rnd 13: Ch 3, dc in same sp, work Shell in next Shell, ch 4, (long dc, ch 6, long dc) **around** sps in previous 3 rnds, ch 4, work Shell in next 2 Shells, ch 4, (long dc, ch 6, long dc) **around** sps in previous 3 rnds, ch 4, 2 dc in same sp as first dc, ch 1, sc in first dc to form last sp; finish off.

Repeat for second side; do **not** finish off.

FINISHING

Slip Covers onto hanger with loops to the center; matching top Shells, slip st through ch-2 sps of all 4 Shells; finish off leaving a long end for wrapping hook of hanger.

Sew remaining Shells together at bottom of hanger and sew center loops together.

Wrap yarn around hook of hanger until hook is completely covered. Using yarn needle and holding yarn tight, weave yarn back and forth through several strands; cut yarn close to work. Glue yarn at end of hook to hold it in place.

Glue flowers to Cover as desired. Tie ribbon in a bow around hanger.

ARGYLE AFGHAN

A classic argyle pattern brings masculine appeal to this stylish afghan. Post stitches form a ridge along each side of the four panels, which are joined with whipstitches and completed with a generous fringe. This handsome throw is an ideal accent for Dad's study or favorite easy chair.

Finished Size: Approximately 56" x 72"

MATERIALS
Worsted Weight Yarn, approximately:
   MC (Tan) - 63 ounces, (1,790 grams, 3,870 yards)
   Color A (Blue) - 14 ounces, (400 grams, 860 yards)
   Color B (Red) - 5 ounces, (140 grams, 310 yards)
Crochet hook, size I (5.50 mm) **or** size needed for gauge
2 Bobbins
Yarn needle

GAUGE: 14 sc and 16 rows = 4"

BOBBINS
Wind Color B onto 2 bobbins. Work each Color B stripe with a separate bobbin and work each MC section on opposite side of diamond with separate balls of yarn. Always keep unused yarn on the **wrong** side of the Panel.

PANEL (Make 4)
With MC, ch 50 **loosely**.

Row 1 (Right side)**:** Sc in second ch from hook and in each ch across: 49 sc.

Note: Loop a short piece of yarn around any stitch to mark last row as **right** side and bottom edge.

Row 2: Ch 1, turn; sc in each sc across.

Note: To work **Front Post double crochet (abbreviated FPdc)**, YO, insert hook from **front** to **back** around post of st indicated *(Fig. 17, page 135)*, YO and pull up a loop **even** with loop on hook, (YO and draw through 2 loops on hook) twice. Skip sc behind FPdc.

Row 3: Ch 1, turn; sc in first sc, work FPdc around sc in row **below** next sc, sc in next 12 sc changing to Color B in last sc worked *(Fig. 31a, page 138)*, sc in next sc changing to MC, sc in next 9 sc changing to Color A in last sc worked, sc in next

sc changing to second ball of MC, sc in next 9 sc changing to second Color B bobbin in last sc worked, sc in next sc changing to MC, sc in next 12 sc, work FPdc around sc in row **below** next sc, sc in last sc.

Row 4: Ch 1, turn; sc in each st across following Chart.

Row 5: Ch 1, turn; sc in first sc, work FPdc around FPdc in row **below** next sc, following Chart, sc in each sc across to last 2 sc, work FPdc around FPdc in row **below** next sc, sc in last sc.

Rows 6-284: Repeating Rows 4 and 5, follow Chart Rows 6-42 once, then follow Rows 3-42, 6 times, then follow Rows 3 and 4 once **more**.

Row 285: Ch 1, turn; sc in first sc, work FPdc around FPdc in row **below** next sc, sc in each sc across to last 2 sc, work FPdc around FPdc in row **below** next sc, sc in last sc.

Row 286: Ch 1, turn; sc in each st across; finish off.

ASSEMBLY

With **wrong** sides and bottom edges together and MC, whipstitch Panels together, matching rows, and working through 2 loops at end of rows, always working from the same direction *(Fig. 35a, page 140)*.

Add fringe using 8 strands of MC, each 11" long *(Figs. 37a & b, page 141)*; spacing evenly, attach across each end of afghan.

CHART

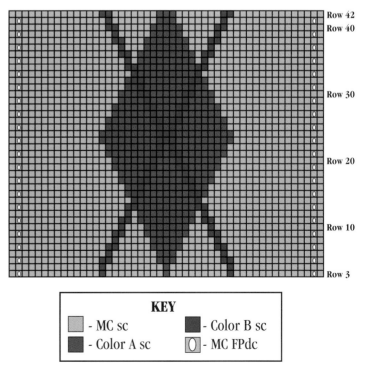

Row 42
Row 40

Row 30

Row 20

Row 10

Row 3

KEY	
▨ - MC sc	■ - Color B sc
■ - Color A sc	Ⓞ - MC FPdc

just for fun

You'll be dazzled by this assortment of crochet projects! We have designs that let you invite the sunshine in, some that can help out in the kitchen, and even one that will get you "egg-cited" about candy keepers! So when you're ready to relax, crochet one of these amusing pieces — just for the fun of it!

HEARTS AND FLOWERS RUG

Featuring alternating blocks with hearts and tulips, our homey rug reflects a love for all things country. The soft floorcloth is worked in single crochets while holding two strands of cotton yarn, and the simple motifs are created as you crochet.

Finished Size: Approximately 25" x 39"

MATERIALS
100% Cotton Worsted Weight Yarn, approximately:
   MC (Off-white) - 32 ounces, (910 grams, 1,370 yards)
   Color A (Blue) - 6 ounces, (170 grams, 255 yards)
   Color B (Green) - 1 ounce, (30 grams, 45 yards)
   Color C (Pink) - 1 ounce, (30 grams, 45 yards)
Crochet hook, size I (5.50 mm) **or** size needed for gauge
Yarn needle

Note: Entire Rug is worked holding 2 strands of yarn together.

GAUGE: 12 sc and 13 rows = 4"

HEART BLOCK (Make 3)
With MC, ch 36.
Row 1 (Right side): Sc in second ch from hook and in each ch across: 35 sc.
Note: Loop a short piece of yarn around any stitch to mark last row as **right** side.
Rows 2-10: Ch 1, turn; sc in each sc across.
Note: When changing colors *(Fig. 31a, page 138)*, keep unused color on **wrong** side of work; do **not** cut yarn until color is no longer needed. Use a separate skein or ball for each color change.

Rows 11-25: Ch 1, turn; sc in each sc across following Chart A; at end of Row 25, cut Color A.
Rows 26-35: Ch 1, turn; sc in each sc across changing to Color A in last sc worked on Row 35; cut MC.

CHART A

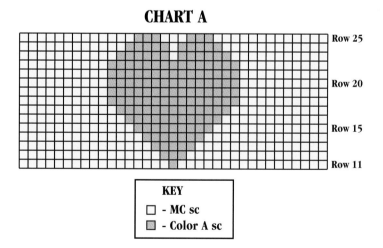

KEY
☐ - MC sc
▨ - Color A sc

BORDER
Rnd 1: Ch 1, sc in end of each row across; working in free loops of beginning ch *(Fig. 28b, page 138)*, 2 sc in first ch, sc in each ch across to last ch, 2 sc in last ch; sc in end of each row across; 2 sc in first sc, sc in each sc across to last sc, 2 sc in last sc; join with slip st to first sc, finish off: 144 sc.

Rnd 2: With **right** side facing, join MC with slip st in same sc as joining; ch 1, sc in same st, ch 1, (skip next sc, sc in next sc, ch 1) 17 times, ★ (sc in next sc, ch 1) twice, (skip next sc, sc in next sc, ch 1) 17 times; repeat from ★ around to last sc, sc in last sc, ch 1; join with slip st to first sc, finish off.

TULIP BLOCK (Make 3)

With MC, ch 36.

Row 1 (Right side): Sc in second ch from hook and in each ch across: 35 sc.

Note: Mark last row as **right** side.

Rows 2-6: Ch 1, turn; sc in each sc across.

Rows 7-29: Ch 1, turn; sc in each sc across following Chart B.

Rows 30-35: Ch 1, turn; sc in each sc across changing to Color A in last sc worked on Row 35; cut MC.

BORDER

Work same as Heart Block, page 63.

ASSEMBLY

With **wrong** sides together and 2 strands of MC, and working through **inside** loops only, whipstitch Blocks together using photo as a guide for placement and forming 2 strips of 3 Blocks each *(Fig. 35b, page 140)*; then whipstitch strips together.

CHART B

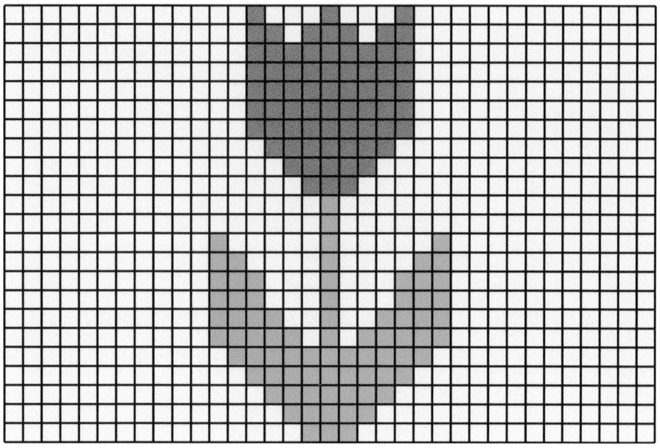

(Chart with rows labeled Row 7, Row 10, Row 15, Row 20, Row 25, Row 29)

KEY
☐ - MC sc
▨ - Color B sc
▨ - Color C sc

EDGING

With **right** side facing, join MC with slip st in any ch-1 sp; ch 1, sc in same sp, ch 3, (sc in next ch-1 sp, ch 3) around working (sc, ch 3) in each joining; join with slip st to first sc, finish off.

Quick SUNCATCHERS

*W*ith these delightful suncatchers, you can let the sun shine in and enjoy a spectrum of radiant colors dancing across the room! The two patterns — both resembling delicate snowflakes — are worked around metal rings using cotton thread. After the accents are stiffened, heart-shaped acrylic prisms are suspended in the centers.

Finished Size: Suncatcher #1 - approximately 4" in diameter
Suncatcher #2 - approximately 4¹⁄₂" in diameter

MATERIALS

For **each** Suncatcher:

Bedspread Weight Cotton Thread (size 10), approximately 16 yards

Steel crochet hook, size 7 (1.65 mm) **or** size needed for gauge

2" metal ring

¹⁄₂ yard of ¹⁄₈" wide ribbon

³⁄₄" prism

Translucent nylon thread

Starching materials: Commercial fabric stiffener, plastic wrap, small paint brush, terry towel, paper towels, cardboard, and stainless steel pins

GAUGE: 18 dc = 2"

SUNCATCHER #1

Rnd 1 (Right side): Join thread with slip st around ring; ch 1, 120 sc in ring; join with slip st to first sc.

Rnd 2: Ch 1, sc in same st, ★ ch 6, skip next 5 sc, sc in next sc; repeat from ★ around to last 5 sc, ch 2, skip last 5 sc, dc in first sc to form last loop: 20 loops.

Rnd 3: Ch 1, sc in same loop, (ch 6, sc in next loop) around, ch 2, dc in first sc to form last loop.

Note: To work **Cluster**, ★ YO 3 times, insert hook in loop indicated, YO and pull up a loop, (YO and draw through 2 loops on hook) 3 times; repeat from ★ 3 times **more**, YO and draw through all 5 loops on hook *(Figs. 13a & b, page 134)*.

Rnd 4: Ch 1, sc in same loop, ch 6, work Cluster in next loop, ch 6, ★ sc in next loop, ch 6, work Cluster in next loop, ch 6; repeat from ★ around; join with slip st to first sc, finish off: 10 Clusters.

SUNCATCHER #2

Rnd 1 (Right side): Join thread with slip st around ring; ch 1, 120 sc in ring; join with slip st to first sc.

Rnd 2: Ch 1, sc in same st, ★ ch 6, skip next 5 sc, sc in next sc; repeat from ★ around to last 5 sc, ch 2, skip last 5 sc, dc in first sc to form last loop: 20 loops.

Rnd 3: Ch 5, 2 dc in same loop, ch 2, sc in next loop, ch 2, ★ (2 dc, ch 2) twice in next loop, sc in next loop, ch 2; repeat from ★ around, dc in same loop as beginning ch-5; join with slip st to third ch of beginning ch-5: 10 sc.

Rnd 4: Slip st in first ch-2 sp, ch 3, (dc, ch 2, 2 dc) in same sp, ch 6, skip next 2 ch-2 sps, ★ (2 dc, ch 2, 2 dc) in next ch-2 sp, ch 6, skip next 2 ch-2 sps; repeat from ★ around; join with slip st to top of beginning ch-3, finish off.

FINISHING

See Starching and Blocking, page 142.
Weave ribbon through Rnd 2 and tie in a bow.
Using nylon thread, add prism and hanger.

This tiny teddy is a sweet little project that's quick to stitch and fun to share on "beary" special occasions. With his posable arms and legs, the fuzzy fellow makes a charming shelf-sitter to enhance an arrangement of nostalgic toys.

Finished Size: Approximately 4¹/₂" tall

MATERIALS

Sport Weight Brushed Acrylic Yarn, approximately:
   MC (Tan) - 45 yards
Sport Weight Yarn, approximately:
   CC (Peach) - 6 yards
Crochet hook, size C (2.75 mm) **or** size needed for gauge
Yarn needle
Soft sculpture needle
Polyester fiberfill
Black embroidery floss
10" length of ¹/₄" wide ribbon

GAUGE: 12 sc and 14 rows = 2"

HEAD AND BODY

Rnd 1 (Right side): With MC, ch 2 **loosely**, 8 sc in second ch from hook; do **not** join, place marker *(see Markers, page 137)*.
Rnd 2: 2 Sc in each sc around: 16 sc.
Rnd 3: (Sc in next sc, 2 sc in next sc) around: 24 sc.
Rnds 4-8: Sc in each sc around.
Rnd 9: (Skip next sc, sc in next 2 sc) around: 16 sc.
Stuff Head with polyester fiberfill.
Rnd 10: (Skip next sc, sc in next sc) around: 8 sc.
Rnds 11 and 12: Sc in each sc around.
Rnd 13: 2 Sc in each sc around: 16 sc.
Rnd 14: (Sc in next 3 sc, 2 sc in next sc) around: 20 sc.
Rnds 15-22: Sc in each sc around.
Rnd 23: (Skip next sc, sc in next sc) around: 10 sc.
Stuff Body with polyester fiberfill.
Rnd 24: (Skip next sc, sc in next sc) 5 times; slip st in next sc, finish off leaving a long end for sewing: 5 sc.
Thread yarn needle with end and weave through remaining sts; gather tightly and secure.

ARM (Make 2)

Rnd 1 (Right side): With MC, ch 2 **loosely**, 9 sc in second ch from hook; do **not** join, place marker.
Rnds 2-5: Sc in each sc around.
Note: To **decrease**, pull up a loop in next 2 sts, YO and draw through all 3 loops on hook **(counts as one sc)**.
Rnd 6: Decrease twice, sc in next 2 sc, 2 sc in each of next 2 sc, sc in next sc: 9 sc.

Rnds 7-10: Sc in each sc around.
Stuff Arm with polyester fiberfill.
Rnd 11: Decrease 4 times, skip next sc; slip st in next sc, finish off: 4 sc.

PAW (Make 2)

With CC, ch 3 **loosely**, 3 hdc in third ch from hook, ch 2, slip st in same ch; finish off leaving a long end for sewing.

LEG (Make 2)

Rnd 1 (Right side): With MC, ch 2 **loosely**, 12 sc in second ch from hook; do **not** join, place marker.
Rnds 2-5: Sc in each sc around.
Rnd 6: Decrease 3 times, sc in next 2 sc, 2 sc in each of next 3 sc, sc in next sc: 12 sc.
Rnds 7-9: Sc in each sc around.
Rnd 10: (Sc in next 2 sc, decrease) 3 times: 9 sc.
Rnd 11: 2 Dc in each of next 4 sc, sc in next 5 sc; slip st in Back Loop Only of next sc *(Fig. 27, page 138)* changing to CC *(Fig. 31b, page 138)*: 13 sts.
Rnd 12: Sc in Back Loop Only of each st around.
Stuff Leg with polyester fiberfill.
Rnd 13: Working in both loops, decrease 6 times, skip next sc: 6 sc.
Rnd 14: (Slip st in next sc, skip next st) around; finish off.

MUZZLE

With CC, ch 3 **loosely**, 8 hdc in third ch from hook; join with slip st to top of beginning ch, finish off leaving a long end for sewing.

EAR (Make 2)

With MC, ch 3 **loosely**, 2 dc in second ch from hook, (2 dc, sc) in last ch; finish off leaving a long end for sewing.

FINISHING

Using photo as a guide for placement, sew Muzzle and Ears to Head.
Sew Paws to Arms, Rnds 10 and 11.

ASSEMBLY

Thread a soft sculpture needle with a doubled 24" length of MC. Insert needle through Arm *(Fig. 1)* between Rnds 1 and 2 (at 1), then back into Arm one stitch over (at 2) and through Arm again (at 1). Insert needle completely through Body between Rnds 13 and 14 and out second side (at 3), through second Arm between Rnds 1 and 2, then back into Arm one stitch over (at 4), through Arm again (at 3) and back through Body (at 5).

Pull both ends of yarn so that Arms fit tightly against the Body but are still able to move freely at sides.

Knot the strands **tightly**, weave the ends under several stitches, and cut close to work.

Attach Legs in same manner, inserting needle between Rnds 3 and 4 on Leg and between Rnds 22 and 23 on Body.

Using embroidery floss, add French Knot eyes *(Fig. 40, page 143)* and Satin St nose *(Fig. 41b, page 143)*. Tie ribbon in a bow around neck.

Fig. 1

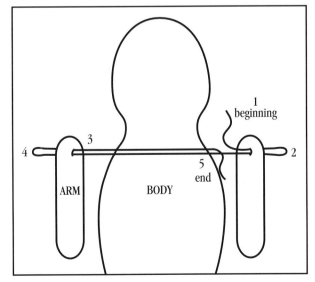

RAINBOW SWIRLS AFGHAN

Bright rainbows swirl around this energetic afghan! A sure-fire kid-pleaser, the cover is worked in blocks featuring centers of blue popcorn stitches surrounded by multicolored chain loops.

Finished Size: Approximately 41" x 58"

MATERIALS
Worsted Weight Yarn, approximately:
 MC (White) - 22 ounces, (620 grams, 1,240 yards)
 Color A (Blue) - 14 ounces, (400 grams, 790 yards)
 Color B (Green) - 4 ounces, (110 grams, 225 yards)
 Color C (Yellow) - 4 ounces, (110 grams, 225 yards)
 Color D (Orange) - 4 ounces, (110 grams, 225 yards)
 Color E (Red) - 4 ounces, (110 grams, 225 yards)
 Color F (Purple) - 4 ounces, (110 grams, 225 yards)
 Crochet hook, size I (5.50 mm) **or** size needed for gauge
 6 yarn bobbins (optional)
 Yarn needle

GAUGE: Rnds 1-3 = 4¹/₄"
 One Square = 8¹/₄"

SQUARE (Make 35)
With Color A, ch 5; join with slip st to form a ring.
Note: To work **Popcorn**, 4 dc in ring, drop loop from hook, insert hook in first dc of 4-dc group, hook dropped loop and draw through *(Fig. 15a, page 134)*.
Rnd 1 (Right side): Ch 3 **(counts as first dc, now and throughout)**, 3 dc in ring, drop loop from hook, insert hook in first dc, hook dropped loop and draw through, ch 3, (work Popcorn in ring, ch 3) 7 times; join with slip st to top of first Popcorn, finish off: 8 ch-3 sps.
Note: Loop a short piece of yarn around any stitch to mark last round as **right** side.
Rnd 2: With **right** side facing, join MC with slip st in any ch-3 sp; ch 3, 5 dc in same sp, 6 dc in next ch-3 sp and in each ch-3 sp around; join with slip st to first dc, finish off: 48 dc.
Rnd 3: With **right** side facing and working in Back Loops Only *(Fig. 27, page 138)*, join Color A with sc in any dc *(see Joining With Sc, page 137)*, sc next dc and in each dc around; join with slip st to both loops of first sc.
Note #1: Join yarn on Rnd 4 in the following Color Sequence: Color B, Color C, Color D, Color E, and Color F.
Note #2: When working with many separate colors at the same time, wind each color on a bobbin to help reduce tangling.

Rnd 4: Ch 1, working in both loops, sc in same st, ch 14, skip next 5 sc, sc in next sc, drop loop from hook leaving yarn to **right** side of work, working in **front** of previous loop, join Color B with sc in first skipped sc, ch 14, sc in sc to **left** of dropped loop, drop loop from hook leaving yarn to **right** side of work *(Fig. 1)*, (working in **front** of previous loop, join next color with sc in next skipped sc, ch 14, sc in sc to **left** of last dropped loop, drop loop from hook leaving yarn to **right** side of work) 4 times; (slip hook into first dropped loop, working in **front** of previous loops, ch 14, sc in sc to **left** of last dropped loop, drop loop from hook leaving yarn to **right** side of work) around; slip hook into first dropped loop, ch 14; join with slip st to first sc of same color, finish off; (slip hook into next dropped loop, working in **front** of previous loops, ch 14; working **behind** beginning loops, join with slip st to first sc of same color, finish off) 5 times: 48 loops.

Fig. 1

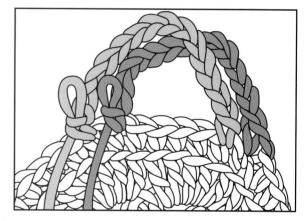

Rnd 5: With **right** side facing, join MC with sc in any loop; 2 sc in next loop, (sc in next loop, 2 sc in next loop) around; join with slip st to first sc: 72 sc.
Rnd 6: Ch 3, dc in next sc, 3 tr in each of next 2 sc, dc in next 2 sc, hdc in next sc, sc in next 10 sc, hdc in next sc, ★ dc in next 2 sc, 3 tr in each of next 2 sc, dc in next 2 sc, hdc in next sc, sc in next 10 sc, hdc in next sc; repeat from ★ around; join with slip st to first dc, finish off: 88 sts.
Rnd 7: With **right** side facing and working in Back Loops Only, join Color A with sc in first dc; sc in next 3 sts, 2 sc in each of next 2 tr, (sc in next 20 sts, 2 sc in each of next 2 tr) 3 times, sc in last 16 sts; join with slip st to first sc, finish off: 96 sc.

Rnd 8: With **right** side facing and working in both loops, join MC with sc in first sc; sc in next 4 sc, (sc, dc) in next sc, (dc, sc) in next sc, ★ sc in next 22 sc, (sc, dc) in next sc, (dc, sc) in next sc; repeat from ★ 2 times **more**, sc in last 17 sc; join with slip st to first sc, finish off.

ASSEMBLY

With **wrong** sides together and MC, and working through **inside** loops only, whipstitch Squares together, forming 5 vertical strips of 7 Squares each *(Fig. 35b, page 140)*; then whipstitch strips together, securing seam at each joining.

Quick ROUND DISHCLOTHS

Colorful accents for the kitchen, our three round dishcloths make handy cleanup helpers! Each design is stitched with worsted weight cotton for long-lasting use.

Finished Size: Approximately 10" in diameter

MATERIALS

100% Cotton Worsted Weight Yarn, approximately:

Dishcloth #1 (Blue) - 75 yards

Dishcloth #2 (Red) - 75 yards

Dishcloth #3

MC (White) - 30 yards

CC (Yellow) - 40 yards

Crochet hook, size H (5.00 mm) **or** size needed for gauge

GAUGE: Rnds 1 and 2 = 2¹/₂"

DISHCLOTH #1

Ch 5; join with slip st to form a ring.

Rnd 1: Ch 4 **(counts as first dc plus ch 1, now and throughout)**, (dc in ring, ch 1) 7 times; join with slip st to first dc: 8 ch-1 sps.

Note: To work **V-St**, (dc, ch 1, dc) in sp indicated.

Rnd 2: Slip st in first ch-1 sp, ch 4, dc in same sp, ch 1, (work V-St in next ch-1 sp, ch 1) around; join with slip st to first dc: 16 ch-1 sps.

Rnd 3: Slip st in first ch-1 sp, ch 4, dc in same sp, ch 2, skip next ch-1 sp, ★ work V-St in next V-St (ch-1 sp), ch 2, skip next ch-1 sp; repeat from ★ around; join with slip st to first dc: 8 V-Sts.

Rnd 4: Slip st in first ch-1 sp, ch 4, dc in same sp, ch 1, work (V-St, ch 1) in next ch-2 sp and in each V-St and ch-2 sp around; join with slip st to first dc: 32 ch-1 sps.

Rnd 5: Repeat Rnd 3: 16 V-Sts.

Rnd 6: Slip st in first ch-1 sp, ch 4, dc in same sp, work V-St in next ch-2 sp and in each V-St and each ch-2 sp around; join with slip st to first dc: 32 V-Sts.

Rnd 7: Slip st in first ch-1 sp, ch 4, dc in same sp, ch 1, (work V-St in next V-St, ch 1) around; join with slip st to first dc: 64 ch-1 sps.

Rnds 8 and 9: Slip st in first ch-1 sp, ch 4, dc in same sp, ch 1, skip next ch-1 sp, ★ work V-St in next V-St, ch 1, skip next ch-1 sp; repeat from ★ around; join with slip st to first dc.

Rnd 10: Slip st in first ch-1 sp, ch 1, sc in same sp, ch 1, (sc in next ch-1 sp, ch 1) around; join with slip st to first sc, finish off.

DISHCLOTH #2

Ch 4; join with slip st to form a ring.

Rnd 1: Ch 3 **(counts as first dc, now and throughout)**, 11 dc in ring; join with slip st to first dc: 12 dc.

Rnd 2: Working in sps **between** dc *(Fig. 29, page 138)*, slip st in first sp, ch 3, dc in same sp, 2 dc in next sp and in each sp around; join with slip st to first dc: 24 dc.

Rnd 3: Working in sps **between** dc, slip st in first sp, ch 2, dc in next sp, ch 3, ★ (YO, insert hook in **next** sp, YO and pull up a loop, YO and draw through 2 loops on hook) twice, YO and draw through all 3 loops on hook, ch 3; repeat from ★ around; skip beginning ch-2 and join with slip st to first dc: 12 ch-3 sps.

Rnd 4: Slip st in first ch-3 sp, ch 3, 6 dc in same sp, ch 1, sc in next ch-3 sp, ch 1, ★ 7 dc in next ch-3 sp, ch 1, sc in next ch-3 sp, ch 1; repeat from ★ around; join with slip st to first dc: 6 dc groups.

Rnd 5: Working in sps **between** dc, slip st in first sp, ch 1, sc in same sp, ch 2, (sc in next sp, ch 2) 5 times, skip next 2 ch-1 sps, ★ (sc in next sp, ch 2) 6 times, skip next 2 ch-1 sps; repeat from ★ around; join with slip st to first sc: 36 ch-2 sps.

Rnd 6: Slip st in first ch-2 sp, ch 1, sc in same sp, ch 3, (sc in next ch-2 sp, ch 3) around; join with slip st to first sc: 36 ch-3 sps.

Rnd 7: Slip st in first ch-3 sp, ch 2, dc in next ch-3 sp, ch 2, ★ YO, insert hook in **same** sp, † YO and pull up a loop, YO and draw through 2 loops on hook †, YO, insert hook in **next** ch-3 sp, repeat from † to † once, YO and draw through all 3 loops on hook, ch 2; repeat from ★ around working last st in same sp as beginning ch-2; skip beginning ch-2 and join with slip st to first dc: 36 ch-2 sps.

Rnd 8: Slip st in first ch-2 sp, ch 1, 3 sc in same sp and in each ch-2 sp around; join with slip st to first sc: 108 sc.

Rnd 9: Slip st in next sc, ch 1, sc in same st, ch 3, skip next 2 sc, (sc in next sc, ch 3, skip next 2 sc) around; join with slip st to first sc: 36 ch-3 sps.

Rnd 10: Slip st in first ch-3 sp, ch 3, 5 dc in same sp, ch 1, sc in next ch-3 sp, ch 1, ★ 6 dc in next ch-3 sp, ch 1, sc in next ch-3 sp, ch 1; repeat from ★ around; join with slip st to first dc: 18 dc groups.

Note: To **decrease**, pull up a loop in next 2 ch-1 sps, YO and draw through all 3 loops on hook.

Rnd 11: Working in sps **between** dc, slip st in first sp, ch 1, sc in same sp, (ch 1, sc in next sp) 4 times, decrease, ★ sc in next sp, (ch 1, sc in next sp) 4 times, decrease; repeat from ★ around; join with slip st to first sc, finish off.

DISHCLOTH #3

With MC, ch 4; join with slip st to form a ring.

Rnd 1 (Right side)**:** Ch 4 **(counts as first dc plus ch 1, now and throughout)**, (dc in ring, ch 1) 7 times; join with slip st to first dc: 8 ch-1 sps.

Note: Loop a short piece of yarn around any stitch to mark last round as **right** side.

Rnd 2: Ch 3 **(counts as first dc, now and throughout)**, dc in same st, ch 1, (2 dc in next dc, ch 1) around; join with slip st to first dc: 16 dc.

Rnd 3: Ch 4, dc in next dc, ch 1, dc in next ch-1 sp, ch 1, ★ (dc in next dc, ch 1) twice, dc in next ch-1 sp, ch 1; repeat from ★ around; join with slip st to first dc changing to CC **(Fig. 31b, page 138)**: 24 dc.

Rnd 4: Ch 3, dc in same st, ch 1, (2 dc in next dc, ch 1) around; join with slip st to first dc, finish off: 48 dc.

Rnd 5: With **right** side facing, join MC with slip st in any ch-1 sp; ch 4, dc in same sp, ch 1, (dc, ch 1) twice in next ch-1 sp and in each ch-1 sp around; join with slip st to first dc, finish off: 48 ch-1 sps.

Rnd 6: With **right** side facing, join CC with slip st in any ch-1 sp; ch 4, (dc in next ch-1 sp, ch 1) around; join with slip st to first dc, finish off.

Rnd 7: With **right** side facing, join MC with slip st in any ch-1 sp; ch 4, (dc, ch 1) twice in each of next 2 ch-1 sps, ★ dc in next ch-1 sp, ch 1, (dc, ch 1) twice in each of next 2 ch-1 sps; repeat from ★ around; join with slip st to first dc, finish off: 80 ch-1 sps.

Rnd 8: Repeat Rnd 6; do **not** finish off.

Rnd 9: Slip st in first ch-1 sp, ch 2, (slip st in next ch-1 sp, ch 2) around; join with slip st to first st, finish off.

Quick FLOWER BASKET NOTEKEEPER

Keeping up with your message pad is a breeze when you hang it from this pretty magnetic notepad holder. Topped with a ribbon-tied basket of rosy blossoms, the design has a plastic canvas back for added support.

Finished Size: Approximately 5" wide x 4" tall, not including notepad

MATERIALS
Worsted Weight Yarn, approximately:
  Brown - 22 yards
  Green - 10 yards
  Rose - 8 yards
  Light Rose - 6 yards
  White - small amount
Crochet hook, size F (3.75 mm) **or** size needed for gauge
7 mesh plastic canvas - 3" x 3½"
Yarn needle
18" length of ⅛" wide ribbon
Polyester fiberfill
Self-adhesive magnetic strip
3" x 5" notepad

PATTERN STITCHES
FRONT POST HALF DOUBLE CROCHET
(abbreviated FPhdc)
YO, insert hook from **front** to **back** around post of stitch indicated, YO and pull up a loop, YO and draw through all 3 loops on hook *(Fig. 18, page 135)*.
REVERSE SINGLE CROCHET (abbreviated reverse sc)
Working from **left** to **right**, insert hook in sp to right of hook, YO and draw through, under and to left of loop on hook (2 loops on hook), YO and draw through both loops on hook *(Figs. 25a-d, page 136)*.

GAUGE: 8 hdc = 2"

BASKET
With Brown, ch 32 **loosely**; being careful not to twist ch, join with slip st to form a ring.
Rnd 1 (Right side)**:** Ch 2 **(counts as first hdc, now and throughout)**, hdc in next ch and in each ch around; join with slip st to first hdc: 32 hdc.
Rnds 2-4: Ch 2, work FPhdc around next st and each st around; join with slip st to first hdc.
Rnd 5: Ch 3, working in Front Loops Only *(Fig. 27, page 138)*, (hdc in next st, ch 1) around; join with slip st to second ch of beginning ch-3.

Rnd 6: Ch 1, working from **left** to **right**, work reverse sc in next ch-1 sp and in each ch-1 sp around; join with slip st to first st, finish off.

HANDLE
With Brown, ch 30 **loosely**; slip st in second ch from hook and in each ch across; working in free loops of beginning ch *(Fig. 28b, page 138)*, slip st in each ch across; finish off leaving a long end for sewing.

FLOWERS
STEMS
Rnd 1: With **right** side of Basket facing, Rnds 5 and 6 forward, and working in free loops on Rnd 4 *(Fig. 28a, page 138)*, join Green with slip st in any st; ch 1, 2 sc in same st, sc in next st and in each st around; join with slip st to Front Loop Only of first sc: 33 sc.
Rnd 2: Ch 1, working in Front Loops Only, sc in first 3 sc, ch 5 **loosely**, slip st in second ch from hook and in each ch across (Stem), slip st in side of sc just worked *(Fig. 30, page 138)*, ★ sc in next 3 sc, ch 5 **loosely**, slip st in second ch from hook and in each ch across, slip st in side of sc just worked; repeat from ★ around; join with slip st to first sc, finish off: 11 Stems.

BLOSSOM (Make 6 with Rose and 5 with Light Rose)
Rnd 1 (Right side)**:** Ch 4 **loosely**, slip st in second ch from hook, skip next ch, slip st in last ch, ★ ch 3 **loosely**, slip st in second ch from hook, skip last ch, slip st in last ch of beginning ch-4; repeat from ★ 3 times **more**, finish off leaving a long end for sewing.

FINISHING
Fold Basket in half with joining at back.
Working in free loops on Rnd 1 of Stems, sew opening closed.
With **right** side facing toward front, sew Blossoms to Stems.
With White, add French Knot centers to Blossoms *(Fig. 40, page 143)*.
Using photo as a guide for placement, sew Handle to inside edge of Basket.
Weave ribbon through sts on Rnd 4 of Basket; tie in a bow.
Stuff Basket lightly with polyester fiberfill.

PLASTIC CANVAS FRAME

Carefully cut plastic canvas following pattern on this page.
Insert top 3 rows of Frame in bottom opening of Basket until
Row 3 is even with beginning ch.
Using Brown, working in free loops of beginning ch **and** in
Row 3 of Frame, sew opening closed.

Attach long magnetic strips to back of Basket.

With **right** side facing, weave cardboard back of notepad
through slots A and B of Frame.

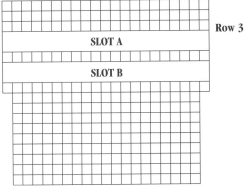

Row 3

SLOT A

SLOT B

Quick NESTING HEN CANDY DISH

*This plucky little chicken is just the thing for those who get "egg-cited" about country decorating!
Made using a two-liter soda bottle, our nesting hen decoration doubles as a whimsical candy dish.
You simply lift the barnyard beauty off her nest of fluffy loop stitches to reveal the treats inside.*

Finished Size: Approximately 9" high x 6½" in diameter

MATERIALS
Worsted Weight Yarn, approximately:
White - 1½ ounces, (40 grams, 85 yards)
Gold - 2 ounces, (60 grams, 155 yards)
Red - 3 yards
Orange - 2 yards
Crochet hook, size H (5.00 mm) **or** size needed for gauge
2 liter plastic soft drink bottle with cap and flat bottom
Tape measure
Craft knife
Yarn needle
Polyester fiberfill
Black felt
Craft glue

GAUGE: 11 sc and 11 rows = 3"

PREPARING BOTTLE
Rinse empty bottle and replace cap. Measure along side of bottle and draw a line around bottle 3" up from bottom and another line 4½" down from cap. Cut along both lines and discard middle.

HEN
HEAD AND BODY
With White, ch 4 **loosely**; being careful not to twist ch, join with slip st to form a ring.
Rnd 1 (Right side)**:** 2 Sc in each ch around; do **not** join, place marker *(see Markers, page 137)*: 8 sc.
Rnd 2: 2 Sc in each sc around: 16 sc.
Rnds 3-5: Sc in each sc around.
Rnd 6: (Sc in next sc, 2 sc in next sc) around: 24 sc.
Rnds 7 and 8: Sc in each sc around.
Rnd 9: (Skip next sc, sc in next 2 sc) around: 16 sc.
Rnds 10 and 11: (Sc in next sc, 2 sc in next sc) around: 36 sc.
Rnd 12: (Sc in next 2 sc, 2 sc in next sc) around: 48 sc.
Rnds 13-20: Sc in each sc around.
Rnd 21: Slip st in Back Loop Only of each sc around *(Fig. 27, page 138)*; finish off.

TAIL
With White, ch 9 **loosely**.
Row 1: Sc in second ch from hook and in next 6 chs, 3 sc in last ch; working in free loops of beginning ch *(Fig. 28b, page 138)*, sc in next 7 chs: 17 sc.

Row 2 (Right side)**:** Ch 1, turn; sc in first 8 sc, 3 sc in next sc, sc in each sc across: 19 sc.
Note: Loop a short piece of yarn around any stitch to mark last row as **right** side.
Row 3: Ch 1, turn; sc in first 9 sc, 3 sc in next sc, sc in each sc across: 21 sc.
Row 4: Ch 1, turn; sc in first 10 sc, 3 sc in next sc, sc in each sc across: 23 sc.
Row 5 (Feathers)**:** Ch 4 **loosely**, turn; slip st in second ch from hook, hdc in next 2 chs, slip st in first 3 sc, ch 5 **loosely**, slip st in second ch from hook, hdc in next 3 chs, slip st in same sc as last slip st and in next 3 sc, ch 6 **loosely**, slip st in second ch from hook, hdc in next 4 chs, slip st in same sc as last slip st and in next 3 sc, ★ ch 7 **loosely**, slip st in second ch from hook, hdc in next 5 chs, slip st in same sc as last slip st and in next 3 sc; repeat from ★ 2 times **more**, ch 6 **loosely**, slip st in second ch from hook, hdc in next 4 chs, slip st in same sc as last slip st and in next 3 sc, ch 5 **loosely**, slip st in second ch from hook, hdc in next 3 chs, slip st in same sc as last slip st and in last 2 sc, ch 4 **loosely**, slip st in second ch from hook, hdc in next 2 chs, slip st in same sc as last slip st; finish off.

WING (Make 2)
With White, ch 15 **loosely**.
Row 1 (Right side)**:** Slip st in second ch from hook, hdc in back ridge of next ch and in each ch across *(Fig. 2a, page 131)*: 14 sts.
Note: Mark last row as **right** side.
Row 2: Ch 1, turn; sc in each hdc across, skip last slip st: 13 sts.
Row 3: Ch 2, turn; slip st in second ch from hook, hdc in each sc across: 14 sts.
Rows 4-9: Repeat Rows 2 and 3, 3 times.
End of Wing: Ch 1, working in end of rows, insert hook in first row, YO and pull up a loop, (insert hook in next row, YO and pull up a loop) across, YO and draw through all 10 loops on hook, ch 1; finish off.

BEAK
Rnd 1 (Right side)**:** With Orange, ch 2, 3 sc in second ch from hook; join with slip st to first sc.
Rnd 2: 2 Sc in each sc around; do **not** join, place marker: 6 sc.
Rnd 3: (Sc in next sc, 2 sc in next sc) around: 9 sc.
Rnd 4: (Sc in next 2 sc, 2 sc in next sc) around changing to Red in last sc *(Fig. 31a, page 138)*: 12 sc.

Wattles: Working in Front Loops Only, (sc, 2 hdc, sc) in next sc, slip st in next sc, (sc, 2 hdc, sc) in next sc, leave remaining sts unworked; finish off.

COMB
With Red, ch 6 **loosely**.
Row 1: (Sc, 2 hdc, sc) in second ch from hook, ★ slip st in next ch, (sc, 2 hdc, sc) in next ch; repeat from ★ once **more**; finish off.

NEST
With Gold, ch 4; being careful not to twist ch, join with slip st to form a ring.
Rnd 1 (Right side): 3 Sc in each ch around; do **not** join, place marker: 12 sc.
Rnd 2: 2 Sc in each sc around: 24 sc.
Rnd 3: (Sc in next sc, 2 sc in next sc) around: 36 sc.
Rnds 4 and 5: Sc in each sc around.
Rnd 6: (Sc in next 2 sc, 2 sc in next sc) around: 48 sc.

Rnd 7: Ch 1, **turn**; work Loop St in each sc around pulling each loop to measure approximately 1¹/₂" *(Figs. 16a-c, page 134)*; do **not** join: 48 Loop Sts.
Rnds 8-18: Work Loop St in each st around.
Rnd 19: Slip st from **front** to **back** around post of each st around *(Fig. 17, page 135)*; finish off.

ASSEMBLY
Using photo as a guide for placement, sew Wings to Hen, leaving back edges free. Sew Tail to center back. Sew Beak and Comb to Head.
Using pattern, cut eyes from felt and glue to Head.
Stuff Head lightly with polyester fiberfill and insert top of bottle into Head, pulling last rnd over edge of bottle.
Insert bottom of bottle into Nest, pulling last rnd over edge of bottle. Set Hen on Nest.

Eye
Cut 2

rock-a-bye collection

The arrival of a newborn is a joyous event, celebrated with gifts from family and friends. For a special gift that will become a favorite keepsake, choose one of the precious designs in this sweet collection. You'll find cuddly afghans, fashion accessories, and decorative accents to brighten baby's room.

DIAMOND CASCADE LAYETTE

Sure to please Mama and baby, this adorable layette features a cascade of diamond motifs created with chain spaces and double crochets. Fashioned with pale lemon sport weight yarn, the set includes an afghan, a sacque, and a bonnet.

Finished Size: Afghan - approximately 41" square
Sacque and Bonnet - 3 and 6 months

MATERIALS
Sport Weight Yarn, approximately:
Complete Set
20 ounces, (570 grams, 2,105 yards)
Afghan
16 ounces, (450 grams, 1,685 yards)
Sacque
3 ounces, (90 grams, 315 yards)
Bonnet
1 ounce, (30 grams, 105 yards)
Crochet hooks, sizes F (3.75 mm) **and** G (4.00 mm) **or** sizes needed for gauge
2 yards of ¼" wide ribbon

AFGHAN
GAUGE: With large size hook (size G), in pattern,
20 sts and 10 rows = 4"

Gauge Swatch: (5½" x 4")
With large size hook, ch 29 **loosely.**
Rows 1-10: Work same as Body.
Finish off.

BODY
With large size hook, ch 197 **loosely.**
Row 1 (Right side)**:** Dc in fourth ch from hook, ch 2, skip next 2 chs, dc in next 7 chs, ch 2, ★ skip next 2 chs, dc in next ch, ch 2, skip next 2 chs, dc in next 7 chs, ch 2; repeat from ★ across to last 4 chs, skip next 2 chs, dc in last 2 chs: 195 sts.
Note: Loop a short piece of yarn around any stitch to mark last row as **right** side.
Row 2: Ch 3 **(counts as first dc, now and throughout),** turn; dc in next 2 sts, ★ ch 2, skip next 2 sts, dc in next 5 sts, ch 2, skip next 2 sts, dc in next 3 sts; repeat from ★ across.
Row 3: Ch 3, turn; dc in next 3 sts, ch 2, skip next 2 sts, dc in next 3 sts, ch 2, ★ skip next 2 sts, dc in next 5 sts, ch 2, skip next 2 sts, dc in next 3 sts, ch 2; repeat from ★ across to last 6 sts, skip next 2 sts, dc in last 4 sts.
Row 4: Ch 3, turn; dc in next 4 sts, ch 2, skip next 2 sts, dc in next st, ch 2, ★ skip next 2 sts, dc in next 7 sts, ch 2, skip next 2 sts, dc in next st, ch 2; repeat from ★ across to last 7 sts, skip next 2 sts, dc in last 5 sts.
Row 5: Repeat Row 3.
Row 6: Repeat Row 2.

Row 7: Ch 3, turn; dc in next st, ch 2, skip next 2 sts, dc in next 7 sts, ch 2, ★ skip next 2 sts, dc in next st, ch 2, skip next 2 sts, dc in next 7 sts, ch 2; repeat from ★ across to last 4 sts, skip next 2 sts, dc in last 2 sts.

Repeat Rows 2-7 for pattern until piece measures approximately 39", ending by working Row 7; do **not** finish off.

EDGING

Rnd 1: Work 195 dc evenly spaced across end of rows; working in free loops of beginning ch *(Fig. 28b, page 138)*, 3 dc in first ch, 2 dc in next ch, dc in each ch across to last 2 chs, 2 dc in next ch, 3 dc in last ch; work 195 dc evenly spaced across end of rows; 3 dc in first dc, 2 dc in next dc, dc in each st across to last 2 dc, 2 dc in next dc, 3 dc in last dc; join with slip st to first dc.

Rnd 2: Slip st in next dc, ch 1, sc in same st, skip next 2 dc, (3 dc, ch 2, 3 dc) in next dc, skip next 2 dc, ★ sc in next dc, skip next 2 dc, (3 dc, ch 2, 3 dc) in next dc, skip next 2 dc; repeat from ★ around; join with slip st to first sc, finish off.

SACQUE

GAUGE: With small size hook (size F), in pattern,
        10 dc = 2" and 4 rows = 1½"

Size Note: Instructions are written for size 3 months with size 6 months in braces { }. Instructions will be easier to read if you circle all the numbers pertaining to your size. If only one number is given, it applies to both sizes.

YOKE

With small size hook, ch 43{47} **loosely**.

Row 1: Dc in fourth ch from hook and next 6 chs, (2 dc, ch 2, 2 dc) in next ch, dc in next 2{4} chs, (2 dc, ch 2, 2 dc) in next ch, dc in next 17 chs, (2 dc, ch 2, 2 dc) in next ch, dc in next 2{4} chs, (2 dc, ch 2, 2 dc) in next ch, dc in last 8 chs.

Row 2: Ch 3 **(counts as first dc, now and throughout)**, turn; ★ dc in next dc and in each dc across to next ch-2 sp, (2 dc, ch 2, 2 dc) in ch-2 sp; repeat from ★ 3 times **more**, dc in each st across: 69{73} dc.

Repeat Row 2, 4{5} times: 133{153} dc.

Next Row: Ch 3, turn; ★ dc in next dc and in each dc across to next ch-2 sp, (dc, ch 2, dc) in ch-2 sp; repeat from ★ 3 times **more**, dc in each dc across: 141{161} dc.

Repeat last row, 3 times; do **not** finish off: 165{185} dc.

Note: Loop a short piece of yarn around any stitch to mark last row as **right** side.

BODY

Row 1: Ch 3, turn; ★ dc in next dc and in each dc across to next ch-2 sp, † YO, insert hook in next ch-2 sp, YO and pull up a loop, YO and draw through 2 loops on hook †, skip next 34{40} dc (armhole), repeat from † to † once, YO and draw through all 3 loops on hook; repeat from ★ once **more**, dc in each dc across: 99{107} sts.

Row 2: Ch 3, turn; dc in next st, ch 2, skip next st, dc in next 5 sts, ch 2, ★ skip next st, dc in next st, ch 2, skip next st, dc in next 5 sts, ch 2; repeat from ★ across to last 3 sts, skip next st, dc in last 2 sts: 24{26} ch-2 sps.

Row 3: Ch 3, turn; dc in next 2 sts, ★ ch 2, skip next 2 sts, dc in next 3 sts; repeat from ★ across.

Row 4: Ch 3, turn; dc in next 3 sts, ch 2, skip next 2 sts, dc in next st, ch 2, ★ skip next 2 sts, dc in next 5 sts, ch 2, skip next 2 sts, dc in next st, ch 2; repeat from ★ across to last 6 sts, skip next 2 sts, dc in last 4 sts.

Row 5: Ch 3, turn; dc in next 2 sts, ★ ch 2, skip next 2 sts, dc in next 3 sts; repeat from ★ across.

Row 6: Ch 3, turn; dc in next st, ch 2, skip next 2 sts, dc in next 5 sts, ch 2, ★ skip next 2 sts, dc in next st, ch 2, skip next 2 sts, dc in next 5 sts, ch 2; repeat from ★ across to last 4 sts, skip next 2 sts, dc in last 2 sts.

Rows 7-14: Repeat Rows 3-6 twice.
Finish off.

SLEEVE

Note: To **decrease** (uses next 2 dc), ★ YO, insert hook in **next** dc, YO and pull up a loop, YO and draw through 2 loops on hook; repeat from ★ once **more**, YO and draw through all 3 loops on hook **(counts as one dc)**.

Size 3 Months Only - Rnd 1: With **wrong** side facing and holding ch-2 sps at armhole together, join yarn with slip st in **both** sps; ch 3, dc in next 5 dc, decrease, (dc in next 9 dc, decrease) twice, dc in last 5 dc; join with slip st to first dc: 32 dc.

Size 6 Months Only - Rnd 1: With **wrong** side facing and holding ch-2 sps at armhole together, join yarn with slip st in **both** sps; ch 3, dc in next 19 dc, decrease, dc in each dc around; join with slip st to first dc: 40 dc.

Both Sizes - Rnd 2: Ch 5, turn; skip next st, dc in next 5 sts, ch 2, skip next st, ★ dc in next st, ch 2, skip next st, dc in next 5 sts, ch 2, skip next st; repeat from ★ around; join with slip st to third ch of beginning ch-5: 40{50} sts.

Rnd 3: Ch 3, turn; dc in next st, ch 2, ★ skip next 2 sts, dc in next 3 sts, ch 2; repeat from ★ around to last 3 sts, skip next 2 sts, dc in last st; join with slip st to first dc.

Continued on page 89.

WATERCOLOR WRAP

Rocking baby to sleep will be extra special with this soft watercolor-look wrap. You work each row with only one color, but the gentle hues are blended when you stitch into the row below. Ridges that form on the back provide additional thickness and warmth.

Finished Size: Approximately 36" x 50"

MATERIALS
  Sport Weight Yarn, approximately:
    Color A (Blue) - 8 ounces, (230 grams, 755 yards)
    Color B (Lavender) - 7 ounces, (200 grams, 660 yards)
    Color C (Pink) - 7 ounces, (200 grams, 660 yards)
    Color D (Green) - 7 ounces, (200 grams, 660 yards)
    Color E (Yellow) - 7 ounces, (200 grams, 660 yards)
  Crochet hook, size F (3.75 mm) **or** size needed for gauge

GAUGE: In pattern, 20 dc and 18 rows = 4"

  Gauge Swatch: (5¹/₂" x 4")
  Ch 28 **loosely.**
  Rows 1-19: Work same as afghan.

Note #1: Each row is worked across length of afghan.

Note #2: Always join yarn and finish off leaving a 6" length to be worked into fringe.

COLOR SEQUENCE
3 Rows Color A, ★ 1 row **each** Color B, Color C, Color D, Color E, Color A; repeat from ★ throughout.

With Color A, ch 248 **loosely.**

Row 1 (Right side)**:** Sc in second ch from hook and in each ch across; finish off: 247 sc.

Note: Loop a short piece of yarn around any stitch to mark last row as **right** side.

Rows 2 and 3: With **right** side facing, join Color A with slip st in BLO of first sc *(Fig. 27, page 138)*; ch 1, sc in BLO of each sc across; finish off.

Row 4: With **right** side facing, join next color with slip st in BLO of first sc; ch 1, sc in BLO of first 7 sc, ★ dc in free loops of each sc in row **below** next 3 sc **(Fig. 1)**, skip sts behind dc **(now and throughout)**, sc in BLO of next 7 sc; repeat from ★ across; finish off.

Fig. 1

Row 5: With **right** side facing, join next color with slip st in free loop of st **below** first sc; ch 3 **(counts as first dc, now and throughout)**, dc in free loop of each st in row **below** next 6 sc, ★ sc in BLO of next 3 dc, dc in free loop of each st in row **below** next 7 sc; repeat from ★ across; finish off.
Row 6: With **right** side facing, join next color with slip st in BLO of first dc; ch 1, sc in BLO of first 7 dc, ★ dc in free loop of each dc in row **below** next 3 sc, sc in BLO of next 7 dc; repeat from ★ across; finish off.
Repeat Rows 5 and 6 for pattern until afghan measures approximately 35½", ending by working Row 5 with Color E.
Last 3 Rows: With **right** side facing, join Color A with slip st in BLO of first st; ch 1, sc in BLO of each st across; finish off.

Add fringe using one strand of matching color, each 12" long **(Figs. 37a & b, page 141)**; attach in end of each row on each end of afghan.

Quick DELIGHTFUL NURSERY SET

*B*righten the nursery with these easy handmade additions! Our lampshade and boutique tissue box cover are stitched in white brushed acrylic yarn and trimmed with borders of baby blue shells. The matching pacifier holder is also created using a shell pattern that's worked in white cotton thread.

MATERIALS
Boutique Tissue Box Cover
Worsted Weight Brushed Acrylic Yarn, approximately:
    MC (White) - 1½ ounces, (40 grams, 95 yards)
    CC (Blue) - 1 ounce, (30 grams, 65 yards)
Crochet hook, size I (5.50 mm) **or** size needed for gauge
Lampshade Cover
Worsted Weight Brushed Acrylic Yarn, approximately:
    MC (White) - 2 ounces, (60 grams, 125 yards)
    CC (Blue) - ½ ounce, (15 grams, 30 yards)
Crochet hook, size I (5.50 mm) **or** size needed for gauge
21" length of ¼" wide ribbon
Yarn needle
Lampshade - 4½" top diameter, 8" bottom diameter, and 6¼" tall
Pacifier Holder
Bedspread Weight Cotton Thread (size 10), approximately 22 yards
Steel crochet hook, size 6 (1.80 mm) **or** size needed for gauge
10" length of ¼" wide ribbon
Sewing needle and thread
¼" Snap
Suspender clip

PATTERN STITCHES
REVERSE SINGLE CROCHET *(abbreviated reverse sc)*
Working from **left** to **right**, insert hook in stitch to right of hook, YO and draw through, under and to left of loop on hook, YO and draw through both loops on hook **(Figs. 25a-d, page 136)**.
DECREASE
Pull up a loop in next 2 sts, YO and draw through all 3 loops on hook **(counts as one sc)**.

BOUTIQUE TISSUE BOX COVER
GAUGE: 10 sts and 11 rows = 3"

TOP
With CC, ch 15 **loosely**.
Row 1: Sc in second ch from hook and in each ch across: 14 sc.
Rows 2-7: Ch 1, turn; sc in each sc across.
Row 8 (opening): Ch 1, turn; sc in first 4 sc, ch 6 **loosely**, skip next 6 sc, sc in last 4 sc: 8 sc.
Rows 9-15: Ch 1, turn; sc in each st across; do **not** finish off: 14 sc.

TRIM

Rnd 1 (Right side)**:** Ch 1, turn; 3 sc in first sc, sc in each sc across to last sc, 3 sc in last sc; 14 sc evenly spaced across end of rows; working in free loops of beginning ch *(Fig. 28b, page 138)*, 3 sc in first ch, sc in each ch across to last ch, 3 sc in last ch; 14 sc evenly spaced across end of rows; join with slip st to Back Loop Only of first sc *(Fig. 27, page 138)*: 64 sc.

Rnd 2: Ch 3, dc in Back Loop Only of next sc and in each sc around; join with slip st to top of beginning ch-3.

Rnd 3: Ch 1, working in Front Loops Only, sc in same st, skip next 3 dc, tr in next dc, (ch 1, tr) 6 times in same st, skip next 3 dc, ★ sc in next dc, skip next 3 dc, tr in next dc, (ch 1, tr) 6 times in same st, skip next 3 dc; repeat from ★ around; join with slip st to first sc: 8 sc.

Rnd 4: Slip st in next tr and in next ch-1 sp, ch 1, sc in same sp, ch 3, (sc in next ch-1 sp, ch 3) around; join with slip st to first sc, finish off.

SIDES

Rnd 1: With **right** side facing, Rnds 3 and 4 of Trim forward, and working in free loops of Rnd 2, join MC with slip st in first st; ch 1, (decrease, sc in next 14 sts) around; join with slip st to first sc: 60 sc.

Rnd 2: Ch 1, sc in both loops of each sc around; join with slip st to first sc.

Repeat Rnd 2 until Sides measure approximately 4³/₄"; finish off.

Bottom Edging: With **right** side facing, join CC with slip st in first sc; ch 1, work reverse sc in each sc around; join with slip st to first st, finish off.

TOP EDGING

With **right** side facing and working in free loops of Rnd 1 on Trim, join MC with slip st in first st; ch 1, work reverse sc in each st around; join with slip st to first st, finish off.

81

LAMPSHADE COVER

GAUGE: 10 sts and 11 rows = 3"

BODY

With MC, ch 56 **loosely**; being careful not to twist ch, join with slip st to form a ring.

Rnd 1 (Right side): Ch 1, sc in each ch around; join with slip st to first sc: 56 sc.

Note: Loop a short piece of yarn around any stitch to mark last round as **right** side.

Rnd 2 (Eyelet rnd): Ch 1, sc in same st, ch 1, skip next sc, (sc in next sc, ch 1, skip next sc) around; join with slip st to first sc: 28 ch-1 sps.

Rnd 3: Ch 1, sc in same st and in each ch-1 sp and each sc around; do **not** join, place marker *(see Markers, page 137)*: 56 sc.

Rnd 4: Sc in each sc around.

Rnd 5: 2 Sc in next sc, (sc in next 18 sc, 2 sc in next sc) twice, sc in each sc around: 59 sc.

Rnd 6: Sc in each sc around.

Rnd 7: Sc in next 9 sc, 2 sc in next sc, (sc in next 19 sc, 2 sc in next sc) twice, sc in next 9 sc: 62 sc.

Rnd 8: Sc in each sc around.

Rnd 9: Sc in next 20 sc, (2 sc in next sc, sc in next 20 sc) twice: 64 sc.

Rnd 10: Sc in each sc around.

Rnd 11: Sc in next 8 sc, 2 sc in next sc, (sc in next 20 sc, 2 sc in next sc) twice, sc in next 13 sc: 67 sc.

Rnd 12: Sc in next 4 sc, 2 sc in next sc, (sc in next 21 sc, 2 sc in next sc) twice, sc in next 18 sc: 70 sc.

Rnd 13: Sc in next 20 sc, 2 sc in next sc, (sc in next 22 sc, 2 sc in next sc) twice, sc in next 3 sc: 73 sc.

Rnd 14: Sc in next 5 sc, 2 sc in next sc, (sc in next 23 sc, 2 sc in next sc) twice, sc in next 19 sc: 76 sc.

Rnd 15: Sc in next 8 sc, 2 sc in next sc, (sc in next 24 sc, 2 sc in next sc) twice, sc in next 17 sc: 79 sc.

Rnd 16: Sc in next 19 sc, 2 sc in next sc, (sc in next 25 sc, 2 sc in next sc) twice, sc in next 7 sc: 82 sc.

Rnd 17: Sc in each sc around.

Rnd 18: Sc in next sc, (2 sc in next sc, sc in next 26 sc) 3 times: 85 sc.

Rnd 19: Sc in each sc around.

Rnd 20: Sc in next 14 sc, 2 sc in next sc, (sc in next 27 sc, 2 sc in next sc) twice, sc in next 14 sc: 88 sc.

Rnds 21-23: Sc in each sc around; at end of Rnd 23, slip st in next sc, finish off.

SCALLOP TRIM

Rnd 1: With **right** side facing, join CC with slip st in first sc; ch 1, sc in each sc around; join with slip st to first sc: 88 sc.

Rnd 2: Ch 1, sc in same st, skip next 3 sc, tr in next sc, (ch 1, tr) 6 times in same st, skip next 3 sc, ★ sc in next sc, skip next 3 sc, tr in next sc, (ch 1, tr) 6 times in same st, skip next 3 sc; repeat from ★ around; join with slip st to first sc: 11 sc.

Rnd 3: Slip st in next tr and in next ch-1 sp, ch 1, sc in same sp, ch 3, (sc in next ch-1 sp, ch 3) around; join with slip st to first sc, finish off.

TOP EDGING

With **right** side facing and working in free loops of beginning ch *(Fig. 28b, page 138)*, join CC with slip st in first ch; ch 1, work reverse sc in each ch around; join with slip st to first st, finish off.

FINISHING

Weave ribbon through Eyelet rnd. Tie ribbon in a bow to secure.

PACIFIER HOLDER

GAUGE: 8 sts = 1"

Ch 3; join with slip st to form a ring.

Rnd 1: Ch 4, (dc in ring, ch 1) 11 times; join with slip st to third ch of beginning ch-4: 12 ch-1 sps.

Rnd 2: Slip st in first ch-1 sp, ch 1, sc in same sp, (ch 3, sc in next ch-1 sp) around, ch 1, hdc in first sc to form last sp.

Note: Begin working in rows.

Row 1 (Right side): Ch 3, skip next ch-3 sp, dc in next ch-3 sp, (ch 1, dc) 6 times in same sp, skip next ch-3 sp, tr in next ch-3 sp, leave remaining 7 ch-3 sps unworked.

Note: Loop a short piece of thread around any stitch to mark last row as **right** side.

Row 2: Ch 3, turn; sc in first ch-1 sp, (ch 3, sc in next ch-1 sp) 5 times, tr in last dc.

Row 3: Turn; slip st in first sc and in next ch-3 sp, ch 3, skip next ch-3 sp, dc in next ch-3 sp, (ch 1, dc) 6 times in same sp, skip next ch-3 sp, tr in next ch-3 sp.

Repeat Rows 2 and 3 until piece measures approximately 10", ending by working Row 2; finish off.

FINISHING

See Washing and Blocking, page 140.

Weave ribbon through center spaces of Pacifier Holder and sew each end to wrong side.

Sew base of suspender clip to Pacifier Holder.

With **wrong** side facing, sew one side of snap ¼" away from bottom end and the other side of snap 3" away from bottom end.

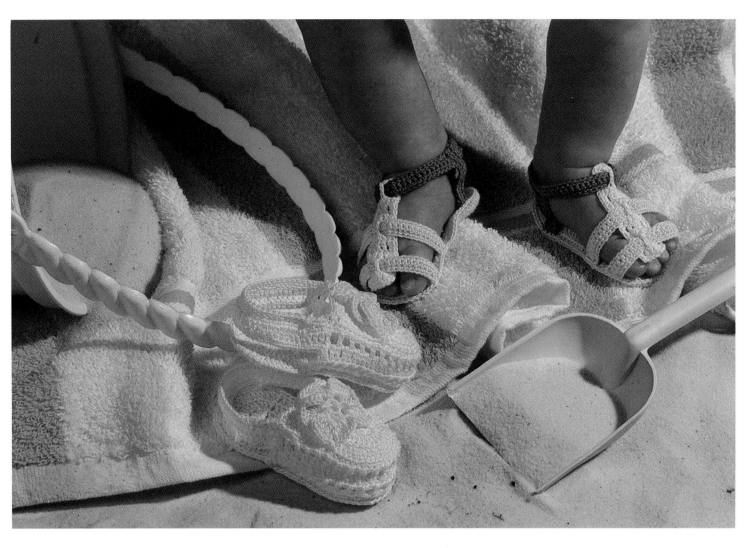

$\mathcal{Q}$uick SUMMER SANDALS

These soft summertime shoes are perfect for a newborn's tiny toes. Fashioned in open-toe and sling-back styles, both slippers are worked with size 10 cotton thread and have double soles for added comfort. A button closure accents the open-toe sandals, and the sling-backs are embellished with tiny three-dimensional pansies.

Finished Size: Newborn

MATERIALS
  Bedspread Weight Cotton Thread (size 10), approximately:
  Pansy Sandals
    White - 36 yards
    Yellow - 66 yards
  Open-Toe Sandals
    Yellow - 60 yards
    Blue - 15 yards
    White - 8 yards
  Steel crochet hook, size 7 (1.65 mm) **or** size needed for gauge
  Sewing needle and thread
  2 - ¹/₄" buttons for each pair

GAUGE: 10 dc = 1"

PANSY SANDAL
PANSY
With Yellow, ch 6; join with slip st to form a ring.
Rnd 1 (Right side)**:** Ch 1, (sc in ring, ch 5) 5 times; join with slip st to first sc: 5 loops.
Note: Loop a short piece of thread around any stitch to mark last round as **right** side.
Rnd 2: (Slip st, ch 2, 12 dc, ch 2, slip st) in each of first 3 loops (Small Petals), (slip st, ch 3, 7 tr, ch 1, 7 tr, ch 3, slip st) in each of last 2 loops (Large Petals); join with slip st to first st, finish off.

INSTEP

With White, ch 13 **loosely**.

Row 1 (Right side)**:** Dc in fourth ch from hook and in next 8 chs **(3 skipped chs count as first dc)**, 8 dc in last ch; working in free loops of beginning ch **(Fig. 28b, page 138)**, dc in next 10 chs: 28 dc.

Note: Mark last row as **right** side.

Row 2: Ch 3 **(counts as first dc, now and throughout)**, turn; dc in next 9 dc, 2 dc in each of next 8 dc, dc in last 10 dc: 36 dc.

Row 3: Ch 3, turn; dc in next 9 dc; with **wrong** side of Pansy against **right** side of Instep, slip st in ch-1 sp on first Large Petal, 2 dc in next dc, (dc in next dc, 2 dc in next dc) 7 times, slip st in ch-1 sp on next Large Petal, dc in last 11 dc; ch 38 **loosely** (Strap); being careful not to twist ch, join with slip st to Back Loop Only of first dc **(Fig. 27, page 138)**: 44 dc.

Note: Begin working in rounds.

Rnd 1: Ch 1, do **not** turn; sc in Back Loop Only of first 44 dc, sc in each ch around; join with slip st to both loops of first sc: 82 sc.

Rnd 2: Ch 4 **(counts as first dc plus ch 1, now and throughout)**, working in both loops, (skip next sc, dc in next sc, ch 1) 21 times, skip next sc, dc in next sc and in each sc around; join with slip st to first dc: 60 dc.

Note: Begin working in rows.

Row 1: Ch 3, (dc in next ch-1 sp, dc in next dc) 22 times, leave remaining dc unworked: 45 dc.

Row 2: Ch 4, turn; skip next dc, dc in next dc, (ch 1, skip next dc, dc in next dc) across: 22 ch-1 sps.

Row 3: Ch 1, turn; sc in first dc and in each ch-1 sp and each dc across; finish off: 45 sc.

TOP EDGING

Rnd 1: With **right** side facing and working in free loops of beginning ch of Strap, join Yellow with slip st in same st as joining; ch 1, sc in each ch around; work 8 sc evenly spaced across end of first 3 rows, slip st in sixth dc of center Small Petal, work 8 sc evenly spaced across end of last 3 rows; join with slip st to first sc, finish off.

BOTTOM EDGING

Row 1: With **right** side facing, join Yellow with slip st in end of first row on Instep; ch 1, sc evenly across end of rows, sc in each dc across Strap, sc evenly across end of rows; finish off.

SOLE

With Yellow, ch 22 **loosely**.

Rnd 1 (Right side)**:** 7 Dc in fourth ch from hook, dc in each ch across to last ch, 8 dc in last ch; working in free loops of beginning ch, dc in next 17 chs; join with slip st to top of beginning ch: 50 sts.

Note: Mark last round as **right** side.

Rnd 2: Ch 3, dc in same st, 2 dc in each of next 7 dc, dc in next 17 dc, 2 dc in each of next 8 dc, dc in each dc around; join with slip st to first dc: 66 dc.

Rnd 3: Ch 3, dc in same st, (dc in next dc, 2 dc in next dc) 7 times, dc in next 18 dc, 2 dc in next dc, (dc in next dc, 2 dc in next dc) 7 times, dc in each dc around; join with slip st to first dc, finish off: 82 dc.

Repeat for top Sole; do **not** finish off.

Joining Rnd: Ch 1, with **wrong** sides of Soles together, matching sts, and working through **both** loops of **both** pieces, sc in first 30 dc; with **wrong** side of Instep against **right** side of top Sole and working through **both** loops of all 3 pieces, sc in next 45 sts, sc in last 7 dc; join with slip st to first sc, finish off.

OPEN-TOE SANDAL
INSTEP

With White, ch 6 **loosely**.

Row 1: Sc in second ch from hook and in each ch across: 5 sc.

Row 2 (Right side)**:** Ch 4 **(counts as first dc plus ch 1)**, turn; skip next sc, dc in next sc, ch 1, skip next sc, dc in last sc: 2 ch-1 sps.

Note: Loop a short piece of thread around any stitch to mark last row as **right** side and top edge.

Row 3: Ch 1, turn; sc in each dc and in each sp across: 5 sc.

Row 4: Ch 3 **(counts as first dc, now and throughout)**, turn; dc in next sc and in each sc across.

Row 5: Ch 1, turn; sc in each dc across.

Rows 6-11: Repeat Rows 2-5 once, then repeat Rows 2 and 3 once **more**.

Edging: Ch 1, turn; sc evenly around; join with slip st to first sc, finish off.

BOTTOM STRAP

With Yellow, ch 22 **loosely**.

Row 1 (Right side)**:** Sc in back ridge of second ch from hook and in each ch across **(Fig. 2a, page 131)**: 21 sc.

Note: Mark last row as **right** side.

Rows 2 and 3: Ch 1, turn; sc in each sc across. Finish off.

MIDDLE STRAP

With Yellow, ch 29 **loosely**.

Row 1 (Right side)**:** Sc in back ridge of second ch from hook and in each ch across: 28 sc.

Note: Mark last row as **right** side.

Rows 2 and 3: Ch 1, turn; sc in each sc across. Finish off.

ANKLE STRAP - RIGHT SANDAL

FRONT

With Blue, ch 32 **loosely**.

Row 1 (Right side)**:** Sc in back ridge of second ch from hook and in each ch across: 31 sc.

Note: Mark last row as **right** side.

Row 2: Ch 1, turn; sc in each sc across to last 5 sc, ch 3, skip next 3 sc (buttonhole), sc in last 2 sc: 28 sc.

Row 3: Ch 1, turn; sc in first 2 sc, 3 sc in next ch-3 sp, sc in each sc across; do **not** finish off: 31 sc.

FIRST SIDE

Ch 10 **loosely**.

Row 1: Sc in back ridge of second ch from hook and in next 8 chs, sc in end of each row across: 12 sc.

Rows 2 and 3: Ch 1, turn; sc in each sc across; do **not** finish off.

BACK

Row 1: Ch 1, turn; sc in first 3 sc, leave remaining 9 sc unworked.

Rows 2-19: Ch 1, turn; sc in each sc across; do **not** finish off.

SECOND SIDE

Ch 10 **loosely**.

Row 1: Sc in back ridge of second ch from hook and in each ch across, sc in next 3 sc: 12 sc.

Rows 2 and 3: Ch 1, turn; sc in each sc across. Finish off.

ANKLE STRAP - LEFT SANDAL

FIRST SIDE

With Blue, ch 13 **loosely**.

Row 1 (Right side)**:** Sc in back ridge of second ch from hook and in each ch across: 12 sc.

Note: Mark last row as **right** side.

Rows 2 and 3: Ch 1, turn; sc in each sc across; do **not** finish off.

BACK

Row 1: Ch 1, turn; sc in first 3 sc, leave remaining 9 sc unworked.

Rows 2-19: Ch 1, turn; sc in each sc across; do **not** finish off.

SECOND SIDE

Ch 10 **loosely**.

Row 1: Sc in back ridge of second ch from hook and in each ch across, sc in next 3 sc: 12 sc.

Row 2: Ch 1, turn; sc in each sc across.

Row 3: Ch 1, turn; sc in each sc across to last 2 sc, leave last 2 sc unworked; do **not** finish off: 10 sc.

FRONT

Ch 32 **loosely**.

Row 1: Sc in back ridge of second ch from hook and in each ch across, sc in 2 unworked sc on Second Side: 33 sc.

Row 2: Turn; skip first 2 sc, sc in next sc and in each sc across to last 5 sc, ch 3, skip next 3 sc (buttonhole), sc in last 2 sc: 28 sc.

Row 3: Ch 1, turn; sc in first 2 sc, 3 sc in next ch-3 sp, sc in each sc across, slip st in last sc on Second Side; finish off.

ASSEMBLY

With **right** sides facing, weave Front Ankle Strap through ch-1 sps at top of Instep (marked edge), Middle Strap through ch-1 sps at center of Instep, and Bottom Strap through ch-1 sps at bottom of Instep.

SOLE

Work same as Pansy Sandal, page 84, to Joining Rnd.

Joining Rnd: Ch 1, with **wrong** sides of Soles together, matching sts, and working through **both** loops of **both** pieces (**now and throughout**), sc in first 2 dc; with **right** side of Bottom Strap facing and working in end of rows, sc in next 3 sts of all 3 pieces (**now and throughout**), sc in next 14 dc of Soles; working in end of rows of opposite end of Bottom Strap, sc in next 3 sts, sc in next 3 dc of Soles; with **right** side of Middle Strap facing and working in end of rows, sc in next 3 sts, sc in next 10 dc of Soles; with **right** side of First Side facing and working in end of rows, sc in next 3 sts, sc in next 24 dc of Soles; with **right** side of Second Side facing and working in end of rows, sc in next 3 sts, sc in next 10 dc of Soles; working in end of rows on opposite end of Middle Strap, sc in next 3 sts, sc in last dc of Soles; join with slip st to first sc, finish off.

Sew buttons to side straps.

CRISSCROSS COVER-UP

Cradle a little girl in the lap of luxury with this dreamy creation! The cloud-soft cover-up features a diamond lattice pattern that's formed when pink slip stitches are woven through a white background of extended single crochets.

Finished Size: Approximately 35" x 47"

MATERIALS

Worsted Weight Yarn, approximately:
    MC (White) - 29 ounces, (820 grams, 1,690 yards)
    CC (Pink) - 4 ounces, (110 grams, 235 yards)
    Crochet hook, size I (5.50 mm) **or** size needed for gauge

GAUGE: 10 Ex sc = 3" and 10 rows = 4"

PATTERN STITCHES
EXTENDED SINGLE CROCHET (*abbreviated Ex sc*)
Insert hook in st indicated, YO and pull up a loop, YO and draw through one loop on hook, YO and draw through both loops on hook (***Fig. 1***).

Fig. 1

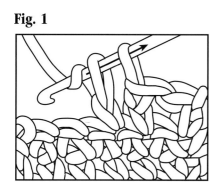

DECREASE (uses next 2 sc)
★ Insert hook in **next** sc, YO and pull up a loop, YO and draw through one loop on hook; repeat from ★ once **more**, YO and draw through all 3 loops on hook.

CLUSTER
★ Insert hook in ch-1 sp indicated, YO and pull up a loop, YO and draw through one loop on hook; repeat from ★ once **more**, YO and draw through all 3 loops on hook (***Figs. 13a & b, page 134***).

BODY

With MC, ch 102 **loosely**.

Row 1: Sc in second ch from hook and in each ch across: 101 sc.

Row 2 (Right side): Ch 1, turn; Ex sc in first 8 sc, ch 1, ★ skip next sc, Ex sc in next 11 sc, ch 1; repeat from ★ across to last 9 sc, skip next sc, Ex sc in last 8 sc: 101 sts.

Note: Loop a short piece of yarn around any stitch to mark last row as **right** side and bottom edge.

Row 3: Ch 1, turn; Ex sc in first 6 sts, ch 1, skip next st, Ex sc in next st, Ex sc in next ch-1 sp and in next st, ★ ch 1, skip next st, Ex sc in next 7 sts, ch 1, skip next st, Ex sc in next st, Ex sc in next ch-1 sp and in next st; repeat from ★ across to last 7 sts, ch 1, skip next st, Ex sc in last 6 sts.

Row 4: Ch 1, turn; Ex sc in first 4 sts, ch 1, skip next st, Ex sc in next st and in next ch-1 sp, Ex sc in next 3 sts, Ex sc in next ch-1 sp and in next st, ★ ch 1, skip next st, Ex sc in next 3 sts, ch 1, skip next st, Ex sc in next st and in next ch-1 sp, Ex sc in next 3 sts, Ex sc in next ch-1 sp and in next st; repeat from ★ across to last 5 sts, ch 1, skip next st, Ex sc in last 4 sts.

Row 5: Ch 1, turn; Ex sc in first 2 sts, ★ ch 1, skip next st, Ex sc in next st and in next ch-1 sp, Ex sc in next 7 sts and in next ch-1 sp, Ex sc in next st; repeat from ★ across to last 3 sts, ch 1, skip next st, Ex sc in last 2 sts.

Row 6: Ch 1, turn; Ex sc in first 2 sts and in next ch-1 sp, ★ Ex sc in next st, ch 1, skip next st, Ex sc in next 7 sts, ch 1, skip next st, Ex sc in next st and in next ch-1 sp; repeat from ★ across to last 2 sts, Ex sc in last 2 sts.

Row 7: Ch 1, turn; Ex sc in first 4 sts, ★ † Ex sc in next ch-1 sp and in next st, ch 1, skip next st, Ex sc in next 3 sts, ch 1, skip next st, Ex sc in next st and in next ch-1 sp †, Ex sc in next 3 sts; repeat from ★ across to last 13 sts, then repeat from † to † once, Ex sc in last 4 sts.

Row 8: Ch 1, turn; Ex sc in first 6 sts, Ex sc in next ch-1 sp and in next st, ch 1, skip next st, Ex sc in next st and in next ch-1 sp, ★ Ex sc in next 7 sts, Ex sc in next ch-1 sp and in next st, ch 1, skip next st, Ex sc in next st and in next ch-1 sp; repeat from ★ across to last 6 sts, Ex sc in last 6 sts.

Repeat Rows 3-8 until afghan measures approximately 42", ending by working Row 8.

Last Row: Ch 1, turn; Ex sc in each st and in each ch-1 sp across; do **not** finish off.

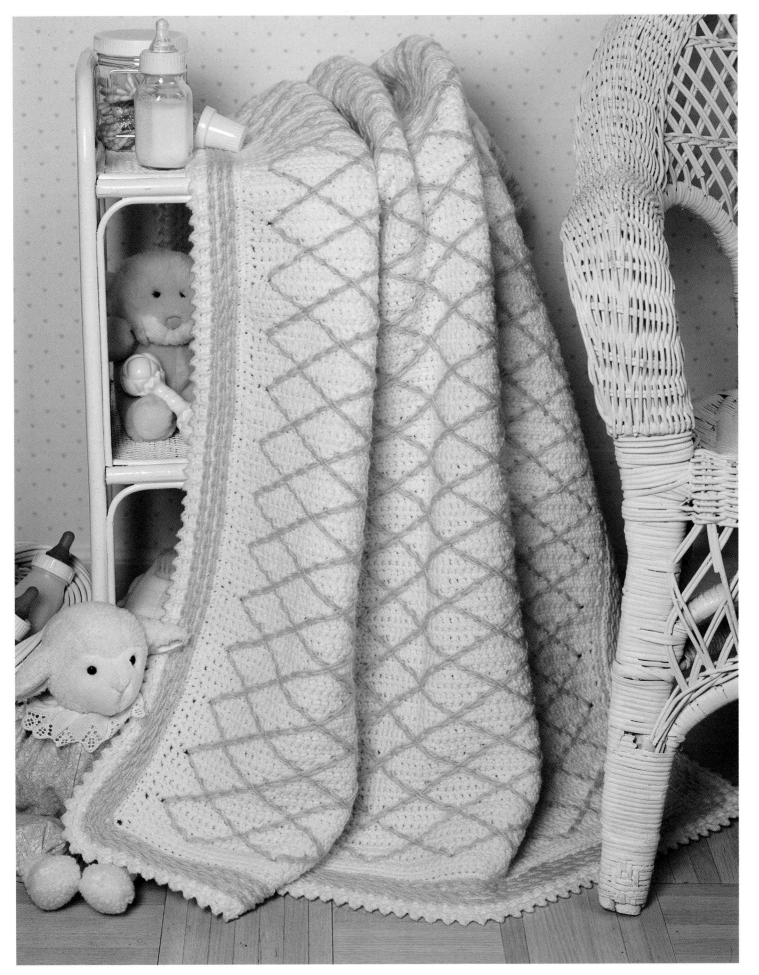

EDGING

Rnd 1: Ch 1, turn; 3 sc in first st, work 100 sc evenly spaced across to last st, 3 sc in last st; work 138 sc evenly spaced across end of rows; working in free loops of beginning ch *(Fig. 28b, page 138)*, 3 sc in first ch, work 100 sc evenly spaced across to last ch, 3 sc in last ch; work 138 sc evenly spaced across end of rows; join with slip st to Back Loop Only of first sc *(Fig. 27, page 138)*: 488 sc.

Rnd 2: Ch 1, working in Back Loops Only, sc in same st, 3 sc in next sc, ★ sc in each sc across to next corner sc, 3 sc in corner sc; repeat from ★ 2 times **more**, sc in each sc across; join with slip st to first sc.

Rnd 3: Ch 2, Ex sc in next sc **(counts as first decrease)**, ch 1, (work Cluster, ch 1) twice in next corner sc, ★ (decrease, ch 1) across to next corner sc, (work Cluster, ch 1) twice in corner sc; repeat from ★ 2 times **more**, (decrease, ch 1) across; join with slip st to first decrease.

Rnds 4 and 5: Slip st in first ch-1 sp, ch 1, Ex sc in same sp, ch 1, (work Cluster, ch 1) twice in next corner ch-1 sp, ★ (work Cluster in next ch-1 sp, ch 1) across to next corner ch-1 sp, (work Cluster, ch 1) twice in corner ch-1 sp; repeat from ★ 2 times **more**, (work Cluster in next ch-1 sp, ch 1) across; join with slip st to first Ex sc.

Rnd 6: Slip st in first ch-1 sp, ch 1, 2 sc in same sp, 3 sc in next corner ch-1 sp, ★ 2 sc in next ch-1 sp and in each ch-1 sp across to next corner ch-1 sp, 3 sc in corner ch-1 sp; repeat from ★ 2 times **more**, 2 sc in next ch-1 sp and in each ch-1 sp across; join with slip st to first sc.

Note: To work **Picot**, ch 2, sc in second ch from hook.

Rnd 7: Work Picot, working **around** sc of previous rnd, work long sc in ch-1 sp in rnd **below** next sc *(Fig. 6, page 131)*, work (Picot, long sc in ch-1 sp in rnd **below** corner 3-sc group) twice, ★ work (Picot, long sc in ch-1 sp in rnd **below** next sc) across to next corner ch-1 sp, work (Picot, long sc in ch-1 sp in rnd **below** corner 3-sc group) twice; repeat from ★ 2 times **more**, work (Picot, long sc in ch-1 sp in rnd **below** next sc) across; join with slip st to first ch, finish off.

CRISSCROSS SLIP STITCHES

With **right** side facing, beginning at bottom edge and working diagonally upward to the right, hold CC at back of work, insert hook from **front** to **back** in first ch-1 sp on Row 2, YO and pull up a loop approximately ³/₄", leaving a 3" end at back; ★ insert hook in next ch-1 sp on next row, YO and draw through loop on hook pulling loop up approximately ³/₄"; repeat from ★ across to last ch-1 sp, insert hook in last ch-1 sp, YO and draw through loop on hook, drop loop from hook, insert hook from **back** to **front** on other side of ch-1 sp, hook dropped loop and pull loop to wrong side; finish off. Work in same manner, beginning in each ch-1 sp across bottom edge, and then beginning in each ch-1 sp along left edge.

CROSSING CHAINS

Working diagonally upward to the left in same manner as before, alternate working over and under slip sts so that they look woven. To work under slip sts, drop loop from hook, insert hook from top to bottom under previous slip st, hook dropped loop and draw through.

BORDER

Rnd 1: With **right** side facing, hold CC at back of work, insert hook from **front** to **back** in first ch-1 sp on Rnd 3 of Edging, YO and pull up a ³/₄" loop; ★ insert hook in next ch-1 sp, YO and draw through loop on hook pulling loop up approximately ³/₄"; repeat from ★ around, insert hook in same sp as first st, YO and draw through loop on hook, remove hook from loop, insert hook from **back** to **front** in next st, hook dropped loop and pull loop to wrong side, ch 1.
Work in same manner on Rnds 4 and 5 of Edging.
Finish off.

DIAMOND CASCADE LAYETTE

Continued from page 78.

Rnd 4: Ch 3, turn; dc in next 2 sts, ch 2, skip next 2 sts, dc in next st, ch 2, ★ skip next 2 sts, dc in next 5 sts, ch 2, skip next 2 sts, dc in next st, ch 2; repeat from ★ around to last 4 sts, skip next 2 sts, dc in last 2 sts; join with slip st to first dc.

Rnd 5: Repeat Rnd 3.

Rnd 6: Ch 5, turn; skip next 2 sts, dc in next 5 sts, ch 2, skip next 2 sts, ★ dc in next st, ch 2, skip next 2 sts, dc in next 5 sts, ch 2, skip next 2 sts; repeat from ★ around; join with slip st to third ch of beginning ch-5.

Rnds 7-11: Repeat Rnds 3-6 once, then repeat Rnd 3 once **more**.

Rnd 12: Ch 3, turn; dc in next 2 sts, skip next 2 sts, dc in next st, ★ skip next 2 sts, dc in next 5 sts, skip next 2 sts, dc in next st; repeat from ★ around to last 4 sts, skip next 2 sts, dc in last 2 sts; join with slip st to first dc: 24{30} dc.

Rnd 13: Ch 1, turn; sc in each dc around; join with slip st to first sc.

Rnd 14: Ch 1, turn; sc in first 4{5} sc, ★ pull up a loop in next 2 sc, YO and draw through all 3 loops on hook, sc in next 3 sc; repeat from ★ around; join with slip st to first sc: 20{25} sts.

Rnd 15: Ch 1, do **not** turn; sc in each st around; join with slip st to first sc, finish off.

Repeat for second Sleeve.

EDGING

Eyelet Row: With **wrong** side facing and beginning at neck edge, join yarn with slip st in first free loop of beginning ch; ch 3, working in sps **between** dc on Row 1 of Yoke *(Fig. 29, page 138)*, dc in first sp, ch 1, (skip next sp, dc in next sp, ch 1) 3 times, † skip next 2 sps, dc in next sp, ch 1, skip next 1{2} sps, dc in next sp, ch 1, skip next sp, dc in next sp, ch 1, skip next 1{2} sps, dc in next sp, ch 1 †, (skip next 2 sps, dc in next sp, ch 1) twice, (skip next sp, dc in next sp, ch 1) 6 times, repeat from † to † once, skip next 2 sps, dc in next sp, ch 1, (skip next sp, dc in next sp, ch 1) 3 times, dc in last st.

Rnd 1: Ch 1, turn; sc in each dc and in each ch-1 sp across neck edge; sc evenly around entire Sacque working 3 sc in each corner; join with slip st to first sc, finish off.

Weave 1 yard of ribbon through Eyelet Row along neck edge.

BONNET

GAUGE: With small size hook (size F), in pattern,
10 dc = 2" and 4 rows = 1½"

Size Note: Instructions are written for size 3 months with size 6 months in braces { }. Instructions will be easier to read if you circle all the numbers pertaining to your size. If only one number is given, it applies to both sizes.

BACK

With small size hook, ch 4; join with slip st to form a ring.

Rnd 1 (Right side)**:** Ch 3 **(counts as first dc, now and throughout)**, 11 dc in ring; join with slip st to first dc: 12 dc.

Rnd 2: Ch 3, dc in same st, 2 dc in next dc and in each dc around; join with slip st to first dc: 24 dc.

Rnd 3: Ch 3, 2 dc in next dc, (dc in next dc, 2 dc in next dc) around; join with slip st to first dc: 36 dc.

Rnd 4: Ch 3, dc in next dc, 2 dc in next dc, (dc in next 2 dc, 2 dc in next dc) around; join with slip st to first dc: 48 dc.

Rnd 5: Ch 3, dc in next 2 dc, 2 dc in next dc, (dc in next 3 dc, 2 dc in next dc) around; join with slip st to first dc: 60 dc.

Size 6 Months Only - Rnd 6: Ch 3, dc in next 3 dc, 2 dc in next dc, (dc in next 4 dc, 2 dc in next dc) around; join with slip st to first dc, do **not** finish off: 72 dc.

BRIM

Row 1: Ch 3, dc in next dc, ch 2, skip next dc, dc in next 5 dc, ch 2, ★ skip next dc, dc in next dc, ch 2, skip next dc, dc in next 5 dc, ch 2; repeat from ★ around to last 12{16} dc, skip next dc, dc in next 2 dc, leave remaining 9{13} dc unworked: 63{73} sts.

Row 2: Ch 3, **turn;** dc in next 2 sts, ★ ch 2, skip next 2 sts, dc in next 3 sts; repeat from ★ across.

Row 3: Ch 3, turn; dc in next 3 sts, ch 2, skip next 2 sts, dc in next st, ch 2, ★ skip next 2 sts, dc in next 5 sts, ch 2, skip next 2 sts, dc in next st, ch 2; repeat from ★ across to last 6 sts, skip next 2 sts, dc in last 4 sts.

Row 4: Ch 3, turn; dc in next 2 sts, ★ ch 2, skip next 2 sts, dc in next 3 sts; repeat from ★ across.

Row 5: Ch 3, turn; dc in next st, ch 2, skip next 2 sts, dc in next 5 sts, ch 2, ★ skip next 2 sts, dc in next st, ch 2, skip next 2 sts, dc in next 5 dc, ch 2; repeat from ★ across to last 4 sts, skip next 2 sts, dc in last 2 sts.

Rows 6-9: Repeat Rows 2-5.

Row 10: Ch 1, turn; sc in each dc and in each ch-2 sp across: 51{59} sc.

Row 11: Ch 1, turn; sc in each sc across; do **not** finish off.

NECKBAND

Row 1: Ch 1, work 16 sc evenly spaced across end of rows, work 7{9} sc evenly spaced across unworked sts on Back, work 16 sc evenly spaced across end of rows: 39{41} sc.

Row 2 (Eyelet row)**:** Ch 4 **(counts as first dc plus ch 1)**, turn; skip next sc, dc in next sc, (ch 1, skip next sc, dc in next sc) across: 19{20} sps.

Row 3: Ch 1, turn; sc in each dc and in each ch-1 sp across; finish off: 39{41} sc.

Weave 1 yard of ribbon through Eyelet Row of Neckband.

fashion corner

Take a look through our fashion corner and you'll discover lots of stylish accessories for your entire family. There are cozy sweaters and gloves for cold days, a glitzy evening bag for a night on the town, and a delicate lapel pin to dress up an everyday outfit. It's fun to create high fashion with this exciting collection!

SUNFLOWER SWEATERS

Everything's coming up sunflowers on these bright pullovers for little girls! Designed for sizes small, medium, and large, the crewneck sweaters feature fields of bold sunflower granny squares blooming against red or blue backgrounds. What perky tops for Grandma's little rays of sunshine!

Size:	Small	Medium	Large
Finished Chest			
Measurement:	21"	24"	28"

Size Note: Instructions are written for size Small with sizes Medium and Large in braces { }. Instructions will be easier to read if you circle all the numbers pertaining to your size. If only one number is given, it applies to all sizes.

MATERIALS
Sport Weight Yarn, approximately:
  MC (Red or Blue) - 6{8-10} ounces,
    [170{230-280} grams, 615{825-1,030} yards]
  Color A (Green) - 38{38-68} yards
  Color B (Yellow) - 24{24-42} yards
  Color C (Brown) - 20{20-34} yards
Crochet hooks, sizes D (3.25 mm) **and** F (3.75 mm) **or**
  sizes needed for gauge
Yarn needle

GAUGE: One Square = 3½"
  With large size hook (size F), 3 3-dc groups
  and 5 rows = 2"
  With small size hook (size D), 12 sc and 12 rows = 2"

FRONT
SQUARE [Make 9{9-16}]
With large size hook and Color C, ch 4; join with slip st to form a ring.

Rnd 1 (Right side): Ch 3 **(counts as first dc, now and throughout)**, work 15 dc in ring; join with slip st to first dc, finish off: 16 dc.

Note: Loop a short piece of yarn around any stitch to mark last round as **right** side.

Rnd 2: With **right** side facing, join Color B with slip st in any dc; ch 4 **(counts as first dc plus ch 1, now and throughout)**, (dc in next dc, ch 1) around; join with slip st to first dc, finish off: 16 ch-1 sps.

Rnd 3: With **right** side facing, join Color A with slip st in any ch-1 sp; ch 3, (2 dc, ch 1, 3 dc) in same sp, skip next ch-1 sp, 3 dc in next ch-1 sp, skip next ch-1 sp, ★ (3 dc, ch 1, 3 dc) in next ch-1 sp, skip next ch-1 sp, 3 dc in next ch-1 sp, skip next ch-1 sp; repeat from ★ around; join with slip st to first dc, finish off: 36 dc.

Rnd 4: With **right** side facing, join MC with slip st in any corner ch-1 sp; ch 3, (2 dc, ch 1, 3 dc) in same sp, 3 dc in each sp **between** 3-dc groups across to next corner ch-1 sp *(Fig. 29, page 138)*, ★ (3 dc, ch 1, 3 dc) in corner ch-1 sp, 3 dc in each sp **between** 3-dc groups across to next corner ch-1 sp; repeat from ★ around; join with slip st to first dc, finish off: 48 dc.

JOINING

With **wrong** sides together and MC, and working through **inside** loops only, whipstitch Squares together, forming 3{3-4} strips of 3{3-4} Squares each *(Fig. 35b, page 140)*; then whipstitch strips together.

SIZE SMALL ONLY

Neck Foundation Row: With **right** side facing and large size hook, join MC with slip st in any corner ch-1 sp; ch 3, 3 dc in same sp, 3 dc in each of next 3 sps **between** 3-dc groups, ch 2, skip next 2 dc, sc in next dc, sc in next joining, sc in next 12 dc, sc in next joining, sc in next dc, ch 2, skip next 2 dc, 3 dc in each of next 3 sps **between** 3-dc groups, 4 dc in next corner ch-1 sp; do **not** finish off: 16 sc.

SIZE MEDIUM ONLY

Rnd 1: With **right** side facing and large size hook, join MC with slip st in any corner ch-1 sp; ch 4, 3 dc in same sp, 3 dc in each sp **between** 3-dc groups and in each joining across to next corner ch-1 sp, ★ (3 dc, ch 1, 3 dc) in corner ch-1 sp, 3 dc in each sp **between** 3-dc groups and in each joining across to next corner ch-1 sp; repeat from ★ 2 times **more**, 2 dc in same sp as first dc; join with slip st to first dc: 52 3-dc groups.
Rnd 2: Slip st in first corner ch-1 sp, ch 3, (2 dc, ch 1, 3 dc) in same sp, 3 dc in each sp **between** 3-dc groups around working (3 dc, ch 1, 3 dc) in each corner ch-1 sp; join with slip st to first dc: 56 3-dc groups.
Neck Foundation Row: Slip st in next 2 dc and in next corner ch-1 sp, ch 3, 3 dc in same sp, 3 dc in each of next 3 sps **between** 3-dc groups, ch 2, skip next 2 dc, sc in next 20 dc, ch 2, skip next 2 dc, 3 dc in each of next 3 sps **between** 3-dc groups, 4 dc in next corner ch-1 sp, leave remaining sts unworked; do **not** finish off: 20 sc.

SIZE LARGE ONLY

Neck Foundation Row: With **right** side facing and large size hook, join MC with slip st in any corner ch-1 sp; ch 3, 3 dc in same sp, 3 dc in each of next 3 sps **between** 3-dc groups, 3 dc in next joining, ch 2, skip next 3 dc, sc in next 9 dc, sc in next sp, sc in next joining and in next sp, sc in next 9 dc, ch 2, skip next 3 dc, 3 dc in next joining, 3 dc in each of next 3 sps **between** 3-dc groups, 4 dc in next corner ch-1 sp; do **not** finish off: 21 sc.

RIGHT SHOULDER SHAPING

Row 1: Ch 4, turn; 3 dc in each of next 3{3-4} sps **between** 3-dc groups, ch 1, dc in last ch-2 sp, leave remaining sts unworked: 3{3-4} 3-dc groups.
Row 2: Ch 3, turn; 3 dc in next ch-1 sp, 3 dc in each of next 2{2-3} sps **between** 3-dc groups, 3 dc in next ch-1 sp, dc in last dc: 4{4-5} 3-dc groups.
Row 3: Ch 4, turn; 3 dc in each of next 3{3-4} sps **between** 3-dc groups, ch 1, dc in last dc: 3{3-4} 3-dc groups.
Row 4: Repeat Row 2.
Row 5: Turn; skip first dc, slip st in next 2 dc, sc in next dc, hdc in next sp **between** 3-dc groups, (2 hdc, dc) in next sp **between** 3-dc groups, 3 dc in each of next 1{1-2} sps **between** 3-dc groups, ch 1, dc in last dc.
Sizes Small and Meduim Only - Row 6: Ch 3, turn; 3 dc in next ch-1 sp, (dc, hdc, sc) in next sp **between** groups, skip next 3 sts, sc in sp **before** next hdc, slip st in next hdc, leave remaining sts unworked; finish off.
Size Large Only - Row 6: Ch 3, turn; 3 dc in next ch-1 sp, 3 dc in next sp **between** 3-dc groups, (dc, hdc, sc) in next sp **between** groups, skip next 3 sts, sc in sp **before** next hdc, slip st in next hdc, leave remaining sts unworked; finish off.

LEFT SHOULDER SHAPING

Row 1: With **wrong** side facing and large size hook, join MC with slip st in ch-2 sp to **left** of Neck; ch 4, 3 dc in each of next 3{3-4} sps **between** 3-dc groups, ch 1, dc in last dc.
Rows 2-4: Work same as Right Shoulder Shaping.
Row 5: Ch 4, turn; 3 dc in each of next 1{1-2} sps **between** 3-dc groups, (dc, 2 hdc) in next sp **between** 3-dc groups, hdc in next sp **between** 3-dc groups, sc in next dc, leave remaining 3 dc unworked.
Sizes Small and Meduim Only - Row 6: Turn; skip first sc, slip st in next hdc, sc in sp **before** next hdc, (sc, hdc, dc) in next sp **between** groups, 3 dc in next ch-1 sp, dc in last dc; finish off.
Size Large Only - Row 6: Turn; skip first sc, slip st in next hdc, sc in sp **before** next hdc, (sc, hdc, dc) in next sp **between** groups, 3 dc in next sp **between** 3-dc groups, 3 dc in next ch-1 sp, dc in last dc; finish off.

BOTTOM RIBBING

Foundation Row: With **right** side facing and large size hook, join MC with slip st in corner ch-1 sp on bottom edge; ch 1, sc in same sp, work 50{56-64} sc evenly spaced across to next corner ch-1 sp, sc in corner ch-1 sp: 52{58-66} sc.
Change to small size hook.
Ch 9{9-12} **loosely**.

Row 1: Sc in back ridge of second ch from hook and in each ch across *(Fig. 2a, page 131)*, with **right** side facing, slip st in first 2 sc on Foundation Row: 10{10-13} sts.
Row 2: Turn; skip first 2 slip sts, sc in Back Loop Only of each sc across *(Fig. 27, page 138)*: 8{8-11} sc.
Row 3: Ch 1, turn; sc in Back Loop Only of each sc across, slip st in next 2 sc on Foundation Row: 10{10-13} sts.
Repeat Rows 2 and 3 across, ending by working Row 2. Finish off.

BACK
RIBBING
With small size hook and MC, ch 9{9-12} **loosely**.
Row 1: Sc in back ridge of second ch from hook and in each ch across: 8{8-11} sc.
Row 2: Ch 1, turn; sc in Back Loop Only of each sc across. Repeat Row 2 until 26{29-33} ribs [52{58-66} rows] are complete; do **not** finish off.

BODY
Change to large size hook.
Row 1 (Right side)**:** Ch 1, working in end of rows, 1{1-2} sc in first row, sc in next row and in each row across: 52{58-67} sc.
Note: Mark last row as **right** side.
Row 2: Ch 3, turn; (skip next 2 sc, 3 dc in next sc) across to last 3 sc, skip next 2 sc, dc in last sc: 16{18-21} 3-dc groups.
Row 3: Ch 4, turn; skip next 3 dc, 3 dc in each sp **between** 3-dc groups across to last 4 dc, ch 1, skip next 3 dc, dc in last dc: 15{17-20} 3-dc groups.
Row 4: Ch 3, turn; 3 dc in next ch-1 sp, 3 dc in each sp **between** 3-dc groups across to last ch-1 sp, 3 dc in last ch-1 sp, dc in last dc: 16{18-21} 3-dc groups.
Repeat Rows 3 and 4 for pattern until Back measures approximately 14{15½-18}" from bottom edge, ending by working Row 4; do **not** finish off.

SHOULDER SHAPING
Row 1: Turn; skip first dc, slip st in next 2 dc, sc in next dc, hdc in next sp **between** 3-dc groups, (2 hdc, dc) in next sp **between** 3-dc groups, 3 dc in each of next 11{13-16} sps **between** 3-dc groups, (dc, 2 hdc) in next sp **between** 3-dc groups, hdc in next sp **between** 3-dc groups, sc in next dc, leave remaining 3 dc unworked: 11{13-16} 3-dc groups.
Row 2: Turn; skip first sc, slip st in next hdc, sc in sp **before** next hdc, (sc, hdc, dc) in next sp **between** groups, 3 dc in each of next 10{12-15} sps **between** 3-dc groups, (dc, hdc, sc) in next sp **between** groups, skip next 3 sts, sc in sp **before** next hdc, slip st in next hdc, leave remaining sts unworked; finish off.

SLEEVE (Make 2)
RIBBING
With small size hook, MC, and leaving a long end for sewing, ch 9{9-12} **loosely**.
Row 1: Sc in back ridge of second ch from hook and in each ch across: 8{8-11} sc.
Row 2: Ch 1, turn; sc in Back Loop Only of each sc across. Repeat Row 2 until 15{15-17} ribs [30{30-34} rows] are complete; do **not** finish off.

BODY
Change to large size hook.
Row 1 (Right side)**:** Ch 1, work 34{34-37} sc evenly spaced across end of rows.
Note: Mark last row as **right** side.
Row 2: Ch 3, turn; (skip next 2 sc, 3 dc in next sc) across to last 3 sc, skip next 2 sc, dc in last sc: 10{10-11} 3-dc groups.
Row 3 (Increase row)**:** Ch 3, turn; 3 dc in sp **before** first 3-dc group, 3 dc in each sp **between** 3-dc groups across, 3 dc in sp **before** last dc, dc in last dc: 11{11-12} 3-dc groups.
Rows 4 and 5: Ch 3, turn; 3 dc in each sp **between** 3-dc groups across, 3 dc in sp **before** last dc, dc in last dc.
Repeat Rows 3-5, 5 times, then repeat Row 3, 0{1-1} time **more**: 16{17-18} 3-dc groups.
Repeat Row 4 until Sleeve measures approximately 10{11½-12½}" from bottom edge; finish off.

FINISHING
Sew shoulder seams.

NECK RIBBING
Foundation Rnd: With **right** side facing and small size hook, join MC with slip st at center back neck edge; ch 1, work 56{62-68} sc evenly spaced around; join with slip st to first sc. Ch 6 **loosely**.
Row 1: Sc in back ridge of second ch from hook and in each ch across, with **right** side facing, slip st in first 2 sc on Foundation Rnd: 7 sts.
Row 2: Turn; skip first 2 slip sts, sc in Back Loop Only of each sc across: 5 sc.
Row 3: Ch 1, turn; sc in Back Loop Only of each sc across, slip st in next 2 sc on Foundation Rnd: 7 sts.
Repeat Rows 2 and 3 around, ending by working Row 2; finish off leaving a long end for sewing.
Sew seam.

Sew Sleeves to sweater, matching center of Sleeve to shoulder seam and beginning 5½{6-6¼}" down from seam.

Weave underarm and side in one continuous seam.

Quick CHIC EVENING BAG

An ideal size for holding necessities, this chic purse is a must for an elegant evening! Crocheted with double strands of black or natural cotton thread and metallic gold cord, the clutch includes a shoulder strap and a button closure.

Finished Size: Approximately 8" wide x 4³/4 " deep

MATERIALS

For **each** Bag:
Bedspread Weight Cotton Thread (size 10),
   approximately 400 yards
Metallic Gold 1-ply cord, approximately 400 yards
Steel crochet hooks, sizes 0 (3.25 mm) **and** 4 (2.00)
   or sizes needed for gauge
Straight pins
1 - 1" button
1 - size 4 snap
Tapestry needle

Note: Entire Evening Bag is worked holding 2 strands of thread and 2 strands of metallic cord together, unless otherwise specified.

GAUGE: With large size hook (size 0),
        in pattern, 19 sts and 11 rows = 3"
        With small size hook (size 4), 7 sc and 7 rows = 1"

       Gauge Swatch: (3" x 3")
       With large size hook, ch 21 **loosely**.
       Rows 1-11: Work same as Body.
       Finish off.

BODY

With large size hook, ch 45 **loosely**.
Row 1: 2 Dc in third ch from hook, ★ skip next 2 chs, (sc, 2 dc) in next ch; repeat from ★ across to last 3 chs, skip next 2 chs, sc in last ch: 43 sts.
Row 2 (Right side): Ch 2, turn; 2 dc in first sc, ★ skip next 2 dc, (sc, 2 dc) in next sc; repeat from ★ across to last 3 sts, skip next 2 dc, sc in top of beginning ch.
Note: Loop a short piece of thread around any stitch to mark last row as **right** side.
Row 3: Ch 2, turn; 2 dc in first sc, ★ skip next 2 dc, (sc, 2 dc) in next sc; repeat from ★ across to last 3 sts, skip next 2 dc, sc in top of beginning ch-2.
Repeat Row 3 for pattern until piece measures approximately 12" from beginning ch, ending by working a **wrong** side row; do **not** finish off.
Note: Loop short pieces of thread around first and around last stitch on row 8" from beginning ch to mark Gusset placement.

SHAPING

Rows 1-5: Turn; slip st in first 4 sts, ch 2, 2 dc in same st, ★ skip next 2 dc, (sc, 2 dc) in next sc; repeat from ★ across to last 6 sts, skip next 2 dc, sc in next sc, leave remaining 3 sts unworked: 13 sts.
Finish off.

GUSSET (Make 2)

With small size hook and holding one strand of thread and one strand of metallic together, ch 7 **loosely**.
Row 1: Sc in second ch from hook and in each ch across: 6 sc.
Rows 2-16: Ch 1, turn; sc in each sc across.
Note: Mark last row as **right** side.
Row 17: Ch 1, turn; 2 sc in first sc, sc in next 4 sc, 2 sc in last sc: 8 sc.
Rows 18-24: Ch 1, turn; sc in each sc across.
Row 25: Ch 1, turn; 2 sc in first sc, sc in next 6 sc, 2 sc in last sc: 10 sc.
Rows 26-32: Ch 1, turn; sc in each sc across.
Finish off.

FINISHING

With **wrong** side of Body facing and beginning ch toward you, place **wrong** side of each Gusset on Body, matching corner of last row to markers; pin in place at corner.
Fold lower edge of Body up until beginning ch of Body matches free corner of last row of each Gusset; pin Gusset in place along both sides.

Joining Rnd: With **right** side of front facing, large size hook and working through **both** thicknesses, join threads and metallics with slip st in front right corner; ch 1, working from **left** to **right**, work reverse sc evenly around to first marked stitch *(Figs. 25a-d, page 136)*, easing in Gusset as necessary; working on Body only, work reverse sc evenly around to next marked stitch; working through **both** thicknesses, work reverse sc evenly around to beginning ch, easing in Gusset as necessary; working in free loops of beginning ch *(Fig. 28b, page 138)*, work reverse sc in each ch across; join with slip st to first st, finish off.

STRAP

With large size hook, ch 177 **loosely**.

Rnd 1: 3 Sc in second ch from hook, sc in each ch across to last ch, 3 sc in last ch; working in free loops of beginning ch, sc in each ch across; join with slip st to first sc, finish off. Sew one end of strap to inside of each Gusset, 1/4" below upper edge.

With tapestry needle and one strand of thread, sew back of snap to **right** side of center front of Body 2 1/2" below beginning ch. Sew front of snap to center of **wrong** side of flap 1/4" below last rnd.

Sew button to **right** side of Body over snap front.

HANDSOME CARDIGAN

When the weather turns cool, a special gentleman will appreciate the warmth of this handsome cardigan. Stylishly designed, the button-front sweater has a ribbed V-neck and ribbing at the sleeves and waist. Instructions are provided for sizes small, medium, and large.

Size:	Small	Medium	Large
Finished Chest			
Measurement:	42"	46"	49"

Size Note: Instructions are written for size Small with sizes Medium and Large in braces { }. Instructions will be easier to read if you circle all the numbers pertaining to your size. If only one number is given, it applies to all sizes.

MATERIALS
Worsted Weight Yarn, approximately:
   MC (Dark Brown) - 18{20-22} ounces,
      [510{570-620} grams, 1,235{1,370-1,510} yards]
   Color A (Brown) - 5{5-6} ounces,
      [140{140-170} grams, 345{345-410} yards]
   Color B (Light Brown) - 4{4¹/₂-5} ounces,
      [110{130-140} grams, 275{310-345} yards]
Crochet hooks, sizes G (4.00 mm) **and** J (6.00 mm) **or** sizes needed for gauge
Yarn needle
Sewing needle and thread
5 - ⁵/₈" buttons

GAUGE: With large size hook (size J),
      in pattern for Sleeves and Back,
      13 sts = 4" and 9 rows = 3"
      In pattern for Fronts, 13 sc and 17 rows = 4"
      With small size hook (size G), 8 sc and 8 rows = 2"

PATTERN STITCHES
FRONT POST DOUBLE TREBLE CROCHET (abbreviated FPdtr)
YO 3 times, insert hook from **front** to **back** around post of st indicated *(Fig. 23, page 136)*, YO and pull up a loop, (YO and draw through 2 loops on hook) 4 times. Skip st behind FPdtr.

FRONT POST QUADRUPLE TREBLE CROCHET (abbreviated FPqtr)
YO 5 times, insert hook from **front** to **back** around post of st indicated *(Fig. 24, page 136)*, YO and pull up a loop, (YO and draw through 2 loops on hook) 6 times. Skip st behind FPqtr.

DECREASE
Pull up a loop in next 2 sts, YO and draw through all 3 loops on hook **(counts as one sc)**.

SLEEVE (Make 2)
RIBBING
With small size hook and MC, ch 14 **loosely**.
Row 1: Sc in back ridge of second ch from hook and in each ch across *(Fig. 2a, page 131)*: 13 sc.
Row 2: Ch 1, turn; sc in Back Loop Only of each sc across *(Fig. 27, page 138)*.
Repeat Row 2 until 15{16-17} ribs [30{32-34} rows] are complete.

BODY
Change to large size hook.
Row 1 (Right side): Ch 1, sc in end of each row across: 30{32-34} sc.
Note: Loop a short piece of yarn around any stitch to mark last row as **right** side.
Row 2: Ch 2 **(counts as first hdc, now and throughout)**, turn; hdc in next sc and in each sc across to last sc, skip last sc, hdc in turning ch.
Row 3 (Increase row): Ch 1, turn; sc in each hdc across to last hdc, 2 sc in last hdc: 31{33-35} sc.
Row 4 (Increase row): Ch 2, turn; hdc in next sc and in each sc across to last sc, skip last sc, 2 hdc in turning ch: 32{34-36} hdc.
Repeat Rows 3 and 4, 19{20-21} times: 70{74-78} hdc.
Next Row: Ch 1, turn; sc in each hdc across.
Next Row: Ch 2, turn; hdc in next sc and in each sc across to last sc, skip last sc, hdc in turning ch.
Repeat last 2 rows until Sleeve measures approximately 17¹/₂{18-18¹/₂}" from beginning; finish off.

BACK
RIBBING
With small size hook and MC, ch 14 **loosely**.
Row 1: Sc in back ridge of second ch from hook and in each ch across: 13 sc.
Row 2: Ch 1, turn; sc in Back Loop Only of each sc across.
Repeat Row 2 until 34{37-40} ribs [68{74-80} rows] are complete.

BODY
Change to large size hook.
Row 1 (Right side): Ch 1, sc in end of each row across: 68{74-80} sc.
Note: Mark last row as **right** side.

Row 2: Ch 2, turn; hdc in next sc and in each sc across to last sc, skip last sc, hdc in turning ch.
Row 3: Ch 1, turn; sc in each hdc across.
Repeat Rows 2 and 3 for pattern until Back measures approximately 26{27-28}" from beginning, ending by working a **right** side row; finish off.

LEFT FRONT

RIBBING

With small size hook and MC, ch 14 **loosely.**
Row 1: Sc in back ridge of second ch from hook and in each ch across: 13 sc.
Row 2: Ch 1, turn; sc in Back Loop Only of each sc across.
Repeat Row 2 until 17{18-19} ribs [34{36-38} rows] are complete.

BODY

Change to large size hook.
Row 1 (Right side): Ch 1, sc in end of each row across: 34{36-38} sc.
Note: Mark last row as **right** side.
Row 2: Ch 1, turn; sc in each sc across changing to Color A in last sc worked *(Fig. 31a, page 138).*
Rows 3 and 4: Ch 1, turn; sc in each sc across; at end of Row 4, change to Color B in last sc worked.
Rows 5-8: Ch 1, turn; sc in each sc across; at end of Row 8, change to Color A in last sc worked.
Row 9: Ch 1, turn; sc in first sc, work FPdtr around sc 4 rows **below** each of next 2 sc, ★ sc in next 4 sc, work FPdtr around sc 4 rows **below** each of next 2 sc, sc in next 2 sc, work FPdtr around sc 4 rows **below** each of next 2 sc; repeat from ★ across to last 1{3-5} sc, sc in last 1{3-5} sc.
Row 10: Ch 1, turn; sc in each st across changing to MC in last sc worked.
Row 11: Ch 1, turn; sc in first 9 sc, work FPqtr around sc 8 rows **below** each of next 2 sc, ★ sc in next 8 sc, work FPqtr around sc 8 rows **below** each of next 2 sc; repeat from ★ across to last 3{5-7} sc, sc in last 3{5-7} sc.
Row 12: Ch 1, turn; sc in each st across changing to Color A in last sc worked.
Repeat Rows 3-12 for pattern until Left Front measures approximately 16" from beginning, ending by working a **right** side row.

NECK SHAPING

Decrease Row: Ch 1, turn; decrease, sc in each st across: 33{35-37} sc.
Continue to work in pattern, working a decrease row every other row, 3{1-1} times more, then decrease every fourth row, 7{9-9} times: 23{25-27} sts.
Work even until Left Front measures same as Back, ending by working a **right** side row; finish off.

RIGHT FRONT

Work same as Left Front through Row 2.
Rows 3 and 4: Ch 1, turn; sc in each sc across; at end of Row 4, change to Color B in last sc worked.
Rows 5-8: Ch 1, turn; sc in each sc across; at end of Row 8, change to Color A in last sc worked.
Row 9: Ch 1, turn; sc in first 1{3-5} sc, work FPdtr around sc 4 rows **below** each of next 2 sc, ★ sc in next 2 sc, work FPdtr around sc 4 rows **below** each of next 2 sc, sc in next 4 sc, work FPdtr around sc 4 rows **below** each of next 2 sc; repeat from ★ across to last sc, sc in last sc.
Row 10: Ch 1, turn; sc in each st across changing to MC in last sc worked.
Row 11: Ch 1, turn; sc in first 3{5-7} sts, work FPqtr around sc 8 rows **below** each of next 2 sc, ★ sc in next 8 sc, work FPqtr around sc 8 rows **below** each of next 2 sc; repeat from ★ across to last 9 sc, sc in last 9 sc.
Row 12: Ch 1, turn; sc in each st across changing to Color A in last sc worked.
Repeat Rows 3-12 for pattern until Right Front measures same as Left Front to Neck Shaping, ending by working a **right** side row.

NECK SHAPING

Decrease Row: Ch 1, turn; sc in each st across to last 2 sts, decrease: 33{35-37} sc.
Complete same as Left Front.

FINISHING

With **wrong** sides together, MC, and working through **both** loops, whipstitch shoulder seams *(Fig. 35a, page 140).*

BAND

Row 1: With **right** side facing and small size hook, join MC with slip st in BLO of first sc on Right Front Ribbing; ch 1, sc in BLO of first 13 sc, work 60 sc evenly spaced across end of rows to Neck Shaping, work 42{46-50} sc evenly spaced across end of rows to Shoulder seam, sc in BLO of each st across Back, work 42{46-50} sc evenly spaced across end of rows of Neck Shaping, work 60 sc evenly spaced across end of rows to Left Front Ribbing, sc in BLO of last 13 sts: 252{262-272} sc.
Rows 2 and 3: Ch 1, turn; sc in BLO of each sc across.
Row 4: Ch 1, turn; sc in BLO of first 3 sc, ch 2 **loosely** (buttonhole), (skip next 2 sc, sc in BLO of next 14 sc, ch 2 **loosely**) 4 times, skip next 2 sc, sc in BLO of each sc across.
Row 5: Ch 1, turn; sc in BLO of each sc and in each ch across; finish off.

Sew Sleeves to sweater, matching center of Sleeve to shoulder seam and beginning 10³⁄₄{11¹⁄₂-12}" down from seam.
Weave underarm and side in one continuous seam.
Sew buttons to Right Front Band opposite buttonholes.

Quick RIBBED GLOVES

*Stay outside and play in the snowy weather — your hands will stay warm and toasty
in our comfortable ribbed gloves! Instructions for these quick-to-stitch designs are given
for small and large sizes, so you can make a pair for each of your fun-loving friends.*

Finished Size: Small   Large

Length of Hand: 7"   8"

Size Note: Measure hand from wrist to tip of middle finger.
Instructions are written for size Small with size Large in braces
{ }. Instructions will be easier to read if you circle all the
numbers pertaining to your size. If only one number is given, it
applies to both sizes.

MATERIALS

Worsted Weight Yarn, approximately:
   3 ounces, (90 grams, 200 yards) **each** pair
Crochet hook, size G (4.00 mm) **or** size needed for gauge
Yarn needle

GAUGE: In pattern, 8 sc = 2" and 5 rows = 1½"

Leaving a long end for sewing, ch 82{88} **loosely.**
Note: Work in back ridge of chs *(Fig. 2a, page 131)* or in
Back Loops Only of sc and slip sts throughout *(Fig. 27, page 138).*
Row 1 (Right side): Sc in second ch from hook and in next
11 chs, slip st in next 5 chs, sc in next 22{25} chs, slip st in
next 3 chs, sc in next 22{25} chs, slip st in next 5 chs, sc in
last 12 chs: 81{87} sts.
Note: Loop a short piece of yarn around any stitch to mark last
row as **right** side.
Rows 2 and 3: Ch 1, turn; sc in first 12 sc, slip st in next
5 slip sts, sc in next 22{25} sc, slip st in next 3 slip sts, sc in
next 22{25} sc, slip st in next 5 slip sts, sc in last 12 sc.

Row 4: Ch 1, turn; slip st in first 30{32} sts, hdc in next sc, ch 23{25} **loosely**, skip next 19{21} sts, hdc in next sc, slip st in last 30{32} sts: 85{91} sts.

Row 5: Ch 1, turn; sc in first 12 sts, slip st in next 5 slip sts, sc in next 14{16} sts, sc in next 10{11} chs, slip st in next 3 chs, sc in next 10{11} chs, sc in next 14{16} sts, slip st in next 5 slip sts, sc in last 12 sts.

Rows 6 and 7: Ch 1, turn; sc in first 12 sc, slip st in next 5 slip sts, sc in next 24{27} sc, slip st in next 3 slip sts, sc in next 24{27} sc, slip st in next 5 slip sts, sc in last 12 sc.

Row 8: Ch 1, turn; slip st in first 30{32} sts, hdc in next sc, ch 27{29} **loosely**, skip next 23{25} sts, hdc in next sc, slip st in last 30{32} sts: 89{95} sts.

Row 9: Ch 1, turn; sc in first 12 sts, slip st in next 5 slip sts, sc in next 14{16} sts, sc in next 12{13} chs, slip st in next 3 chs, sc in next 12{13} chs, sc in next 14{16} sts, slip st in next 5 slip sts, sc in last 12 sts.

Rows 10 and 11: Ch 1, turn; sc in first 12 sc, slip st in next 5 slip sts, sc in next 26{29} sc, slip st in next 3 slip sts, sc in next 26{29} sc, slip st in next 5 slip sts, sc in last 12 sts.

Row 12: Ch 1, turn; slip st in first 30{32} sts, hdc in next sc, ch 23{25} **loosely**, skip next 27{29} sts, hdc in next sc, slip st in last 30{32} sts: 85{91} sts.

Rows 13-15: Repeat Rows 5-7.

Row 16: Ch 1, turn; slip st in first 26{28} sts, hdc in next sc, ch 19{21} **loosely**, skip next 31{33} sts, hdc in next sc, slip st in last 26{28} sts: 73{79} sts.

Row 17: Ch 1, turn; sc in first 12 sts, slip st in next 5 sts, sc in next 10{12} sts, sc in next 8{9} chs, slip st in next 3 chs, sc in next 8{9} chs, sc in next 10{12} sts, slip st in next 5 sts, sc in last 12 sts.

Rows 18 and 19: Ch 1, turn; sc in first 12 sc, slip st in next 5 sts, sc in next 18{21} sc, slip st in next 3 sts, sc in next 18{21} sc, slip st in next 5 sts, sc in last 12 sc.
Finish off leaving a long end for sewing.

With **wrong** side together, working through **inside** loops only, and matching sts, whipstitch seams between fingers and on outside edges *(Fig. 35b, page 140)*.

Quick ROSE LAPEL PIN

A classic fashion accent, our delicate rose pin can dress up your lapel or hold a scarf in place. The flower is crocheted with cotton thread in one continuous round piece, which is folded and rolled to create a perfect bud. Silk florals enhance the rose's natural beauty.

Finished Size: Approximately 2½" wide x 4" tall

MATERIALS
Bedspread Weight Cotton Thread (size 10), approximately 23 yards
Steel crochet hook, size 6 (1.80) **or** size needed for gauge
Florist tape
3" length of 22 gauge florist wire
Silk flowers and leaves

GAUGE: 8 sts = 1"

ROSE

Rnd 1 (Right side): Leaving a 3" end, wind thread around finger once to form a ring, insert hook in ring, YO and draw through ring forming a loop on hook *(Fig. 1a)*, ch 3, work 43 dc in ring *(Fig. 1b)*; join with slip st to top of beginning ch-3, pull end tightly to close ring: 44 sts.

Note: Loop a short piece of thread around any stitch to mark last round as **right** side.

Fig. 1a

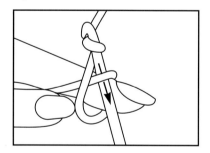

Fig. 1b

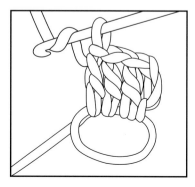

Rnd 2: Ch 1, sc in same st, (ch 4, skip next dc, sc in next dc) around to last dc, ch 2, skip last dc, hdc in first sc to form last loop: 22 loops.

Rnd 3: Ch 1, sc in same loop, ch 3, (2 dc, ch 1, 2 dc) in next loop, ch 3, ★ sc in next loop, ch 3, (2 dc, ch 1, 2 dc) in next loop, ch 3; repeat from ★ around; join with slip st to first sc.

Rnd 4: Ch 1, sc in same st, ch 4, (2 dc, ch 1, 2 dc) in next ch-1 sp, ch 4, ★ sc in next sc, ch 4, (2 dc, ch 1, 2 dc) in next ch-1 sp, ch 4; repeat from ★ around; join with slip st to first sc.

Rnds 5 and 6: Ch 1, sc in same st, ch 5, (2 dc, ch 1, 2 dc) in next ch-1 sp, ch 5, ★ sc in next sc, ch 5, (2 dc, ch 1, 2 dc) in next ch-1 sp, ch 5; repeat from ★ around; join with slip st to first sc. Finish off.

FINISHING

Fold circle in half with **wrong** side together.
Beginning at one corner, roll piece to form a rose.
Insert wire through bottom of rose (Rnd 1) and bend end to secure.
Wrap florist tape around bottom of rose and around wire.
Add leaves and flowers and wrap again with florist tape, catching stems as you wrap.

TEXTURED CARDIGAN

Fashioned in ecru sport weight yarn, this long-sleeved cardigan will become an indispensable addition to your cool-weather attire. Clusters and V-stitches give the buttoned jacket its textured appeal, and simple ribbing along the neck, sleeves, and waist offers a stylish finish.

Size:	Small	Medium	Large
Finished Chest			
Measurement:	36"	40"	44"

Size Note: Instructions are written for size Small with sizes Medium and Large in braces { }. Instructions will be easier to read if you circle all the numbers pertaining to your size.

MATERIALS

Sport Weight Yarn, approximately:
   30{36-40} ounces,
     [850{1,020-1,140} grams,
       2,570{3,085-3,430} yards]
Crochet hook, size F (3.75 mm) **or** size needed for gauge
Yarn needle
8 - 1/2" buttons

GAUGE: In pattern, 11 V-Sts and 14 rows = 4"

   Gauge Swatch: (4" x 4¼")
   Ch 22 **loosely**.
   Row 1: Sc in second ch from hook and in each ch across: 21 sc.
   Rows 2-15: Work same as Body.
   Finish off.

PATTERN STITCHES

V-ST

(Hdc, ch 1, hdc) in st or sp indicated.

CLUSTER

★ YO, insert hook in sp indicated, YO and pull up a loop, YO and draw through 2 loops on hook; repeat from ★ 2 times **more**, YO and draw through all 4 loops on hook *(Figs. 13a & b, page 134)*.

ENDING CLUSTER

(YO, insert hook in st indicated, YO and pull up a loop, YO and draw through 2 loops on hook) twice, YO and draw through all 3 loops on hook.

BACK

RIBBING

Ch 16 **loosely**.

Row 1: Sc in back ridge of second ch from hook and in each ch across *(Fig. 2a, page 131)*: 15 sc.

Row 2: Ch 1, turn; sc in Back Loop Only of each sc across *(Fig. 27, page 138)*.

Repeat Row 2 until 50{55-60} ribs [100{110-120} rows] are complete.

BODY

Row 1 (Right side)**:** Ch 1, working in end of rows, 2 sc in first row, sc in next row and in each row across: 101{111-121} sc.

Note: Loop a short piece of yarn around any stitch to mark last row as **right** side.

Row 2: Ch 2 **(counts as first hdc, now and throughout)**, turn; hdc in same st, (skip next sc, work V-St in next sc) across to last 2 sc, skip next sc, 2 hdc in last sc: 49{54-59} V-Sts.

Row 3: Ch 2, turn; dc in same st **(counts as first Cluster)**, ch 1, [work Cluster in next V-St (ch-1 sp), ch 1] across, work ending Cluster in last hdc: 50{55-60} ch-1 sps.

Row 4: Ch 2, turn; work V-St in each ch-1 sp across, hdc in last Cluster: 50{55-60} V-Sts.

Row 5: Ch 3 **(counts as first dc, now and throughout)**, turn; work Cluster in next V-St, (ch 1, work Cluster in next V-St) across, dc in last hdc: 49{54-59} ch-1 sps.

Row 6: Ch 2, turn; hdc in same st, work V-St in each ch-1 sp across, 2 hdc in last dc: 49{54-59} V-Sts.

Repeat Rows 3-6 for pattern until Back measures approximately 12½{12½-13½}" from beginning, ending by working Row 6.

ARMHOLE SHAPING

Row 1: Turn; slip st in first 12{15-18} sts, ch 2, dc in same st, ch 1, skip next ch-1 sp, (work Cluster in next V-St, ch 1) across to last 4{5-6} V-Sts, skip next ch-1 sp, work ending Cluster in next hdc, leave remaining sts unworked: 42{45-48} ch-1 sps. Beginning by working Row 4, work even until Armholes measure approximately 8{9-9}", ending by working pattern Row 6.

RIGHT NECK SHAPING

Row 1: Ch 2, turn; dc in same st, ch 1, (work Cluster in next V-St, ch 1) 11{12-13} times, skip next ch-1 sp, work ending Cluster in next hdc, leave remaining sts unworked: 12{13-14} ch-1 sps.

Row 2: Ch 2, turn; work V-St in each ch-1 sp across, hdc in last Cluster; finish off.

LEFT NECK SHAPING

Row 1: With **right** side facing, skip 17{18-19} V-Sts from Right Neck Shaping and join yarn with slip st in next hdc; ch 2, dc in same st, ch 1, skip next ch-1 sp, (work Cluster in next V-St, ch 1) across, work ending Cluster in last hdc: 12{13-14} ch-1 sps.

Row 2: Ch 2, turn; work V-St in each ch-1 sp across, hdc in last Cluster; finish off.

LEFT FRONT

RIBBING

Ch 16 **loosely**.

Row 1: Sc in back ridge of second ch from hook and in each ch across: 15 sc.

Row 2: Ch 1, turn; sc in Back Loop Only of each sc across. Repeat Row 2 until 23{26-28} ribs [46{52-56} rows] are complete.

BODY

Row 1 (Right side)**:** Ch 1, working in end of rows, 2 sc in first row, sc in next row and in each row across: 47{53-57} sc.
Note: Mark last row as **right** side.

Row 2: Ch 2, turn; hdc in same st, (skip next sc, work V-St in next sc) across to last 2 sc, skip next sc, 2 hdc in last sc: 22{25-27} V-Sts.

Row 3: Ch 2, turn; dc in same st, ch 1, (work Cluster in next V-St, ch 1) across, work ending Cluster in last hdc: 23{26-28} ch-1 sps.

Row 4: Ch 2, turn; work V-St in each ch-1 sp across, hdc in last Cluster: 23{26-28} V-Sts.

Row 5: Ch 3, turn; work Cluster in next V-St, (ch 1, work Cluster in next V-St) across, dc in last hdc: 22{25-27} ch-1 sps.

Row 6: Ch 2, turn; hdc in same st, work V-St in each ch-1 sp across, 2 hdc in last dc.

Repeat Rows 3-6 for pattern until Front measures same as Back to Armhole Shaping, ending by working Row 6.

ARMHOLE SHAPING

Row 1: Turn; slip st in first 12{15-18} sts, ch 2, dc in same st, ch 1, skip next ch-1 sp, (work Cluster in next V-St, ch 1) across, work ending Cluster in last hdc: 19{21-22} ch-1 sps.
Beginning by working Row 4, work even until Armhole measures approximately 5³/₄", ending by working pattern Row 6.

NECK SHAPING

Row 1: Ch 2, turn; dc in same st, (ch 1, work Cluster in next V-St) across to last 3{4-4} V-Sts, work ending Cluster in next V-St, leave remaining sts unworked: 15{16-17} ch-1 sps.

Row 2: Ch 2, turn; work V-St in each ch-1 sp across, hdc in last Cluster: 15{16-17} V-Sts.

Row 3: Ch 3, turn; work Cluster in next V-St, (ch 1, work Cluster in next V-St) across to last V-St, skip last V-st, dc in last hdc: 13{14-15} ch-1 sps.

Row 4: Ch 2, turn; work V-St in each ch-1 sp across, 2 hdc in last dc: 13{14-15} V-Sts.

Row 5: Ch 2, turn; dc in same st, (ch 1, work Cluster in next V-St) across to last V-St, work ending Cluster in last V-St: 12{13-14} ch-1 sps.

Row 6: Ch 2, turn; work V-St in each ch-1 sp across, hdc in last Cluster: 12{13-14} V-Sts.

Beginning by working pattern Row 5, work even until Left Front measures same as Back, ending by working pattern Row 4; finish off.

RIGHT FRONT

Work same as Left Front to Armhole Shaping.

ARMHOLE SHAPING

Row 1: Ch 2, turn; dc in same st, ch 1, (work Cluster in next V-St, ch 1) across to last 4{5-6} V-Sts, skip next ch-1 sp, work ending Cluster in next hdc, leave remaining sts unworked: 19{21-22} ch-1 sps.
Beginning by working Row 4, work even until Armhole measures approximately 5³/₄", ending by working pattern Row 6.

NECK SHAPING

Row 1: Turn; slip st in first 10{13-13} sts, ch 2, dc in same st, (work Cluster in next V-St, ch 1) across, work ending Cluster in last hdc: 15{16-17} ch-1 sps.

Row 2: Ch 2, turn; work V-St in each ch-1 sp across, skip next Cluster, hdc in last Cluster: 15{16-17} V-Sts.

Row 3: Ch 3, turn; skip first V-St, work Cluster in next V-St, (ch 1, work Cluster in next V-St) across, dc in last hdc: 13{14-15} ch-1 sps.

Row 4: Ch 2, turn; hdc in same st, work V-St in each ch-1 sp across, hdc in last dc: 13{14-15} V-Sts.

Row 5: Turn; slip st in next hdc and in next ch-1 sp, ch 2, dc in same sp, (work Cluster in next V-St, ch 1) across, work ending Cluster in last hdc: 12{13-14} ch-1 sps.

Row 6: Ch 2, turn; work V-St in each ch-1 sp across, skip next Cluster, hdc in last Cluster: 12{13-14} V-Sts.

Beginning by working Row 5, work even until Right Front measures same as Left Front, ending by working pattern Row 4; finish off.

SLEEVE
RIBBING
Ch 11 **loosely**.
Row 1: Sc in back ridge of second ch from hook and in each ch across: 10 sc.
Row 2: Ch 1, turn; sc in Back Loop Only of each sc across.
Repeat Row 2 until 21{22-24} ribs [42{44-48} rows] are complete.

BODY
Row 1 (Right side)**:** Ch 1, work 49{55-55} sc evenly spaced across end of rows.
Note: Mark last row as **right** side.
Row 2: Ch 2, turn; hdc in same st, (skip next sc, work V-St in next sc) across to last 2 sc, skip next sc, 2 hdc in last sc: 23{26-26} V-Sts.
Row 3: Ch 2, turn; dc in same st, ch 1, (work Cluster in next V-St, ch 1) across, work ending Cluster in last hdc: 24{27-27} ch-1 sps.
Row 4: Ch 2, turn; work V-St in each ch-1 sp across, hdc in last Cluster: 24{27-27} V-Sts.
Row 5 (Increase row)**:** Ch 4 **(counts as first dc plus ch 1, now and throughout)**, turn; (work Cluster in next V-St, ch 1) across, dc in last hdc: 25{28-28} ch-1 sps.
Row 6 (Increase row)**:** Ch 2, turn; hdc in same st, work V-St in each ch-1 sp across, 2 hdc in last dc: 25{28-28} V-Sts.
Repeat Rows 3-6, 11{13-13} times: 47{54-54} V-Sts.
Work same as Rows 3-6 of Back Body for pattern, page 102, until Sleeve measures approximately 19½{20¾-22}" from beginning; finish off.
Note: Mark each end of row approximately 18{19-20}" from beginning.

FINISHING
With **wrong** sides together, and working through **both** loops, whipstitch shoulder seams *(Fig. 35a, page 140)*.

BUTTON BAND
Foundation Row: With **right** side facing, join yarn with slip st in top corner of Left Front; ch 1, work 104{104-108} sc evenly spaced across.
Ch 8 **loosely**.
Row 1: Sc in second ch from hook and in each ch across, sc in first 2 sc on Foundation Row: 9 sc.
Row 2: Turn; skip first 2 sc, sc in BLO of each sc across: 7 sc.
Row 3: Ch 1, turn; sc in BLO of each sc across, sc in next 2 sc on Foundation Row: 9 sc.
Repeat Rows 2 and 3 across, ending by working Row 2.
Finish off.

BUTTONHOLE BAND
Foundation Row: With **right** side facing, join yarn with slip st in bottom corner of Right Front; ch 1, work 104{104-108} sc evenly spaced across to start of Neck Shaping.
Ch 8 **loosely**.
Row 1: Sc in second ch from hook and in each ch across, sc in first 2 sc on Foundation Row: 9 sc.
Row 2: Turn; skip first 2 sc, sc in BLO of each sc across: 7 sc.
Row 3: Ch 1, turn; sc in BLO of each sc across, sc in next 2 sc on Foundation Row: 9 sc.
Repeat Rows 2 and 3, 4{4-1} times.
Buttonhole Row: Turn; skip first 2 sc, sc in BLO of next 2 sc, ch 2, skip next 2 sc, sc in BLO of last 3 sc: 5 sc.
Next Row: Ch 1, turn; sc in BLO of first 3 sc and in next 2 chs, sc in BLO of last 2 sc, sc in next 2 sc on Foundation Row: 9 sc.
Repeat Rows 2 and 3, 6{6-7} times; then repeat Buttonhole Row and Next Row once **more**.
Continue in same manner, working a buttonhole between every 12{12-14} rows.
Finish off.

NECKBAND
Foundation Row: With **right** side facing, join yarn with slip st in first st of Buttonhole Band; ch 1, sc in same st and in free loop of each ch across Band, work 22{28-30} sc evenly spaced along Right Neck edge, work 34{36-38} sc evenly spaced across Back Neck edge, work 22{28-30}sc evenly spaced along Left Neck edge, sc in each sc across Button Band: 92{106-112} sc.
Complete same as Button Band, working buttonhole in line with previous buttonholes.
Finish off.

Sew side seams.
Sew Sleeve seams to marker, then sew rows above marker to short edges of underarm.
Sew Sleeves to cardigan, matching center of Sleeve to shoulder seam.
Sew buttons to Band opposite buttonholes.

hooked on holidays

Holidays are more fun when you decorate your home to reflect the spirit of the occasion! In this festive assortment, there are delightful designs to greet all of your favorite days. You'll find sweet-smelling sachets to help Valentine's Day memories linger, a floral afghan that's as pretty as a basket of Easter eggs, and lifelike fruit to fill a Thanksgiving cornucopia. Just remember, whichever design you choose to create, a handmade decoration becomes a holiday keepsake that you'll cherish!

VALENTINE'S DAY

Crocheted with size 10 cotton thread and filled with fragrant potpourri, these dainty sachets will help you share sweet sentiments on Valentine's Day. The ball features a delicate floral motif, and the bag is made up of shell stitches. Satin ribbon joins the front and back pieces of the heart-shaped sachet.

Quick SENTIMENTAL SACHETS

MATERIALS

Bedspread Weight Cotton Thread (size 10), approximately:
- **Heart** - 55 yards
- **Ball** - 70 yards
- **Bag**
  - Color A (White) - 34 yards
  - Color B (Rose) - 40 yards

Steel crochet hook:
- **Heart** - size 8 (1.50 mm) **or** size needed for gauge
- **Ball** - size 9 (1.40 mm) **or** size needed for gauge
- **Bag** - size 10 (1.30 mm) **or** size needed for gauge

Sewing needle and thread
25" length of ¹/₈" wide ribbon for **each**
Bridal net
Potpourri

HEART

Finished Size: Approximately 4¹/₂" x 4¹/₂"

GAUGE: Rnds 1-4 = 2"

FRONT

Ch 5; join with slip st to form a ring.

Rnd 1 (Right side): Ch 3 **(counts as first dc)**, 19 dc in ring; join with slip st to first dc: 20 dc.

Note: Loop a short piece of thread around any stitch to mark last round as **right** side.

Rnd 2: Ch 1, sc in same st, (ch 5, skip next dc, sc in next dc) around to last dc, ch 2, skip last dc, dc in first sc to form last loop: 10 loops.

Rnd 3: Ch 1, sc in same loop, (ch 5, sc in next loop) around, ch 2, dc in first sc to form last loop.

Note #1: To work **beginning Cluster**, ch 3, ★ YO, insert hook in loop indicated, YO and pull up a loop, YO and draw through 2 loops on hook; repeat from ★ once **more**, YO and draw through all 3 loops on hook *(Figs. 13a & b, page 134)*.

Note #2: To work **Cluster**, ★ YO, insert hook in loop indicated, YO and pull up a loop, YO and draw through 2 loops on hook; repeat from ★ 2 times **more**, YO and draw through all 4 loops on hook.

Rnd 4: Work (beginning Cluster, ch 3, Cluster) in same loop, (ch 3, work Cluster) twice in next loop and in each loop around, ch 1, hdc in top of beginning Cluster to form last sp: 20 sps.

Rnd 5: Ch 1, sc in same sp, (ch 3, work Cluster) twice in next ch-3 sp, ch 3, ★ sc in next ch-3 sp, (ch 3, work Cluster) twice in next ch-3 sp, ch 3; repeat from ★ around; join with slip st to first sc: 30 sps.

Rnd 6: Ch 1, sc in same st, ch 7, skip next ch-3 sp, sc in next ch-3 sp, (ch 7, sc in next sc, ch 7, skip next ch-3 sp, sc in next ch-3 sp) around, ch 4, dc in first sc to form last loop: 20 loops.

Rnd 7: Ch 1, sc in same loop, (ch 5, dc) twice in next loop, (ch 5, sc in next loop) 3 times, ch 5, dc in next loop, ch 5, tr in next loop, ch 5, dtr in next loop, ch 5, (tr tr, ch 5) 4 times in next loop, tr in next loop, ch 5, sc in next loop, (ch 3, sc in next loop) twice, ch 5, tr in next loop, ch 5, (tr tr, ch 5) 4 times in next loop, dtr in next loop, ch 5, tr in next loop, ch 5, dc in next loop, (ch 5, sc in next loop) twice, ch 2, dc in first sc to form last loop: 27 loops.

Rnd 8: Ch 1, sc in same loop, ch 5, sc in next loop, (ch 5, sc) twice in next loop, (ch 5, sc in next loop) 13 times, ch 1, sc in next loop, (ch 5, sc in next loop) 10 times, ch 2, dc in first sc to form last loop.

Rnd 9 (Eyelet rnd): Ch 1, sc in same loop, ch 3, (sc in next sc, ch 3, sc in next loop, ch 3) 16 times, sc in next ch-1 sp, (ch 3, sc in next loop, ch 3, sc in next sc) 10 times, ch 1, hdc in first sc to form last sp: 54 sps.

Rnd 10: Ch 1, sc in same sp, (ch 3, sc in next ch-3 sp) 32 times, ch 1, pull up a loop in each of next 2 ch-3 sps, YO and draw through all 3 loops on hook, ch 1, sc in next ch-3 sp, (ch 3, sc in next ch-3 sp) 18 times, ch 1, hdc in first sc to form last sp.

Rnd 11: Ch 1, sc in same sp, (ch 3, dc in third ch from hook, sc in next ch-3 sp) 32 times, (slip st in next st and in next ch-1 sp) twice, slip st in next sc, (sc in next ch-3 sp, ch 3, dc in third ch from hook) around; join with slip st to first sc, finish off.

BACK

Work same as Front through Rnd 8.

Rnd 9 (Eyelet rnd): Ch 1, sc in same loop, ch 3, (sc in next sc, ch 3, sc in next loop, ch 3) 16 times, sc in next ch-1 sp, ch 3, (sc in next loop, ch 3, sc in next sc, ch 3) 10 times; join with slip st to first sc, finish off: 54 sps.

FINISHING

See Washing and Blocking, page 140.
Using Back for pattern and adding 1/4" seam allowance, cut 2 hearts from bridal net.
For pouch, sew pieces of net together, leaving a 2" opening for turning.
Turn right side out.
Fill pouch with potpourri; sew opening closed.
With **wrong** sides of crocheted pieces together, matching sps, and beginning at center top, weave ribbon through eyelet round, inserting pouch before closing; tie ribbon in a bow.

BALL

Finished Size: Approximately 4" long x 3" in diameter

GAUGE: Each Motif = 1 1/2"

FIRST MOTIF

Ch 8; join with slip st to form a ring.
Rnd 1 (Right side): Ch 1, 16 sc in ring; join with slip st to first sc.
Note #1: Loop a short piece of thread around any stitch to mark last round as **right** side.
Note #2: To work **beginning Cluster**, ch 4, ★ YO twice, insert hook in **next** sc, YO and pull up a loop, (YO and draw through 2 loops on hook) twice; repeat from ★ once **more**, YO and draw through all 3 loops on hook *(Figs. 14a & b, page 134)*.
Note #3: To work **Cluster**, YO twice, insert hook in **same** st as last st worked, YO and pull up a loop, (YO and draw through 2 loops on hook) twice, ★ YO twice, insert hook in **next** sc, YO and pull up a loop, (YO and draw through 2 loops on hook) twice; repeat from ★ once **more**, YO and draw through all 4 loops on hook.
Rnd 2: Work beginning Cluster, ch 7, (work Cluster, ch 7) around working last Cluster in same st as beginning Cluster; join with slip st to top of beginning Cluster, finish off: 8 Clusters.

SECOND MOTIF

Ch 8; join with slip st to form a ring.
Rnd 1 (Right side): Ch 1, 16 sc in ring; join with slip st to first sc.
Rnd 2: Work beginning Cluster, (ch 7, work Cluster) 6 times, ch 3, with **wrong** sides together, slip st in center ch of any loop on **First Motif** *(Fig. 32, page 138)*, ch 3, work Cluster on **new** Motif working in same st as beginning Cluster, ch 3, slip st in center ch of next loop on **First Motif**, ch 3; join with slip st to top of beginning Cluster, finish off: 8 Clusters.

NEXT 3 MOTIFS

Ch 8; join with slip st to form a ring.
Rnd 1 (Right side): Ch 1, 16 sc in ring; join with slip st to first sc.
Rnd 2: Work beginning Cluster, (ch 7, work Cluster) 6 times, ch 3, with **wrong** sides together, skip next 2 loops on **previous** Motif, slip st in center ch of next loop, ch 3, work Cluster on **new** Motif working in same st as beginning Cluster, ch 3, slip st in center ch of next loop on **previous** Motif, ch 3; join with slip st to top of beginning Cluster, finish off: 8 Clusters.

LAST MOTIF

Ch 8; join with slip st to form a ring.
Rnd 1 (Right side): Ch 1, 16 sc in ring; join with slip st to first sc.
Rnd 2: Work beginning Cluster, (ch 7, work Cluster) twice, ch 3, with **wrong** sides together, skip next 2 loops on **previous** Motif, slip st in center ch of next loop, ch 3, work Cluster on **new** Motif, ch 3, slip st in center ch of next loop on **previous** Motif, ch 3, work Cluster on **new** Motif, (ch 7, work Cluster) twice, ch 3, with **wrong** sides together, skip next 2 loops on **First Motif**, slip st in center ch of next loop, ch 3, work Cluster on **new** Motif working in same st as beginning Cluster, ch 3, slip st in center ch of next loop on **First Motif**, ch 3; join with slip st to top of beginning Cluster, finish off: 8 Clusters.

Continued on page 128.

ST. PATRICK'S DAY

*You'll spread the luck of the Irish when you use these shamrock-shaped coasters!
They're quick to stitch holding two strands of cotton worsted weight yarn together.*

Quick SHAMROCK COASTER

Finished Size: Approximately 5" in diameter

MATERIALS

100% Cotton Worsted Weight Yarn, approximately 22 yards **each**
Crochet hook, size H (5.00 mm) **or** size needed for gauge

Note: Entire Coaster is worked holding 2 strands of yarn together.

GAUGE: Rnd 1 = 1³/₄" (from side to side)

COASTER

Ch 4; join with slip st to form a ring.
Row 1 (Right side): (Ch 2, 2 dc in ring, ch 2, slip st in ring) 3
times: 6 dc.
Row 2: Ch 3, turn; working in Back Loops Only *(Fig. 27, page 138)*, 2 dc in each of next 2 dc, ch 3, (slip st in next
slip st, ch 3, 2 dc in each of next 2 dc, ch 3) twice, slip st in
beginning ring: 12 dc.

Row 3: Ch 2, turn; ★ † working **around** next ch-3, dc in st at
base of next 2 dc *(Fig. 1)*, working in Front Loops Only, 2 dc
in each of next 4 dc, working **around** next ch-3, dc in st at
base of last 2 dc just worked into, ch 2 †, slip st in **both** loops
of next slip st, ch 2; repeat from ★ once **more**, then repeat
from † to † once, slip st in beginning ring; ch 7 **loosely**
(stem), hdc in third ch from hook and in next ch, sc in next
2 chs, slip st in last ch and in beginning ring; finish off.

Fig. 1

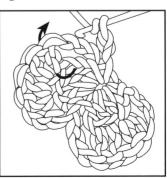

EASTER

Look at the treasures we discovered on the bunny trail! (Below) This little cottontail hopped right into our hearts. Just the thing for perking up an Easter basket, the stuffed rabbit is stitched with huggably soft brushed acrylic yarn. (Opposite) Decorated Easter eggs inspired the colors of this pretty afghan. Featuring spring-fresh floral motifs, the throw has a richly textured appearance that's created using popcorns and front post stitches.

Quick CHARLIE COTTONTAIL

Finished Size: Approximately 10" tall

MATERIALS

Worsted Weight Brushed Acrylic Yarn, approximately:
    White - 1¼ ounces, (35 grams, 96 yards)
    Pink - 6 yards
    Gray - small amount
Crochet hook, size F (3.75 mm) **or** size needed for gauge
Polyester fiberfill
2 - 6 mm beads (eyes)
Yarn needle
Sewing needle and thread
18" length of ¼" wide ribbon

GAUGE: 9 sc and 9 rows = 2"

HEAD AND BODY

With White, ch 3 **loosely**; join with slip st to form a ring.

Rnd 1 (Right side)**:** 2 Sc in each ch around; do **not** join, place marker *(see Markers, page 137)*: 6 sc.

Rnd 2: 2 Sc in each sc around: 12 sc.

Rnd 3: (Sc in next sc, 2 sc in next sc) around: 18 sc.

Rnd 4: (Sc in next 2 sc, 2 sc in next sc) around: 24 sc.

Rnds 5-9: Sc in each sc around.

Note: To **decrease**, pull up a loop in next 2 sc, YO and draw through all 3 loops on hook **(counts as one sc)**.

Rnd 10: (Sc in next 2 sc, decrease) around: 18 sc.

Rnd 11: (Sc in next sc, decrease) around: 12 sc.

Rnds 12 and 13: Sc in each sc around.

Stuff Head with polyester fiberfill.

Rnd 14: (Sc in next 3 sc, 2 sc in next sc) around: 15 sc.

Rnd 15: (Sc in next 4 sc, 2 sc in next sc) around: 18 sc.

Rnd 16: (Sc in next 5 sc, 2 sc in next sc) around: 21 sc.

Rnd 17: (Sc in next 6 sc, 2 sc in next sc) around: 24 sc.

Rnds 18-22: Sc in each sc around.

Stuff Body with polyester fiberfill.

Joining: Slip st in next sc, ch 1, flatten Rnd 22 with slip st at side; working through **both** loops of **both** thicknesses, sc in each sc across; do **not** finish off: 12 sc.

LEFT LEG

Rnd 1: Ch 1, turn; sc in Front Loop Only of first 6 sc *(Fig. 27, page 138)*, turn; sc in free loop of each sc across *(Fig. 28a, page 138)*; do **not** join, place marker: 12 sc.

Rnds 2-11: Sc in each sc around.

Stuff Leg with polyester fiberfill.

Rnd 12: Decrease around: 6 sc.

Rnd 13: (Skip next sc, slip st in next sc) around; finish off: 3 sts.

RIGHT LEG

Rnd 1: With back of Body facing and working in Front Loops Only, join White with slip st in first sc on Body; sc in each sc across, **turn**; sc in free loop of each sc across; do **not** join, place marker: 12 sc.

Rnds 2-13: Work same as Left Leg.

FOOT (Make 2)

With White, ch 3 **loosely**; join with slip st to form a ring.

Rnd 1 (Right side)**:** 2 Sc in each ch around; do **not** join, place marker: 6 sc.

Rnd 2: 2 Sc in each sc around: 12 sc.

Rnd 3: (Sc in next 2 sc, 2 sc in next sc) around: 16 sc.

Rnd 4: Sc in each sc around; slip st in next sc, finish off leaving a long end for sewing.

ARM (Make 2)

With White, ch 3 **loosely**; join with slip st to form a ring.

Rnd 1 (Right side)**:** 2 Sc in each ch around; do **not** join, place marker: 6 sc.

Rnd 2: (Sc in next sc, 2 sc in next sc) around: 9 sc.

Rnds 3-14: Sc in each sc around.

Stuff Arm with polyester fiberfill.

Joining: Decrease, slip st in next sc, flatten Rnd 14 with slip st at side; working through **both** loops of **both** thickness, sc in each sc across; finish off leaving a long end for sewing: 4 sc.

EAR (Make 2)
INNER EAR

Row 1 (Right side)**:** With Pink, ch 2, 2 sc in second ch from hook.
Note: Loop a short piece of yarn around any stitch to mark last row as **right** side.

Rows 2-4: Ch 1, turn; sc in each sc across: 2 sc.

Row 5: Ch 1, turn; 2 sc in first sc, sc in last sc: 3 sc.

Rows 6 and 7: Ch 1, turn; sc in each sc across.

Row 8: Ch 1, turn; 2 sc in first sc, sc in last 2 sc: 4 sc.

Rows 9 and 10: Ch 1, turn; sc in each sc across.

Row 11: Ch 1, turn; decrease, sc in last 2 sc: 3 sc.

Row 12: Ch 1, turn; decrease, sc in last sc; finish off: 2 sc.

BACK EAR

With White, work same as Inner Ear; do **not** finish off.

Joining: With **wrong** sides together, Inner Ear facing, and working through **both** pieces, sc evenly across end of rows, 3 sc in free loop of beginning ch *(Fig. 28b, page 138)*, sc evenly across end of rows; finish off leaving a long end for sewing.

CHEEK (Make 2)

With White, ch 3 **loosely**; join with slip st to form a ring.

Rnd 1 (Right side)**:** 2 Sc in each ch around; do **not** join, place marker: 6 sc.

Rnd 2: 2 Sc in each sc around: 12 sc.

Rnd 3: Sc in each sc around; slip st in next sc, finish off leaving a long end for sewing.

FINISHING

Stuff each Foot with polyester fiberfill and sew to Legs.

Sew Arms to side of Body.

Sew Ears to top of Head, ½" apart.

Sew Cheeks to Head, with edges touching, lightly stuffing with polyester fiberfill before closing.

Sew beads to Head for eyes.

With Pink, add Satin Stitch nose *(Fig. 41b, page 143)*.

Attach a White 1½" diameter pom-pom to Body for tail *(Figs. 36a & b, page 141)*.

Using photo as a guide for placement, with Gray, add 4 Straight Stitches to each Arm and Foot *(Fig. 39, page 143)*.

Tie ribbon in a bow around neck.

EASTER EGG AFGHAN

Finished Size: Approximately 47" x 63"

MATERIALS

Worsted Weight Yarn, approximately:
Color A (White) - 18 ounces, (510 grams, 1,185 yards)
6 Pastel colors (green, orange, purple, pink, blue, and yellow) - 7 ounces, (200 grams, 460 yards) **each**
Crochet hook, size G (4.00 mm) **or** size needed for gauge
Yarn needle

GAUGE: One Square = 5½" x 5½"

PATTERN STITCHES

POPCORN

5 Dc in ring, drop loop from hook, insert hook in first dc of 5-dc group, hook dropped loop and draw through *(Fig. 15b, page 134)*.

FRONT POST TREBLE CROCHET (abbreviated FPtr)

YO twice, insert hook from **front** to **back** around post of st indicated *(Fig. 17, page 135)*, YO and pull up a loop **even** with last st worked, (YO and draw through 2 loops on hook) 3 times. Skip st behind FPtr.

SQUARE (Make 77)

Note: Each Square is made using one pastel color for Rnds 1, 2, and 4, another pastel color for Rnd 3, and Color A for Rnd 5.

With first color, ch 8; join with slip st to form a ring.

Rnd 1 (Right side): Ch 3 **(counts as first dc, now and throughout)**, 4 dc in ring, drop loop from hook, insert hook in first dc of 5-dc group, hook dropped loop and draw through, ch 5, (work Popcorn in ring, ch 5) 3 times; join with slip st to top of first Popcorn: 4 Popcorns.

Rnd 2: Ch 3, (3 dc, ch 2, 3 dc) in next loop, ★ dc in next Popcorn, (3 dc, ch 2, 3 dc) in next loop; repeat from ★ around; join with slip st to first dc, finish off: 28 dc.

Rnd 3: With **right** side facing, join next color with slip st in any corner ch-2 sp; ch 3, (dc, ch 2, 2 dc) in same sp, dc in next 3 dc, work FPtr around top of Popcorn on rnd **below** next dc, dc in next 3 dc, ★ (2 dc, ch 2, 2 dc) in next corner ch-2 sp, dc in next 3 dc, work FPtr around top of Popcorn on rnd **below** next dc, dc in next 3 dc; repeat from ★ around; join with slip st to first dc, finish off.

Rnd 4: With **right** side facing, join first color with slip st in any corner ch-2 sp; ch 3, (dc, ch 2, 2 dc) in same sp, ★ † dc in next 4 dc, work FPtr around dc on rnd **below** next dc, dc in next FPtr, work FPtr around dc on rnd **below** next dc, dc in next 4 dc †, (2 dc, ch 2, 2 dc) in next corner ch-2 sp; repeat from ★ 2 times **more**, then repeat from † to † once; join with slip st to first dc, finish off.

Rnd 5: With **right** side facing, join Color A with slip st in any corner ch-2 sp; ch 6, dc in same sp, dc in each st across to next corner ch-2 sp, ★ (dc, ch 3, dc) in corner ch-2 sp, dc in each st across to next corner ch-2 sp; repeat from ★ around; join with slip st to third ch of beginning ch-6, finish off: 68 dc.

ASSEMBLY

With **wrong** sides together and Color A, and working through **both** loops, whipstitch Squares together. Form 7 vertical strips of 11 Squares each using desired color placement *(Fig. 35a, page 140)*; do **not** join strips.

PLACEMENT DIAGRAM

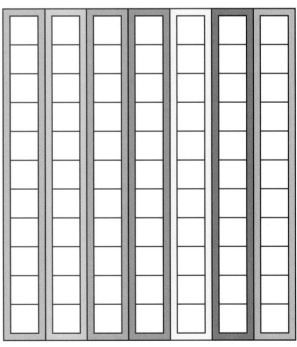

Continued on page 129.

INDEPENDENCE DAY

Display your all-American spirit with this smart red, white, and blue table rug! A great accent for the Fourth of July (or any patriotic occasion), the checkerboard-look rug is fashioned with cotton thread yo-yos using a join-as-you-go stitching method.

AMERICAN TABLE RUG

Finished Size: Approximately 11" x 30½"

MATERIALS
Cotton Crochet Thread (size 8), approximately:
    Red - 3 ounces, (90 grams, 190 yards)
    Cream - 3 ounces (90 grams, 190 yards)
    Blue - 2 ounces, (60 grams, 130 yards)
Crochet hook, size C (2.75 mm) **or** size needed for gauge

GAUGE: One Yo-Yo = 1½" in diameter

FIRST YO-YO
With Blue, ch 3; join with slip st to form a ring.
Rnd 1 (Right side)**:** Ch 3 **(counts as first dc, now and throughout)**, 11 dc in ring; join with slip st to first dc: 12 dc.
Note: Loop a short piece of yarn around any stitch to mark last round as **right** side.
Rnd 2: Ch 1, sc in same st, ch 3, (sc in next dc, ch 3) around; join with slip st to first sc, finish off.

ADDITIONAL YO-YOS
Work same as First Yo-Yo through Rnd 1, using color as indicated on Placement Diagram, beginning with bottom row and working from left to right.
Note: Mark last round as **right** side.
Work One-Sided or Two-Sided Joining, following Placement Diagram as a guide.
Note: Yo-Yos are joined with **wrong** sides together and new Yo-Yo facing throughout *(Fig. 32, page 138)*.

ONE-SIDED JOINING
Rnd 2: Ch 1, sc in same st, (ch 3, sc in next dc) 8 times, ★ ch 1, sc in corresponding ch-3 sp on **adjacent Yo-Yo**, ch 1, sc in next dc on **new Yo-Yo**; repeat from ★ 2 times **more**, ch 3; join with slip st to first sc, finish off.

TWO-SIDED JOINING
Rnd 2: Ch 1, sc in same st, (ch 3, sc in next dc) 5 times, ★ ch 1, sc in corresponding ch-3 sp on **adjacent Yo-Yo**, ch 1, sc in next dc on **new Yo-Yo**; repeat from ★ 5 times **more**, ch 3; join with slip st to first sc, finish off.

EDGING
With **right** side facing, join Cream with slip st from **front** to **back** around post of joining sc as indicated on Placement Diagram *(Fig. 17, page 135)*; ch 1, sc around same st, ch 3, (sc in next ch-3 sp, ch 3) across next Yo-Yo, ★ sc around next joining sc, ch 3, (sc in next ch-3 sp, ch 3) across next Yo-Yo; repeat from ★ around working across Blue Yo-Yo's with Blue; join with slip st to first sc, finish off.

PLACEMENT DIAGRAM

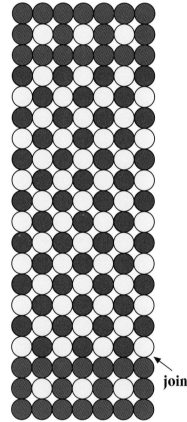

join for edging

HALLOWEEN

Halloween will be a scream when you decorate with these frightful friends! (Below) Our jack-o'-lantern pillows are quick to crochet with fabric strips. The features are simply cut from felt and glued on. (Opposite) This bewitching little miss will have you spellbound with her Halloween charm! Crocheted holding two strands of thread, the stuffed doll sports wavy locks created from unraveled worsted weight yarn. Her beguiling smile will enchant boys and "ghouls" of all ages.

JACK-O'-LANTERN PILLOWS

Finished Size: Large - approximately 16" wide x 17" tall
Small - approximately 13" wide x 15" tall

MATERIALS

100% Cotton Fabric, 44/45" wide, approximately:

Large Pillow
Orange - 12 yards
Brown - 1/4 yard

Small Pillow
Orange - 9 yards
Brown - 1/4 yard

Crochet hook, size P (10.00 mm) **or** size needed for gauge
Polyester fiberfill
Black felt
Craft glue

Prepare fabric except 2/3 yard of Orange for each pillow form and tear into 1 1/2" wide strips **(see Preparing Fabric Strips and Joining Fabric Strips, page 139)**.

GAUGE: 3 sc and 2 rows = 2"

PATTERN STITCHES

SC DECREASE (uses next 2 sts)
Pull up a loop in next 2 sts, YO and draw through all 3 loops on hook **(counts as one sc)**.

DC DECREASE (uses next 2 sts)
★ YO, insert hook in **next** st, YO and pull up a loop, YO and draw through 2 loops on hook; repeat from ★ once **more**, YO and draw through all 3 loops on hook **(counts as one dc)**.

LARGE PILLOW

FRONT

With Orange, ch 15 **loosely**.

Row 1: Dc in fourth ch from hook, hdc in next ch, sc in next ch, (work sc decrease, sc in next ch) twice, hdc in next ch, dc in last 2 chs: 11 sts.

Row 2 (Right side): Ch 3 **(counts as first dc, now and throughout)**, turn; dc in same st, (dc, hdc) in next dc, hdc in next hdc, sc in next 5 sc, hdc in next hdc, (hdc, dc) in next dc, 2 dc in last st: 15 sts.

Note: Loop a scrap piece of fabric around any stitch to mark last row as **right** side.

Row 3: Ch 3, turn; dc in same st, (dc, hdc) in next dc, hdc in next 11 sts, (hdc, dc) in next dc, 2 dc in last dc: 19 sts.

Row 4: Ch 3, turn; dc in same st, dc in next 2 dc, hdc in next 13 sts, dc in next 2 dc, 2 dc in last dc: 21 sts.

Large Pillow
Eyes and Nose Pattern

Row 5: Ch 2 **(counts as first hdc, now and throughout)**, turn; hdc in same st and in each st across to last dc, 2 hdc in last dc: 23 hdc.

Rows 6-11: Ch 2, turn; hdc in next hdc and in each hdc across.

Row 12: Ch 3, turn; work dc decrease, hdc in next 8 hdc, sc in next hdc, hdc in next 8 hdc, work dc decrease, dc in last hdc: 21 sts.

Row 13: Ch 3, turn; dc in next dc, hdc in next 8 hdc, sc in next sc, hdc in next 8 hdc, dc in last 2 dc.

Row 14: Ch 3, turn; work dc decrease, hdc in next 6 hdc, sc in next 3 sts, hdc in next 6 hdc, work dc decrease, dc in last dc: 19 sts.

Row 15: Ch 3, turn; work dc decrease, dc in next 2 hdc, hdc in next 4 sts, sc in next sc, hdc in next 4 sts, dc in next 2 hdc, work dc decrease, dc in last dc: 17 sts.

Row 16: Ch 1, turn; sc in each st across.

Row 17: Ch 1, turn; work sc decrease, sc in next sc, hdc in next 4 sc, dc in next sc, (dc, slip st, dc) in next sc, dc in next sc, hdc in next 4 sc, sc in next sc, work sc decrease: 17 sts.

Row 18: Ch 1, turn; work sc decrease, sc in next hdc, hdc in next 2 hdc, sc in next hdc, slip st in next 5 sts, sc in next hdc, hdc in next 2 hdc, sc in next hdc, work sc decrease: 15 sts.

Edging: Ch 1, work 20 sc evenly spaced across end of rows; working in free loops of beginning ch **(Fig. 28b, page 138)**, 2 sc in first ch, sc in each ch across to last ch, 2 sc in last ch; work 20 sc evenly spaced across end of rows; 2 sc in first sc, sc in each st across to last sc, 2 sc in last sc; join with slip st to first sc, finish off: 72 sts.

BACK

Work same as Front; do **not** finish off.

FINISHING

Using Orange, make pillow form, page 140.

JOINING

Ch 1, turn; holding Front and Back with **wrong** sides together, Front facing, and working through **both** loops of **both** pieces, slip st in each sc around, matching sts and inserting pillow form before closing; join with slip st to first slip st, finish off.

STEM

Row 1: With Front facing, join Brown with slip st in third slip st to the **right** of center; ch 1, sc in same st and in next 2 slip sts, hdc in next slip st, sc in next 3 slip sts: 7 sts.

Row 2: Ch 1, turn; skip first sc, sc in next sc, hdc in next 3 sts, sc in next sc, leave remaining sc unworked: 5 sts.

Row 3: Turn; slip st in first sc, sc in next 3 hdc, slip st in last sc; finish off.

Using patterns, cut eyes, nose, and mouth from felt and glue to Front.

Large Pillow
Mouth Pattern

SMALL PILLOW

FRONT

With Orange, ch 12 **loosely**.

Row 1: Hdc in third ch from hook, sc in next ch, (work sc decrease, sc in next ch) twice, hdc in next ch, dc in last ch: 9 sts.

Row 2 (Right side): Ch 3 **(counts as first dc, now and throughout)**, turn; dc in same st, (dc, hdc) in next hdc, hdc in next sc, sc in next 3 sc, hdc in next sc, (hdc, dc) in next hdc, 2 dc in last st: 13 sts.

Note: Loop a scrap piece of fabric around any stitch to mark last row as **right** side.

Row 3: Ch 3, turn; dc in same st, hdc in next 11 sts, 2 dc in last dc: 15 sts.

Rows 4 and 5: Ch 2 **(counts as first hdc, now and throughout)**, turn; hdc in same st, hdc in next st and in each st across to last st, 2 hdc in last st: 19 hdc.

Rows 6-9: Ch 2, turn; hdc in next hdc and in each hdc across.

Row 10: Ch 2, turn; work dc decrease, hdc in next 6 hdc, sc in next hdc, hdc in next 6 hdc, work dc decrease, hdc in last hdc: 17 sts.

Row 11: Ch 3, turn; work dc decrease, hdc in next 4 hdc, sc in next 3 sts, hdc in next 4 hdc, work dc decrease, dc in last hdc: 15 sts.

Row 12: Ch 1, turn; sc in each st across.

Row 13: Ch 1, turn; work sc decrease, sc in next sc, hdc in next 3 sc, dc in next sc, (dc, slip st, dc) in next sc, dc in next sc, hdc in next 3 sc, sc in next sc, work sc decrease: 15 sts.

Row 14: Ch 1, turn; work sc decrease, sc in next 3 hdc, slip st in next 5 sts, sc in next 3 hdc, work sc decrease: 13 sts.

Edging: Ch 1, work 16 sc evenly spaced across end of rows; working in free loops of beginning ch *(Fig. 28b, page 138)*, 2 sc in first ch, sc in each ch across to last ch, 2 sc in last ch; work 16 sc evenly spaced across end of rows; 2 sc in first sc, sc in each st across to last sc, 2 sc in last sc; join with slip st to first sc, finish off: 60 sts.

BACK

Work same as Front; do **not** finish off.

FINISHING

Work same as Large Pillow.

Small Pillow
Mouth Pattern

Small Pillow
Eyes and Nose Pattern

LITTLE MISS MAGIC

Finished Size: Approximately 6" tall

MATERIALS

Bedspread Weight Cotton Thread (size 10), approximately:
MC (Purple) - 175 yards
Color A (Black) - 80 yards
Color B (Ecru) - 50 yards
Color C (Tan) - 14 yards
Red - small amount
Worsted Weight Yarn, approximately: Gold - 1½ yards
Steel crochet hook, size 7 (1.65 mm) **or** size needed for gauge
Safety pin
Polyester fiberfill
Tapestry needle
Craft glue
2 - 4 mm black beads (eyes)

Note: Entire Witch is worked holding 2 strands of thread together.

GAUGE: 15 sc and 15 rows = 2"

PATTERN STITCHES

SC DECREASE (uses next 2 sts)
Pull up a loop in next 2 sts, YO and draw through all 3 loops on hook **(counts as one sc)**.

HDC DECREASE (uses next 2 sts)
(YO, insert hook in **next** st, YO and pull up a loop) twice, YO and draw through all 5 loops on hook **(counts as one hdc)**.

DC DECREASE (uses next 2 sts)
★ YO, insert hook in **next** st, YO and pull up a loop, YO and draw through 2 loops on hook; repeat from ★ once **more**, YO and draw through all 3 loops on hook **(counts as one dc)**.

HAT

Rnd 1 (Right side): With Color A, ch 2, 4 sc in second ch from hook; do **not** join, place marker *(see Markers, page 137)*.

Note: Loop a short piece of thread around any stitch to mark last round as **right** side.

Rnd 2: (Sc in next sc, 2 sc in next sc) twice: 6 sc.

Rnds 3 and 4: Sc in each sc around.

Rnd 5: (Sc in next sc, 2 sc in next sc) around: 9 sc.

Rnd 6: Sc in each sc around.

Rnd 7: (Sc in next 2 sc, 2 sc in next sc) around: 12 sc.

Rnd 8: Sc in each sc around.

Rnd 9: (Sc in next 2 sc, 2 sc in next sc) around: 16 sc.

Rnd 10: Sc in each sc around.

Rnd 11: (Sc in next 3 sc, 2 sc in next sc) around: 20 sc.

Rnd 12: (Sc in next 9 sc, 2 sc in next sc) twice: 22 sc.

Rnd 13: Sc in each sc around; slip st in Front Loop Only of next sc *(Fig. 27, page 138)*, remove marker, do **not** finish off.

BRIM

Rnd 1: Ch 1, turn; working in Back Loops Only, sc in first sc, 2 sc in next sc, (sc in next sc, 2 sc in next sc) around; join with slip st to both loops of first sc: 33 sc.

Rnd 2: Ch 1, turn; working in both loops, sc in first 2 sc, 2 sc in next sc, (sc in next 2 sc, 2 sc in next sc) around; join with slip st to first sc: 44 sc.

Rnd 3: Ch 1, turn; sc in first 4 sc, (2 sc in next sc, sc in next 4 sc) around; join with slip st to first sc: 52 sc.

Rnd 4: Ch 1, turn; sc in first 7 sc, (2 sc in next sc, sc in next 8 sc) around; join with slip st to first sc: 57 sc.

Rnd 5: Ch 1, do **not** turn; sc in first 8 sc, 2 sc in next sc, (sc in next 9 sc, 2 sc in next sc) around to last 8 sc, sc in last 8 sc; join with slip st to first sc, finish off: 62 sc.

HEAD

Rnd 1: With **right** side facing, point of Hat down, and working **behind** Brim in free loops on Rnd 13 *(Fig. 28a, page 138)*, join Color B with slip st in any sc; ch 1, sc in same st and in next 4 sc, hdc in next 3 sc, 2 dc in each of next 6 sc, hdc in next 3 sc, sc in last 5 sc; join with slip st to first sc: 28 sts.

Rnd 2: Ch 1, sc in same st and in next 4 sc, hdc in next 2 hdc, 2 dc in next hdc, dc in next 12 dc, 2 dc in next hdc, hdc in next 2 hdc, sc in last 5 sc; join with slip st to first sc: 30 sts.

Rnd 3: Ch 1, sc in same st and in next 2 sc, hdc in next sc, 2 dc in each of next 2 sts, dc in next 18 sts, 2 dc in each of next 2 sts, hdc in next sc, sc in last 3 sc; join with slip st to first sc: 34 sts.

Rnd 4: Ch 1, sc in same st and in next 2 sc, hdc in next 2 sts, 2 dc in each of next 2 dc, dc in next 20 dc, 2 dc in each of next 2 dc, hdc in next 2 sts, sc in last 3 sc: 38 sts.

Rnd 5: Ch 1, sc in same st and in next 4 sts, hdc in next 2 dc, dc in next 2 dc, 2 dc in each of next 2 dc, (dc in next 7 dc, 2 dc in each of next 2 dc) twice, dc in next 2 dc, hdc in next 2 dc, sc in last 5 sts; join with slip st to first sc: 44 sts.

Rnd 6: Ch 1, sc in same st and in next sc, sc decrease, hdc in next 4 sts, hdc decrease, dc decrease twice, dc in next 3 dc, dc decrease twice, dc in next 2 dc, dc decrease twice, dc in next 3 dc, dc decrease twice, hdc decrease, hdc in next 4 sts, sc decrease, sc in last 2 sc; join with slip st to first sc: 32 sts.

Rnd 7: Ch 1, sc in same st and in next 2 sc, sc decrease, hdc in next hdc, dc decrease twice, dc in next 2 dc, dc decrease 4 times, dc in next 2 dc, dc decrease twice, hdc in next hdc, sc decrease, sc in last 3 sc; join with slip st to first sc: 22 sts.

Rnd 8: Ch 1, sc in same st and in next 2 sc, hdc in next sc, dc in next 5 sts, hdc in next 4 dc, dc in next 5 sts, hdc in next sc, sc in last 3 sc; join with slip st to first sc, do **not** finish off. Stuff Hat and Head with polyester fiberfill.

NECK

Rnd 1: Ch 1, 2 sc in same st, sc in next 4 sts, skip next 12 sts (chin opening), sc in last 5 sts; join with slip st to first sc, slip loop onto safety pin to keep piece from unraveling while forming chin: 11 sc.
To form chin, flatten chin opening from Neck to center front of Head, then sew seam.

Rnd 2: Remove safety pin and slip loop onto hook; ch 3 **(counts as first dc, now and throughout)**, dc in next 3 sc, hdc in next 4 sc, dc in last 3 sc; join with slip st to first dc.

Rnd 3: Ch 1, sc in each st around; join with slip st to first sc, do **not** finish off.

SUPPORT

Rnd 1: Ch 3, 2 dc in same st, 3 dc in next sc and in each sc around; join with slip st to first dc: 33 dc.

Rnd 2: Ch 3, dc in next dc, 2 dc in next dc, (dc in next 2 dc, 2 dc in next dc) around; join with slip st to first dc: 44 dc.

Rnd 3: Ch 1, sc in same st and in each dc around; join with slip st to first sc: 44 sc.
Stuff Support with polyester fiberfill.

Rnds 4 and 5: Ch 1, sc decrease around; join with slip st to first sc: 11 sc.

Rnd 6: Ch 1, skip first sc, sc decrease around; join with slip st to first sc, finish off leaving a long end for sewing: 5 sc.
Thread tapestry needle with end and weave through remaining sts; gather tightly and secure.

NOSE

Rnd 1 (Right side)**:** With Color B, ch 2, 6 sc in second ch from hook; do **not** join, place marker.

Rnd 2: (Sc in next sc, 2 sc in next sc) around: 9 sc.

Rnd 3: Sc in next sc, hdc in next sc, 2 dc in next sc, hdc in next sc, sc in next sc, sc decrease twice; slip st in next sc, finish off leaving a long end for sewing: 8 sts.
Stuff Nose lightly with polyester fiberfill.

DRESS

Rnd 1 (Right side)**:** With MC, ch 2, 6 sc in second ch from hook; do **not** join, place marker.
Note: Mark last round as **right** side.

Rnd 2: 2 Sc in each sc around: 12 sc.

Rnds 3 and 4: (Sc in next sc, 2 sc in next sc) around: 27 sc.

Rnd 5: Sc in next 2 sc, 2 sc in next sc, (sc in next sc, 2 sc in next sc) around: 40 sc.

Rnd 6: Sc in each sc around.

Rnd 7: (Sc in next 3 sc, 2 sc in next sc) around: 50 sc.

Rnd 8: (Sc in next 4 sc, 2 sc in next sc) around: 60 sc.

Rnds 9 and 10: Sc in each sc around.

Rnd 11: Sc in Back Loop Only of each sc around.

Rnds 12-30: Sc in both loops of each sc around.
Rnd 31: (Sc in next 3 sc, sc decrease) around: 48 sc.
Rnd 32: Sc in next 3 sc, (sc decrease, sc in next 3 sc) around: 39 sc.
Rnd 33: Sc in next 4 sc, (sc decrease, sc in next 3 sc) around; slip st in next sc, remove marker: 32 sc.
Rnd 34: Ch 3, dc in next 10 sc changing to Color A in last dc worked *(Fig. 31a, page 138)*, dc in Back Loop Only of next 21 sc; join with slip st to both loops of first dc.
Rnd 35: Ch 3, dc in both loops of next dc and in each dc around; join with slip st to first dc.
Rnd 36: Ch 3, dc in same st, 2 dc in next dc and in each dc around; join with slip st to first dc, finish off: 64 dc.

CAPE

Row 1: With **right** side of Dress facing, opening toward you and working in free loops on Rnd 33, join Color A with slip st in first sc; ch 5 **(counts as first dc plus ch 2, now and throughout)**, dc in next sc, (ch 2, dc in next sc) across: 21 dc.
Rows 2-6: Ch 5, turn; dc in next dc, (ch 2, dc in next dc) across. Finish off.

BOTTOM RUFFLE

With **right** side of Dress facing, opening toward you and working in free loops on Rnd 10, join MC with slip st in sc at center back; ch 3, 2 dc in same st, 3 dc in next sc and in each sc around; join with slip st to first dc, finish off.

ARM (Make 2)

Rnd 1 (Right side): With Color B and beginning at hand, ch 2, 6 sc in second ch from hook; join with slip st to first sc.
Rnd 2: Ch 1, sc in each sc around; join with slip st to first sc.
Rnd 3: Ch 1, sc in same st and in next sc, 2 sc in next sc, sc in next 2 sc, 2 sc in next sc; join with slip st to first sc: 8 sc.
Rnd 4: Ch 1, sc in each sc around; join with slip st to first sc.
Rnd 5: Ch 1, sc in same st and in next sc, ch 4 **loosely**, sc in third ch from hook and in last ch (thumb), slip st in side of sc at base of thumb *(Fig. 30, page 138)*, sc in last 6 sc; join with slip st to first sc.
Rnd 6: Ch 1, sc in same st and in next sc, skip thumb pushing it to front, sc in last 6 sc; join with slip st to first sc: 8 sc.
Rnd 7: Ch 1, sc in each sc around; join with slip st to first sc, finish off.
Rnd 8: With **right** side facing, join MC with slip st in first sc; ch 1, sc in same st and in next sc, 2 sc in next sc, sc in next 3 sc, 2 sc in next sc, sc in last sc; join with slip st to first sc: 10 sc.
Rnds 9-13: Ch 1, sc in each sc around; join with slip st to first sc.
Rnd 14: Ch 1, sc in same st and in next 2 sc, 2 sc in next sc, sc in next 4 sc, 2 sc in next sc, sc in last sc; join with slip st to first sc: 12 sc.

Rnds 15-18: Ch 1, sc in each sc around; join with slip st to first sc.
Rnd 19: Ch 1, sc in same st, sc decrease, (sc in next sc, sc decrease) around; join with slip st to first sc, finish off leaving a long end for sewing: 8 sc.

LEG (Make 2)

Rnd 1 (Right side): With Color A and beginning at shoe, ch 2, 6 sc in second ch from hook; join with slip st to first sc.
Rnd 2: Ch 1, sc in each sc around; join with slip st to first sc.
Rnd 3: Ch 1, sc in same st, 2 sc in next sc, (sc in next sc, 2 sc in next sc) twice; join with slip st to first sc: 9 sc.
Rnds 4 and 5: Ch 1, sc in each sc around; join with slip st to first sc.
Rnd 6: Ch 1, sc in same st and in next sc, hdc in next sc, sc in next 2 sc, slip st in last 4 sc; join with slip st to first sc.
Rnds 7-11: Ch 1, sc in same st and in next sc, hdc in next hdc, sc in next 2 sc, slip st in last 4 slip sts; join with slip st to first sc. Finish off.
Rnd 12: With **right** side facing, join Color C with slip st in first sc; ch 1, 2 sc in same st, sc in each st around; join with slip st to first sc: 10 sc.
Rnds 13-18: Ch 1, sc in each sc around; join with slip st to first sc.
Finish off leaving a long end for sewing.

FINISHING

Using photo as a guide for shaping and placement, sew Nose to Head, and glue on beads for eyes.
With Red, add Straight St for mouth *(Fig. 39, page 143)*.
With yarn, add fringe to Rnd 1 of Head for hair, using one strand, each 4" long *(Figs. 37a & b, page 141)*. Unravel plies and trim front as needed for bangs.
Flatten bottom of Arm (hand), with thumb at fold. Working through **both** thicknesses, weave a strand of Color B through Rnd 7; secure ends.
Stuff Arms with polyester fiberfill, then flatten Arms across Rnd 19 and sew to Dress.
Stuff Legs with polyester fiberfill and sew to Dress under Bottom Ruffle.
Tie: Cut three 18" lengths of Color A. Hold all three strands together and tie in a knot at one end. Braid strands, then tie the other end in a knot.
Weave Tie through first round of dc on top of Dress, beginning at center front.
Stuff Dress with polyester fiberfill.
Place Support in top of Dress. Draw Tie tightly around Neck and tie in a bow.

THANKSGIVING

Artfully arranged in a wicker cornucopia, our lifelike crocheted fruit creates a beautiful Thanksgiving centerpiece. The plums, pears, peaches, and grapes are stitched with nylon worsted weight yarn and embellished with silk autumn leaves.

CORNUCOPIA FRUIT

MATERIALS

For **each** fruit:

100% Nylon Worsted Weight Plastic Canvas Yarn, approximately:

Pear
MC (Gold) - 30 yards
Brown - 1 yard

Peach
MC (Flesh) - 27 yards
Brown - 1 yard

Plum
MC (Burgundy) - 25 yards
Brown - 1 yard

Grape Cluster
MC (Purple, Green, or Red) - 95 yards
Brown - 6 yards

Crochet hook, size F (3.75 mm)
Yarn needle
Polyester fiberfill
Cornucopia - 15" long x 9" tall

Note: Gauge is not important. Fruit can be larger or smaller without changing the overall effect.

PATTERN STITCHES

HDC DECREASE (uses next 2 sts)
(YO, insert hook in **next** st, YO and pull up a loop) twice, YO and draw through all 5 loops on hook **(counts as one hdc)**.

SC DECREASE (uses next 2 sts)
Pull up a loop in next 2 sts, YO and draw through all 3 loops on hook **(counts as one sc)**.

BACK POST HALF DOUBLE CROCHET
(abbreviated BPhdc)
YO, insert hook from **back** to **front** around post of st indicated *(Fig. 19, page 135)*, YO and pull up a loop, YO and draw through all 3 loops on hook.

PEAR

Rnd 1 (Right side): With MC, ch 3, 7 hdc in third ch from hook; do **not** join, place marker *(see Markers, page 137)*: 8 sts.
Rnd 2: 2 Hdc in each st around: 16 hdc.
Rnd 3: (2 Hdc in next hdc, hdc in next hdc) around: 24 hdc.
Rnd 4: (2 Hdc in next hdc, hdc in next 2 hdc) around: 32 hdc.
Rnds 5-7: Hdc in each hdc around.

Rnd 8: (Hdc in next 6 hdc, hdc decrease) 4 times: 28 hdc.
Rnd 9: (Hdc in next 5 hdc, hdc decrease) 4 times: 24 hdc.
Rnd 10: (Hdc in next 2 hdc, hdc decrease) 6 times: 18 hdc.
Rnd 11: (Hdc in next 7 hdc, hdc decrease) twice: 16 hdc.
Rnds 12 and 13: Hdc in each hdc around.
Rnd 14: (Hdc in next 2 hdc, hdc decrease) 4 times: 12 hdc. Stuff Pear with polyester fiberfill.
Rnd 15: Hdc decrease 6 times; slip st in next st, finish off leaving a long end for sewing: 6 hdc.
Thread needle with end and weave through remaining sts; gather tightly and secure.

STEM

With Brown, ch 7 **loosely**; slip st in second ch from hook and in each ch across; finish off leaving a long end for sewing. Sew Stem to top of Pear.

PEACH

Rnd 1 (Right side)**:** With MC, ch 2, 8 sc in second ch from hook; do **not** join, place marker *(see Markers, page 137)*.
Rnd 2: 2 Sc in each of next 3 sc, work BPhdc around each of next 2 sc, 2 sc in each of next 3 sc: 14 sts.
Rnd 3: 2 Sc in each of next 6 sc, work BPhdc around each of next 2 BPhdc, 2 sc in each of next 6 sc: 26 sts.
Rnd 4: (Sc in next sc, 2 sc in next sc) 6 times, work BPhdc around each of next 2 BPhdc, (2 sc in next sc, sc in next sc) 6 times: 38 sts.
Rnds 5-7: Sc in next 18 sc, work BPhdc around each of next 2 BPhdc, sc in next 18 sc.
Rnd 8: (Sc decrease, sc in next sc) 6 times, work BPhdc around each of next 2 BPhdc, (sc in next sc, sc decrease) 6 times: 26 sts.
Rnds 9-12: Sc in next 12 sc, work BPhdc around each of next 2 BPhdc, sc in next 12 sc.
Rnd 13: (Sc decrease, sc in next 2 sc) 3 times, work BPhdc around each of next 2 BPhdc, (sc in next 2 sc, sc decrease) 3 times: 20 sts.
Rnds 14 and 15: Sc in next 9 sc, work BPhdc around each of next 2 BPhdc, sc in next 9 sc.
Rnd 16: (Sc decrease, sc in next sc) 3 times, work BPhdc around each of next 2 BPhdc, (sc in next sc, sc decrease) 3 times: 14 sts.
Stuff Peach with polyester fiberfill.

Continued on page 129.

CHRISTMAS

A forest of evergreens grows on this enchanting Christmas afghan (below). Stitched in traditional colors, this is a winter warmer you'll want to display all through the season! (Opposite) Our three-dimensional Christmas blocks make captivating ornaments. They're created with cotton thread squares, which are stiffened and then joined.

YULETIDE THROW

Finished Size: Approximately 49" x 72"

MATERIALS

Worsted Weight Yarn, approximately:
   Color A (Dark Green) - 25 ounces, (710 grams, 1,575 yards)
   Color B (Green) - 15 ounces, (430 grams, 945 yards)
   Color C (Beige) - 8 ounces, (230 grams, 505 yards)
   Color D (Maroon) - 8 ounces, (230 grams, 505 yards)
Crochet hook, size H (5.00 mm) **or** size needed for gauge

GAUGE: Working in pattern, 1 repeat = 3¼" (from point to point)
      8 rows = 5½"

BODY

With Color A, ch 287 **loosely**.

Note: To work **Shell**, (2 dc, ch 2, 2 dc) in st or sp indicated.

Row 1 (Right side): Dc in fourth ch from hook, ch 2, skip next 3 chs, 2 dc in next ch, ch 2, skip next 3 chs, work Shell in next ch, ★ (ch 2, skip next 3 chs, 2 dc in next ch) twice, skip next 2 chs, (2 dc in next ch, ch 2, skip next 3 chs) twice, work Shell in next ch; repeat from ★ 13 times **more**, ch 2, skip next 3 chs, 2 dc in next ch, ch 2, skip next 3 chs, dc in last 2 chs: 15 Shells.

Note: Loop a short piece of yarn around any stitch to mark last row as **right** side.

Row 2: Ch 3 **(counts as first dc, now and throughout)**, turn; working **around** ch-2 of Row 1 and in the beginning ch, dc in first base ch (middle ch of next 3 skipped chs) *(Fig. 1)*, ch 2, 2 dc in next base ch, ch 2, work Shell in next Shell (ch-2 sp), ★ (ch 2, 2 dc in next base ch) twice, do **not** work in next 2 skipped chs at point, (2 dc in next base ch, ch 2) twice, work Shell in next Shell; repeat from ★ 13 times **more**, ch 2, 2 dc in next base ch, ch 2, dc in next base ch, dc in top of turning ch.

Fig. 1

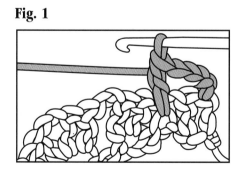

Row 3: Ch 3, turn; working **around** ch-2 of previous row, dc in sp **between** 2-dc group **below** first ch-2 sp *(Fig. 29, page 138)*, ch 2, ★ † 2 dc in sp **between** 2-dc group **below** next ch-2 sp (in first half of Shell), ch 2, work Shell in next Shell on previous row *(Fig. 2)*, ch 2, 2 dc in sp **between** 2-dc group **below** next ch-2 sp (in second half of Shell), ch 2 †, 2 dc in sp **between** 2-dc group **below** next ch-2 sp, skip next two 2-dc groups, 2 dc in sp **between** 2-dc group **below** next ch-2 sp, ch 2; repeat from ★

13 times **more**, then repeat from † to † once, dc in sp **between** 2-dc group **below** next ch-2 sp, dc in last dc.

Fig. 2

Rows 4-6: Repeat Row 3, 3 times changing to Color B in last dc worked on Row 6 *(Fig. 31a, page 138)*.

Rows 7-102: Repeat Row 3, working in the following Color Sequence: ★ 5 rows Color B, 3 rows Color C, 3 rows Color D, 5 rows Color A; repeat from ★ 5 times **more**; do **not** finish off at end of Row 102.

TOP EDGING

Row 1: Ch 3, turn; working **around** ch-2 of previous row, dc in sp **between** 2-dc group **below** first ch-2 sp, sc in next 2 dc on previous row, 2 dc in sp **between** 2-dc group **below** next ch-2 sp, sc in next 2 dc on previous row, (sc, ch 2, sc) in next ch-2 sp, ★ (sc in next 2 dc on previous row, 2 dc in sp **between** 2-dc group **below** next ch-2 sp) twice, skip next two 2-dc groups on row **below** previous row, (2 dc in sp **between** 2-dc group **below** next ch-2 sp, sc in next 2 dc on previous row) twice, (sc, ch 2, sc) in next ch-2 sp; repeat from ★ 13 times **more**, sc in next 2 dc on previous row, 2 dc in sp **between** 2-dc group **below** next ch-2 sp, sc in next 2 dc on previous row, dc in sp **between** 2-dc group **below** next ch-2 sp, dc in turning ch.

Rows 2 and 3: Ch 1, turn; skip first st, sc in next 8 sts, (sc, ch 2, sc) in next ch-2 sp, sc in next 8 sts, ★ skip next 2 sts, sc in next 8 sts, (sc, ch 2, sc) in next ch-2 sp, sc in next 8 sts; repeat from ★ across.
Finish off.

BOTTOM EDGING

Row 1: With **right** side facing and working in free loops of beginning ch *(Fig. 28b, page 138)*, join Color A with slip st in first ch; ch 1, sc in same st and in next 8 chs, ★ skip next ch (where Shell is worked), sc in next 8 chs, (sc, ch 2, sc) in next ch-2 sp (at point), sc in next 8 chs; repeat from ★ 13 times **more**, skip next ch, sc in last 9 chs.

Rows 2 and 3: Ch 1, turn; 2 sc in first sc, sc in next 7 sc, ★ skip next 2 sc, sc in next 8 sc, (sc, ch 2, sc) in next ch-2 sp, sc in next 8 sc; repeat from ★ 13 times **more**, skip next 2 sc, sc in next 7 sc, 2 sc in last sc.
Finish off.

BLOCK ORNAMENTS

Finished Size: Approximately 2" block

MATERIALS
Bedspread Weight Cotton Thread (size 10), approximately:
 Block #1
  Red - 38 yards
  Green - 13 yards
 Block #2
  Ecru - 32 yards
  Red - 13 yards
  Green - 13 yards
 Block #3
  Ecru - 13 yards
  Red - 20 yards
  Green - 20 yards
Steel crochet hook, size 8 (1.50 mm) **or** size needed for gauge
Tapestry needle
Starching materials: Commercial fabric stiffener, cardboard, plastic wrap, small paint brush, terry towel, paper towels, and stainless steel pins

GAUGE: 10 sts = 1"
  One Square = 1³/₄" x 1³/₄"

BLOCK #1

SQUARE (Make 6)
With Red, ch 5; join with slip st to form a ring.

Rnd 1 (Right side)**:** Ch 3 **(counts as first dc, now and throughout)**, 3 dc in ring, ch 3, (4 dc in ring, ch 3) 3 times; join with slip st to first dc, finish off: 16 dc.

Note: Loop a short piece of thread around any stitch to mark last round as **right** side.

Rnd 2: With **right** side facing, join Green with slip st in any ch-3 sp; ch 3, (3 dc, ch 3, 4 dc) in same sp, ch 1, ★ (4 dc, ch 3, 4 dc) in next ch-3 sp, ch 1; repeat from ★ around; join with slip st to first dc, finish off: 32 dc.

Rnd 3: With **right** side facing, join Red with slip st in any corner ch-3 sp; ch 3, (3 dc, ch 3, 4 dc) in same sp, ch 1, 4 dc in next ch-1 sp, ch 1, ★ (4 dc, ch 3, 4 dc) in next corner ch-3 sp, ch 1, 4 dc in next ch-1 sp, ch 1; repeat from ★ around; join with slip st to first dc: 48 dc.

Rnd 4: Ch 1, sc in first 4 dc, 3 sc in next corner ch-3 sp, (sc in next 4 dc, sc in next ch-1 sp) twice, ★ sc in next 4 dc, 3 sc in next corner ch-3 sp, (sc in next 4 dc, sc in next ch-1 sp) twice; repeat from ★ around; join with slip st to first sc, finish off.

BLOCK #2

SQUARE (Make 6)
With Red, ch 5; join with slip st to form a ring.

Rnd 1 (Right side)**:** Ch 1, 8 sc in ring; join with slip st to first sc.

Note: Loop a short piece of thread around any stitch to mark last round as **right** side.

Rnd 2: Ch 3 **(counts as first dc, now and throughout)**, 4 dc in same st, ch 3, skip next sc, (5 dc in next sc, ch 3, skip next sc) around; join with slip st to first dc, finish off: 20 dc.

Rnd 3: With **right** side facing, join Green with slip st in center dc of first 5-dc group; ch 3, (2 dc, ch 3, 3 dc) in same st, 3 dc in next ch-3 sp, ★ (3 dc, ch 3, 3 dc) in center dc of next 5-dc group, 3 dc in next ch-3 sp; repeat from ★ around; join with slip st to first dc, finish off: 36 dc.

Rnd 4: With **right** side facing, join Ecru with slip st in any corner ch-3 sp; ch 3, (2 dc, ch 3, 3 dc) in same sp, 3 dc in center dc on each of next three 3-dc groups, ★ (3 dc, ch 3, 3 dc) in next corner ch-3 sp, 3 dc in center dc on each of next three 3-dc groups; repeat from ★ around; join with slip st to first dc: 60 dc.

Rnd 5: Ch 1, sc in each dc around working 3 sc in each corner ch-3 sp; join with slip st to first sc, finish off: 72 sc.

BLOCK #3

SQUARE (Make 6)
With Green, ch 5; join with slip st to form a ring.

Rnd 1 (Right side)**:** Ch 3 **(counts as first dc, now and throughout)**, 15 dc in ring; join with slip st to first dc: 16 dc.

Note: Loop a short piece of thread around any stitch to mark last round as **right** side.

Rnd 2: Ch 1, sc in same st, ch 5, skip next 3 dc, (sc in next dc, ch 5, skip next 3 dc) around; join with slip st to first sc, finish off: 4 loops.

Rnd 3: With **right** side facing, join Ecru with slip st in any loop; ch 3, 7 dc in same loop, ch 3, (8 dc in next loop, ch 3) around; join with slip st to first dc, finish off: 32 dc.

Rnd 4: With **right** side facing, join Red with slip st in any ch-3 sp; ch 3, (3 dc, ch 2, 4 dc) in same sp, ch 1, skip next 3 dc, 2 sc in each of next 2 dc, ch 1, skip next 3 dc, ★ (4 dc, ch 2, 4 dc) in next ch-3 sp, ch 1, skip next 3 dc, 2 sc in each of next 2 dc, ch 1, skip next 3 dc; repeat from ★ around; join with slip st to first dc, finish off.

Rnd 5: With **right** side facing, join Green with slip st in any corner ch-2 sp; ch 1, 3 sc in same sp, sc in next 4 dc, (sc in next ch-1 sp, sc in next 4 sts) twice, ★ 3 sc in next corner ch-2 sp, sc in next 4 dc, (sc in next ch-1 sp, sc in next 4 sts) twice; repeat from ★ around; join with slip st to first sc, finish off.

FINISHING
See Starching and Blocking, page 142.
With **wrong** sides together, using same color as last round worked, and working through **inside** loops only, whipstitch Squares together to form a block *(Fig. 35b, page 140)*.
Using same color as last round worked, join thread with slip st in any corner; ch 44, slip st in same corner to form hanging loop; finish off.

SENTIMENTAL SACHETS

Continued from page 108.

FIRST SIDE

Note: To **decrease**, pull up a loop in each of next 2 loops (where Motifs were joined), YO and draw through all 3 loops on hook.

Rnd 1: With **right** side of Motifs facing, join thread with slip st in first loop on first Motif; ch 1, sc in same loop, ch 7, sc in next loop, ch 7, decrease, ★ ch 7, (sc in next loop, ch 7) twice, decrease; repeat from ★ around, ch 3, tr in first sc to form last loop: 18 loops.

Note: To work **Shell**, (2 dc, ch 2, 2 dc) in st or sp indicated.

Rnd 2: Ch 3 **(counts as first dc, now and throughout)**, (dc, ch 2, 2 dc) in same st, ch 3, sc in center ch of next loop, ch 3, slip st in side of sc just worked *(Fig. 30, page 138)*, ch 3, ★ work Shell in center ch of next loop, ch 3, sc in center ch of next loop, ch 3, slip st in side of sc just worked, ch 3; repeat from ★ around; join with slip st to first dc: 9 Shells.

Rnd 3: Slip st in next dc and in first ch-2 sp, ch 3, (dc, ch 2, 2 dc) in same sp, ch 7, ★ work Shell in next Shell (ch-2 sp), ch 7; repeat from ★ around; join with slip st to first dc.

Rnd 4: Slip st in next dc and in first ch-2 sp, ch 3, (dc, ch 2, 2 dc) in same sp, ch 3, sc in center ch of next loop, ch 3, slip st in side of sc just worked, ch 3, ★ work Shell in next Shell, ch 3, sc in center ch of next loop, ch 3, slip st in side of sc just worked, ch 3; repeat from ★ around; join with slip st to first dc.

Rnds 5-7: Repeat Rnds 3 and 4 once, then repeat Rnd 3 once **more**.

Rnd 8: Slip st in next dc and in first ch-2 sp, ch 3, (dc, ch 2, 2 dc) in same sp, ch 2, 2 sc in next loop, (ch 3, slip st in side of sc just worked, sc in same loop) 3 times, ch 2, ★ work Shell in next Shell, ch 2, 2 sc in next loop, (ch 3, slip st in side of sc just worked, sc in same loop) 3 times, ch 2; repeat from ★ around; join with slip st to first dc, finish off.

SECOND SIDE

Work same as First Side, working on opposite side of Motifs.

FINISHING

See Washing and Blocking, page 140.
Using flattened crocheted piece for pattern and adding 1/4" seam allowance, cut 2 rectangles from bridal net.
For pouch, sew pieces of net together, leaving a 2" opening for turning.
Turn right side out.
Fill pouch with potpourri; sew opening closed.
Shape into a symmetrical ball.
Cut ribbon into 2 equal lengths. Weave one length of ribbon through Rnd 5 on each end, inserting pouch before closing; tie each ribbon in a bow.

BAG

Finished Size: Approximately 2½" x 5"

GAUGE: In pattern, 3 repeats = 2½"

With Color A, ch 80; being careful not to twist ch, join with slip st to form a ring.

Note: To work **Shell**, (3 dc, ch 1, 3 dc) in st or sp indicated.

Rnd 1 (Right side): Ch 1, sc in same st, ch 1, skip next ch, sc in next ch, skip next 3 chs, work Shell in next ch, skip next 3 chs, ★ sc in next ch, ch 1, skip next ch, sc in next ch, skip next 3 chs, work Shell in next ch, skip next 3 chs; repeat from ★ around; join with slip st to first sc: 8 Shells.

Note: Loop a short piece of thread around any stitch to mark last round as **right** side.

Rnd 2: Slip st in first ch-1 sp, ch 3, hdc in same sp, ch 3, sc in next Shell (ch-1 sp), ch 3, ★ (hdc, ch 1, hdc) in next ch-1 sp, ch 3, sc in next Shell, ch 3; repeat from ★ around; join with slip st to second ch of beginning ch-3, finish off: 8 sc.

Rnd 3: With **right** side facing, skip first ch-1 sp and join next color with slip st in next ch-3 sp; ch 1, sc in same sp, ch 1, sc in next ch-3 sp, work Shell in next ch-1 sp, ★ sc in next ch-3 sp, ch 1, sc in next ch-3 sp, work Shell in next ch-1 sp; repeat from ★ around; join with slip st to first sc: 8 Shells.

Rnds 4-30: Repeat Rnds 2 and 3, 13 times, then repeat Rnd 2 once **more**.

Rnd 31: With **right** side facing, join Color B with slip st in first ch-1 sp; ch 1, sc in same sp, (ch 3, sc in next sp) around, ch 1, hdc in first sc to form last sp: 24 sps.

Rnd 32: Ch 1, sc in same sp, (3 dc, ch 3, slip st in side of dc just worked, 3 dc) in next ch-3 sp *(Fig. 30, page 138)*, ★ sc in next ch-3 sp, (3 dc, ch 3, slip st in side of dc just worked, 3 dc) in next ch-3 sp; repeat from ★ around; join with slip st to first sc, finish off: 12 sc.

BOTTOM EDGING

Row 1: Flatten piece across beginning ch; matching sts and working through **both** thicknesses, join Color B with slip st in first st; work 33 sc evenly spaced across.

Row 2: Ch 2, turn; sc in second ch from hook, skip first 2 sc, slip st in next sc, ★ ch 2, sc in second ch from hook, skip next 2 sc, slip st in next sc; repeat from ★ across; finish off.

FINISHING

See Washing and Blocking, page 140.
Using width of piece and Rnds 1-27 for pattern and adding 1/4" seam allowance, cut 2 rectangles from bridal net.
For pouch, sew pieces of net together, leaving a 2" opening for turning.
Turn right side out.
Fill pouch with potpourri; sew opening closed.
Insert pouch into Bag.
Weave ribbon through Rnd 28; tie ribbon in a bow.

CORNUCOPIA FRUIT
Continued from page 122.

Rnd 17: Sc decrease 3 times, work BPhdc around each of next 2 BPhdc, sc decrease 3 times: 8 sts.

Rnd 18: Sc decrease around; slip st in next sc, finish off leaving a long end for sewing: 4 sc.

Sew opening closed, leaving last sc protruding for bottom tip of Peach; weave end through rnds along BPhdc to top; pull end through Peach to bottom; tighten to shape; secure end.

STEM

With Brown, ch 7 **loosely**; slip st in second ch from hook and in each ch across; finish off leaving a long end for sewing. Sew Stem to top of Peach.

PLUM

Rnd 1 (Right side)**:** With MC, ch 2, 6 sc in second ch from hook; do **not** join, place marker *(see Markers, page 137)*.

Rnd 2: 2 Sc in each sc around: 12 sc.

Rnd 3: 2 Sc in each of next 5 sc, work BPhdc around each of next 2 sc, 2 sc in each of next 5 sc: 22 sts.

Rnd 4: (Sc in next sc, 2 sc in next sc) 5 times, work BPhdc around each of next 2 BPhdc, (2 sc in next sc, sc in next sc) 5 times: 32 sts.

Rnds 5-7: Sc in next 15 sc, work BPhdc around each of next 2 BPhdc, sc in next 15 sc.

Rnd 8: (Sc in next 3 sc, sc decrease) 3 times, work BPhdc around each of next 2 BPhdc, (sc decrease, sc in next 3 sc) 3 times: 26 sts.

Rnds 9 and 10: Sc in next 12 sc, work BPhdc around each of next 2 BPhdc, sc in next 12 sc.

Rnd 11: Sc decrease 3 times, sc in next 6 sc, work BPhdc around each of next 2 BPhdc, sc in next 6 sc, sc decrease 3 times: 20 sts.

Rnd 12: Sc in next 9 sc, work BPhdc around each of next 2 BPhdc, sc in next 9 sc.

Rnd 13: Sc decrease twice, sc in next 5 sc, work BPhdc around each of next 2 BPhdc, sc in next 5 sc, sc decrease twice: 16 sts.
Stuff Plum with polyester fiberfill.

Rnd 14: Sc decrease twice, hdc decrease 4 times, sc decrease twice: 8 sts.

Rnd 15: Sc decrease around; slip st in next sc, finish off leaving a long end for sewing: 4 sc.

Sew opening closed, leaving last sc protruding for bottom tip of Plum; weave end through rnds along BPhdc to top; pull end through Plum to bottom; tighten to shape; secure end.

STEM

With Brown, ch 7 **loosely**; slip st in second ch from hook and in each ch across; finish off leaving a long end for sewing. Sew Stem to top of Plum.

GRAPE CLUSTER
GRAPE (Make 30)

Rnd 1 (Right side)**:** With MC, ch 3, 9 hdc in third ch from hook; do **not** join, place marker *(see Markers, page 137)*: 10 sts.

Rnds 2 and 3: Hdc in each st around.

Rnd 4: Sc decrease 5 times; slip st in next st, finish off leaving a long end for sewing: 5 sc.

Stuff Grape with polyester fiberfill.
Thread needle with end and weave through remaining sts; gather tightly and secure.

STEM

Join Brown with slip st in any sc on Rnd 4 of any Grape, (ch 3, slip st in any sc on Rnd 4 of any unjoined Grape) 29 times, ch 7 **loosely**, slip st in second ch from hook and in next 5 chs, (slip st in slip st at top of third Grape from hook) 9 times, leave remaining 3 Grapes unworked; finish off.

Arrange fruit in cornucopia.

EASTER EGG AFGHAN
Continued from page 113.

BORDER

Note: Work Border around 2 strips using Orange and around 5 strips using each of remaining 5 colors.

Rnd 1: With **right** side facing, join yarn with slip st in top right corner ch-3 sp; ch 3, (dc, ch 2, 2 dc) in same sp, † dc in next 17 dc, (2 dc, ch 2, 2 dc) in next corner ch-3 sp, dc in next 17 dc, (dc in next sp, dc in next joining and in next sp, dc in next 17 dc) across to next corner ch-3 sp †, (2 dc, ch 2, 2 dc) in corner ch-3 sp, repeat from † to † once; join with slip st to first dc, finish off.

With **wrong** sides together and using matching colors as desired, and working through **inside** loops only, whipstitch strips together in order as indicated on Placement Diagram, page 113.

EDGING

With **right** side facing, join Color A with slip st in top right corner ch-2 sp; ch 3, (dc, ch 2, 2 dc) in same sp, † dc in next 21 dc, (dc in next sp, dc in next joining and in next sp, dc in next 21 dc) across to next corner ch-2 sp, (2 dc, ch 2, 2 dc) in corner ch-2 sp, dc in each dc across to next corner ch-2 sp †, (2 dc, ch 2, 2 dc) in corner ch-2 sp, repeat from † to † once; join with slip st to first dc, finish off.

Add fringe using 6 strands of Color A, each 17" long *(Figs. 37a & b, page 141)*; spacing evenly, attach across each end of afghan.

general instructions

basic information

ABBREVIATIONS

Crochet instructions are written in a special language consisting of abbreviations, punctuation marks, and other terms and symbols. This method of writing saves time and space and is actually easy to read once you understand the crochet shorthand.

BLO	Back Loop(s) Only
BPdc	Back Post double crochet(s)
BPhdc	Back Post half double crochet(s)
CC	Contrasting Color
ch(s)	chain(s)
dc	double crochet(s)
dtr	double treble crochet(s)
Ex sc	Extended single crochet(s)
FLO	Front Loop(s) Only
FPdc	Front Post double crochet(s)
FPdtr	Front Post double treble crochet(s)
FPhdc	Front Post half double crochet(s)
FPtr	Front Post treble crochet(s)
FPqtr	Front Post quadruple crochet(s)
hdc	half double crochet(s)
htr	half treble crochet(s)
MC	Main Color
mm	millimeters
Rnd(s)	Round(s)
sc	single crochet(s)
sp(s)	space(s)
st(s)	stitch(es)
tr	treble crochet(s)
tr tr	triple treble crochet(s)
YO	yarn over

SYMBOLS

★ — work instructions following ★ as many **more** times as indicated in addition to the first time.

† to † — work all instructions from first † to second † **as many** times as specified.

( ) or [ ] — work enclosed instructions **as many** times as specified by the number immediately following **or** work all enclosed instructions in the stitch or space indicated **or** contains explanatory remarks.

GAUGE

Gauge is the number of stitches and rows or rounds per inch and is used to determine the finished size. All crochet patterns will specify the gauge that you must match to ensure proper size and to be sure you will have enough yarn to complete the project. Hook sizes given in instructions are merely guides. Because everyone crochets differently – loosely, tightly, or somewhere in between – the finished size can vary even when crocheters use the very same pattern, yarn, and hook.

Before beginning any crocheted item, it is absolutely necessary for you to crochet a gauge swatch in the pattern stitch indicated with the weight of yarn or thread and hook size suggested. Your swatch must be large enough to measure your gauge. Lay your swatch on a hard, smooth, flat surface, then measure it, counting your stitches and rows or rounds carefully. If your swatch is smaller than specified or you have too many stitches per inch, try again with a larger size hook; if your swatch is larger or you don't have enough stitches per inch, try again with a smaller size hook. Keep trying until you find the size that will give you the specified gauge. DO NOT HESITATE TO CHANGE HOOK SIZE TO OBTAIN CORRECT GAUGE. On garments and afghans, once proper gauge is obtained, measure width of piece approximately every 3" to be sure gauge remains consistent.

basic stitch guide

CHAIN

When beginning a first row of crochet in a chain, always skip the first chain from the hook and work into the second chain from hook (for single crochet), third chain from hook (for half double crochet), or fourth chain from hook (for double crochet), etc. *(Fig. 1)*.

Fig. 1

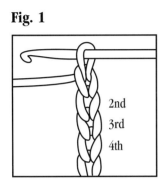

WORKING INTO THE CHAIN

Method 1: Insert hook into back ridge of each chain indicated *(Fig. 2a)*.
Method 2: Insert hook under top two strands of each chain *(Fig. 2b)*.

Fig. 2a   Fig. 2b

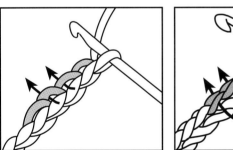

SLIP STITCH *(abbreviated slip st)*

This stitch is used to attach new yarn, to join work, or to move the yarn across a group of stitches without adding height. Insert hook in stitch or space indicated, YO and draw through stitch **and** loop on hook *(Fig. 3)*.

Fig. 3

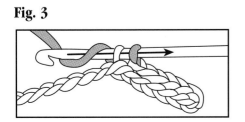

MAKING A BEGINNING RING

Chain amount indicated in instructions. Being careful not to twist chain, slip stitch in first chain to form a ring *(Fig. 4)*.

Fig. 4

SINGLE CROCHET *(abbreviated sc)*

Insert hook in stitch or space indicated, YO and pull up a loop, YO and draw through both loops on hook *(Fig. 5)*.

Fig. 5

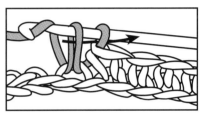

LONG STITCH

Work single crochet *(sc)* or double crochet *(dc)*, inserting hook in stitch or space indicated in instructions *(Fig. 6)* and pulling up a loop **even** with loop on hook; complete stitch.

Fig. 6

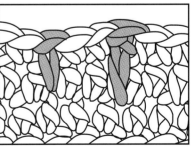

HALF DOUBLE CROCHET
(abbreviated hdc)
YO, insert hook in stitch or space indicated, YO and pull up a loop, YO and draw through all 3 loops on hook (*Fig. 7*).

Fig. 7

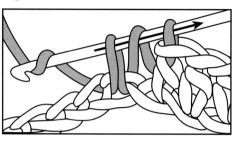

DOUBLE CROCHET (abbreviated dc)
YO, insert hook in stitch or space indicated, YO and pull up a loop, YO and draw through 2 loops on hook (*Fig. 8a*), YO and draw through remaining 2 loops on hook (*Fig. 8b*).

Fig. 8a

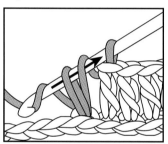

Fig. 8b

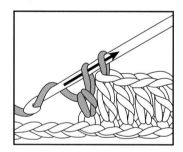

HALF TREBLE CROCHET
(abbreviated htr)
YO twice, insert hook in stitch or space indicated, YO and pull up a loop, YO and draw through 2 loops on hook (*Fig. 9a*), YO and draw through remaining 3 loops on hook (*Fig. 9b*).

Fig. 9a

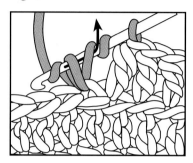

Fig. 9b

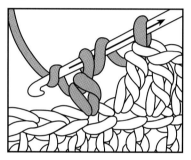

TREBLE CROCHET (abbreviated tr)
YO twice, insert hook in stitch or space indicated, YO and pull up a loop (*Fig. 10a*), (YO and draw through 2 loops on hook) 3 times (*Fig. 10b*).

Fig. 10a

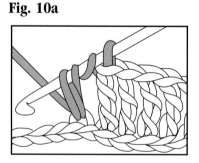

Fig. 10b

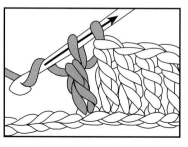

DOUBLE TREBLE CROCHET
(abbreviated dtr)

YO three times, insert hook in stitch or space indicated, YO and pull up a loop *(Fig. 11a)*, (YO and draw through 2 loops on hook) 4 times *(Fig. 11b)*.

Fig. 11a

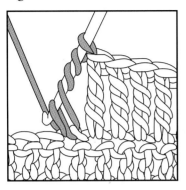

Fig. 11b

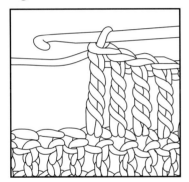

TRIPLE TREBLE CROCHET
(abbreviated tr tr)

YO 4 times, insert hook in stitch or space indicated, YO and pull up a loop *(Fig. 12a)*, (YO and draw through 2 loops on hook) 5 times *(Fig. 12b)*.

Fig. 12a

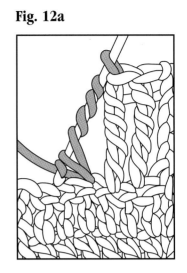

Fig. 12b

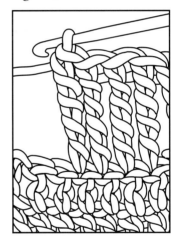

pattern stitches

CLUSTER

A Cluster can be worked all in the same stitch or space *(Figs. 13a & b)* or across several stitches *(Figs. 14a & b)*.

Fig. 13a

Fig. 13b

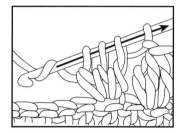

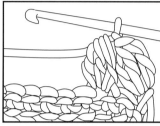

Fig. 14a

Fig. 14b

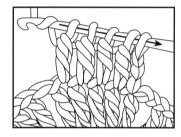

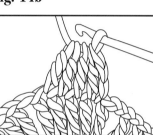

POPCORN

Work specified number of dc in stitch or space indicated, drop loop from hook, insert hook in first dc of dc group, hook dropped loop and draw through *(Figs. 15a & b)*.

Fig. 15a

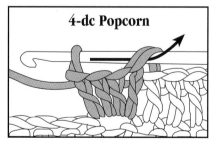

4-dc Popcorn

Fig. 15b

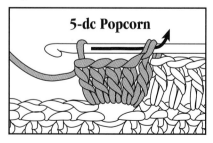

5-dc Popcorn

LOOP STITCH

Insert hook in stitch indicated, wrap yarn around index finger of left hand once **more** and insert hook through loops on finger following direction indicated by arrow *(Fig. 16a)*, being careful to hook all loops *(Fig. 16b)*, draw through stitch pulling each loop to measure approximately 1½", remove finger from loop, YO and draw through all loops on hook **(Loop St made, *Fig. 16c*)**.

Fig. 16a

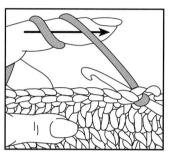

Fig. 16b

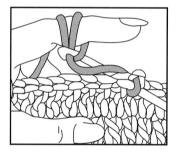

Fig. 16c

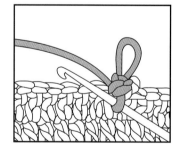

POST STITCH

Work around post of stitch indicated, inserting hook in direction of arrow *(Fig. 17)*.

Fig. 17

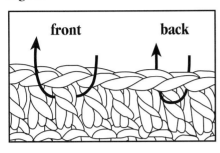

FRONT POST HALF DOUBLE CROCHET
(abbreviated FPhdc)

YO, insert hook from **front** to **back** around post of stitch indicated *(Fig. 17)*, YO and pull up a loop, YO and draw through all 3 loops on hook *(Fig. 18)*.

Fig. 18

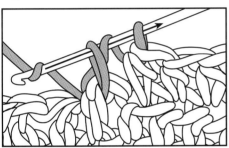

BACK POST HALF DOUBLE CROCHET
(abbreviated BPhdc)

YO, insert hook from **back** to **front** around post of stitch indicated *(Fig. 17)*, YO and pull up a loop, YO and draw through all 3 loops on hook *(Fig. 19)*.

Fig. 19

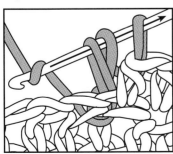

FRONT POST DOUBLE CROCHET
(abbreviated FPdc)

YO, insert hook from **front** to **back** around post of stitch indicated *(Fig. 17)*, YO and pull up a loop *(Fig. 20)*, (YO and draw through 2 loops on hook) twice.

Fig. 20

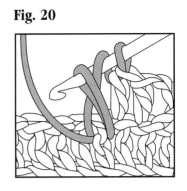

BACK POST DOUBLE CROCHET
(abbreviated BPdc)

YO, insert hook from **back** to **front** around post of stitch indicated *(Fig. 17)*, YO and pull up a loop *(Fig. 21)*, (YO and draw through 2 loops on hook) twice.

Fig. 21

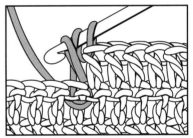

FRONT POST TREBLE CROCHET
(abbreviated FPtr)

YO twice, insert hook from **front** to **back** around post of stitch indicated *(Fig. 17)*, YO and pull up a loop *(Fig. 22)*, (YO and draw through 2 loops on hook) 3 times.

Fig. 22

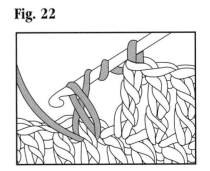

FRONT POST DOUBLE TREBLE CROCHET
(abbreviated FPdtr)

YO 3 times, insert hook from **front** to **back** around post of stitch indicated *(Fig. 17, page 135)*, YO and pull up a loop *(Fig. 23)*, (YO and draw through 2 loops on hook) 4 times.

Fig. 23

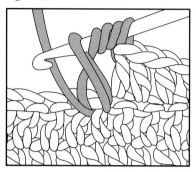

FRONT POST QUADRUPLE TREBLE CROCHET *(abbreviated FPqtr)*

YO 5 times, insert hook from **front** to **back** around post of stitch indicated *(Fig. 17, page 135)*, YO and pull up a loop *(Fig. 24)*, (YO and draw through 2 loops on hook) 6 times.

Fig. 24

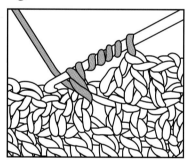

REVERSE SINGLE CROCHET
(abbreviated reverse sc)

Working from **left** to **right**, insert hook in stitch to right of hook *(Fig. 25a)*, YO and draw through, under and to left of loop on hook (2 loops on hook) *(Fig. 25b)*, YO and draw through both loops on hook *(Fig. 25c)* **(reverse sc made, *Fig. 25d*)**.

Fig. 25a

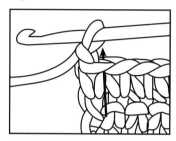

Fig. 25b

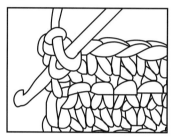

Fig. 25c

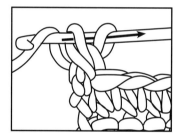

Fig. 25d

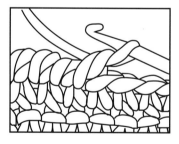

stitching tips

YARN

Yarn weight (type or size) is divided into four basic categories: **Fingering** (baby clothes), **Sport** (lightweight sweaters and afghans), **Worsted** (sweaters, afghans, and toys), and **Bulky** (heavy sweaters, pot holders, and afghans).

Baby yarn may either be classified as Fingering or Sport – check the label for the recommended gauge.

These weights have absolutely nothing to do with the number of plies. Ply refers to the number of strands that have been twisted together to make the yarn. There are fingering weight yarns consisting of four plies – and there are bulky weight yarns made of a single ply.

SUBSTITUTING YARN

Once you know the **weight** of the yarn specified for a particular pattern, **any** brand of the **same** weight may be used for that pattern.

You may wish to purchase a single skein first and crochet a gauge swatch. Compare your gauge to the gauge specified in the pattern and make sure it matches, then compare the way the new yarn looks to the photographed item to be sure that you'll be satisfied with the finished results.

The number of skeins to buy depends on the **yardage**. Compare the labels and don't hesitate to ask the shop owner for assistance. Ounces and grams can vary from one brand of the same weight yarn to another, but the yardage required to make a garment or item, in the size and pattern you've chosen, will always remain the same, provided gauge is met and maintained.

DYE LOTS

Yarn is dyed in large batches. Each batch is referred to as a "dye lot" and is assigned a number which will be listed on the yarn label. The color will vary slightly in shade from one dye lot to another. This color variance may be noticeable if skeins of yarn from different dye lots are used together in the same project.

When purchasing more than one skein of yarn for a particular color in your project, be sure to select skeins of yarn labeled with **identical** dye lot numbers. It is a good practice to purchase an extra skein to be sure that you have enough to complete your project.

HOOKS

Crochet hooks used for working with **yarn** are made from aluminum, plastic, bone, or wood. They are lettered in sizes ranging from size B (2.25 mm) to the largest size Q (15.00 mm) – **the higher the letter, the larger the hook size**. Crochet hooks used for **thread** work are most commonly made of steel. They are numbered in sizes ranging from size 00 (3.50 mm) to a very small size 14 (.75 mm) and, unlike aluminum hooks, **the higher the number, the smaller the hook size**.

HOW TO DETERMINE THE RIGHT SIDE

Many designs are made with the **front** of the stitch as the **right** side. Notice that the **fronts** of the stitches are smooth *(Fig. 26a)* and the **backs** of the stitches are bumpy *(Fig. 26b)*. For easy identification, it may be helpful to loop a short piece of yarn, thread, or fabric around any stitch to mark **right** side.

Fig. 26a

Fig. 26b

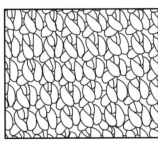 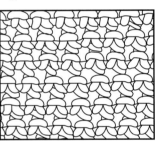

JOINING WITH SC

When instructed to join with sc, begin with a slip knot on hook. Insert hook in stitch or space indicated, YO and pull up a loop, YO and draw through both loops on hook.

MARKERS

Markers are used to help distinguish the beginning of each round being worked. Place a 2" scrap piece of yarn or fabric before the first stitch of each round, moving marker after each round is complete. Remove when no longer needed.

BACK OR FRONT LOOP ONLY

Work only in loop(s) indicated by arrow *(Fig. 27)*.

Fig. 27

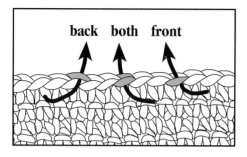

FREE LOOP

After working in Back or Front Loops Only on a row or round, there will be a ridge of unused loops. These are called the free loops. Later, when instructed to work in the free loops of the same row or round, work in these loops *(Fig. 28a)*. When instructed to work in a free loop of a beginning chain, work in loop indicated by arrow *(Fig. 28b)*.

Fig. 28a **Fig. 28b**

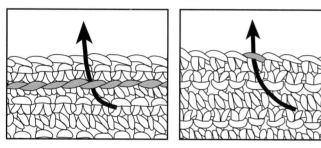

WORKING BETWEEN STITCHES

When instructed to work in spaces **between** stitches or in space **before** a stitch, insert hook in space indicated by arrow *(Fig. 29)*.

Fig. 29

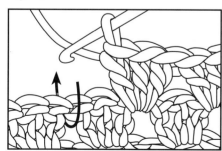

WORKING IN SIDE OF STITCH

When instructed to work in side of stitch just worked, insert hook as indicated by arrow *(Fig. 30)*.

Fig. 30

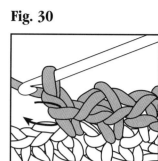

CHANGING COLORS

Work the last stitch to within one step of completion, hook new yarn *(Fig. 31a)* and draw through loops on hook. Cut old yarn and work over both ends unless otherwise specified. When working in rounds, drop old yarn and join with slip stitch to first stitch using new yarn *(Fig. 31b)*.

Fig. 31a **Fig. 31b**

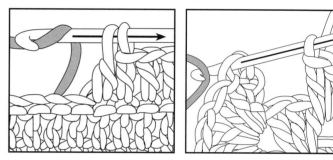

NO-SEW JOINING

Hold Squares, Motifs, or Strips with **wrong** sides together. Work slip stitch or sc into space as indicated *(Fig. 32)*.

Fig. 32

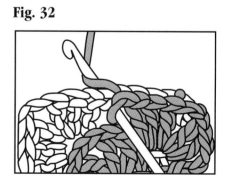

PREPARING FABRIC STRIPS

Fabrics selected should be high quality, evenweave 100% cotton, such as those sold for piecing quilts. Yardages given are based on fabrics 44/45" wide.

If the fabric is not pre-shrunk, it should be gently machine washed and dried. Straighten your fabric by pulling it across the bias. It may be necessary to lightly press the fabric.

To avoid joining strips often, we recommend that your strips be two yards or longer.

TEARING STRIPS

Tear off selvages, then tear fabric into the width of strips specified for pattern.

CUTTING STRIPS

1. Fold the fabric in half, short end to short end, as many times as possible, while still being able to cut through all thicknesses *(Fig. 33a)*.

Fig. 33a

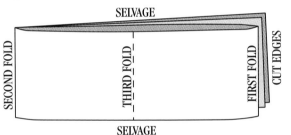

2. Cut off selvages, then cut fabric into 1" wide strips *(Fig. 33b)*. For quick results, a rotary cutter and mat may be used to cut several layers of fabric at one time.

Fig. 33b

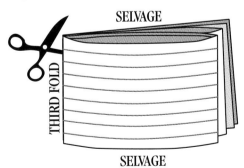

JOINING FABRIC STRIPS

The following is a technique for joining fabric strips without sewing strips together, which eliminates knots or ends to weave in later.

1. To join a new strip of fabric to working strip, cut a ½" slit about ½" from ends of both fabric strips *(Fig. 34a)*.

Fig. 34a

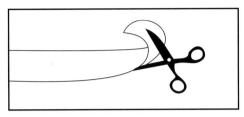

2. With **right** sides up, place end of new strip over end of working strip and match slits *(Fig. 34b)*.

Fig. 34b

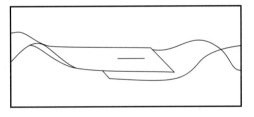

3. Pull free end of new strip through both slits from bottom to top *(Fig. 34c)*.

Fig. 34c

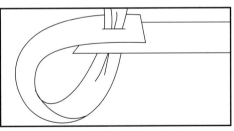

4. Pull new strip firmly to form a small knot *(Fig. 34d)*. Right sides of both strips should be facing up. Continue working with new strip.

Fig. 34d

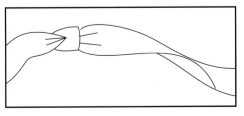

MAKING PILLOW FORM

Using crocheted piece for pattern and adding ¼" seam allowance, cut 2 pieces of fabric.

With **right** sides together, sew seam, leaving a 2" opening for turning.

Turn form right side out; stuff firmly and sew opening closed.

WASHING AND BLOCKING

Blocking "sets" a crocheted item and smooths the stitches to give your work a professional appearance. Before blocking, check the yarn label for any special instructions because many acrylics and some blends may be damaged during blocking. *Note:* Always use stainless steel pins.

Thread projects should be washed before blocking. Using a mild detergent and warm water, gently squeeze suds through the piece, being careful not to rub, twist, or wring. Rinse several times in cool, clear water. Roll piece in a clean terry towel and gently press out the excess moisture. Lay piece on a flat surface and shape to proper size; where needed, pin in place. Allow to dry **completely**. Doilies can be spray starched for extra crispness.

On fragile **acrylics** that can be blocked, pin the item to the correct size on a towel-covered board and cover the item with dampened bath towels. When the towels are dry, the item is blocked.

If the item is **hand washable**, carefully launder it using a mild soap or detergent. Rinse it without wringing or twisting. Remove any excess moisture by rolling it in a succession of dry towels. If you prefer, you may put it in the final spin cycle of your washer – but do not use water. Lay the item on a large towel on a flat surface out of direct sunlight. Gently smooth and pat it to the desired size and shape, comparing the measurements to the pattern instructions as necessary. When the item is completely dry, it is blocked.

Steaming is an excellent method of blocking crochet items, especially those made with **wool or wool blends**. Turn the item wrong side out and pin it to the correct size on a board covered with towels. Hold a steam iron or steamer just above the item and steam it thoroughly. Never let the weight of the iron touch your item because it will flatten the stitches. Leave the garment pinned until it is completely dry.

WHIPSTITCH

With **wrong** sides together and beginning in corner stitch, sew through both pieces once to secure the beginning of the seam, leaving an ample yarn end to weave in later. Insert needle from **front** to **back** through **both** loops of **each** piece *(Fig. 35a)* or through **inside** loops *(Fig. 35b)*. Bring needle around and insert it from **front** to **back** through the next loops of **both** pieces. Continue in this manner across to corner, keeping the sewing yarn fairly loose.

Fig. 35a

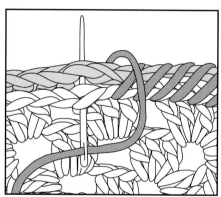

Fig. 35b

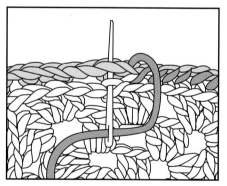

POM-POM

Cut a piece of cardboard 1½" square.
Wind the yarn around the cardboard until it is approximately ½" thick in the middle *(Fig. 36a)*; cut yarn end.
Carefully slip the yarn off the cardboard and firmly tie an 18" length of yarn around the middle *(Fig. 36b)*. Leave the yarn ends long enough to attach the pom-pom.
Cut the loops on both ends and trim the pom-pom into a smooth ball.

Fig. 36a

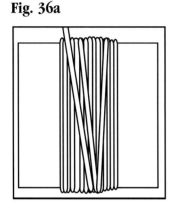

Fig. 36b

FRINGE

Cut a piece of cardboard 8" wide and half as long as specified in instructions for finished strands. Wind the yarn **loosely** and **evenly** around the length of the cardboard until the card is filled, then cut across one end; repeat as needed.
Align the number of strands specified and fold in half.
With **wrong** side facing and using a crochet hook, draw the folded end up through a row or stitch and pull the loose ends through the folded end *(Fig. 37a)*; draw the knot **tightly** *(Fig. 37b)*. Repeat, spacing as specified. Lay flat on a hard surface and trim the ends.

Fig. 37a

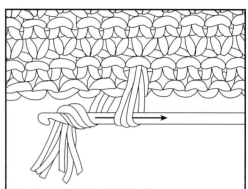

Fig. 37b

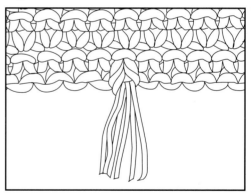

TASSEL

Cut a piece of cardboard 3" wide by the desired length of the finished tassel. Wind a double strand of yarn around the length of the cardboard approximately 20 times; cut yarn end. Cut an 18" length of yarn and insert it under all of the strands at the top of the cardboard; pull **tightly** and tie securely. Leave the yarn ends long enough to attach the tassel. Cut the yarn at the opposite end of the cardboard **(Fig. 38a)** and then remove it. Cut a 6" length of yarn and wrap it **tightly** around the tassel twice ¹/₂" below the top **(Fig. 38b)**; tie securely. Trim the ends.

Fig. 38a

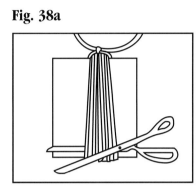

Fig. 38b

STARCHING & BLOCKING

TIPS

1. If using the same fabric stiffener for both white and colored items, starch the white items first in case thread dye bleeds into the solution.
2. A good blocking board can make pinning easier. You can use heavy cardboard, an ironing board, ceiling tile, etc.
3. Use stainless steel pins to prevent rusting. (Pins with balls on the end are easier on the fingertips.) Fabric stiffener will permanently damage pins used for sewing. These can be set aside for all starching projects.
4. Fabric stiffener can be returned to the bottle after starching if it has not been contaminated with particles and dye. Clip one corner of the bag, then squeeze the bag, forcing the solution to flow back into the bottle.
5. An acrylic spray can be used after starching to protect the piece from heat and humidity.

Note: Refer to the following instructions for each specific project.

BASKET OF CHEER (Shown on page 55.)

Read the following instructions before beginning.

1. Wash Basket using a mild detergent and warm water. Gently squeeze suds through the piece, being careful not to rub, twist, or wring. Rinse several times in cool, clear water. Roll piece in a clean terry towel and gently press out the excess moisture.
2. Lay piece flat and allow to dry **completely**.
3. Pour fabric stiffener in a resealable plastic bag. Do not dilute stiffener. **Note:** This method is permanent and will not wash out.
4. Immerse dry piece in fabric stiffener, remove air, and seal the bag. Work solution thoroughly into piece. Let soak several hours or overnight.
5. Remove Basket from solution and squeeze gently to remove as much excess stiffener as possible. Blot with a paper towel several times to remove excess from holes.
6. With **right** side facing, pin bottom of Basket to plastic-covered blocking board, forming a 6" circle.
7. Place a strip of cardboard covered with plastic wrap into Basket, forming a tube. Pin Side to cardboard.
8. Shape Handles as desired.
9. Allow to dry **completely**.

SUNCATCHERS (Shown on page 65.)

Read the following instructions before beginning.

1. Follow Step 1 of Basket to wash each Suncatcher.
2. With **wrong** side facing, pin Suncatcher to plastic-covered cardboard, forming a 4" or 4¹/₂" circle. Be careful not to split the thread when inserting pins between the stitches.
3. Allow to dry **completely**.
4. Do **not** immerse Suncatcher in fabric stiffener, as metal ring can rust. Instead, brush stitches with stiffener, leaving stitches around ring unstarched. Blot with a paper towel to remove stiffener from holes.
5. Allow to dry **completely**.

BLOCK ORNAMENTS (Shown on page 125.)

Read the following instructions before beginning.

1. Follow Step 1 of Basket to wash each Square.
2. With **wrong** side facing, pin each Square to measure 1³/₄" on a plastic-covered cardboard, being careful not to split the thread when inserting pins between the stitches.
3. Allow to dry **completely**.
4. Brush stitches with fabric stiffener, leaving the top loops of the last round unstarched so they can be used to whipstitch the Squares together. Blot Squares with a paper towel to remove excess stiffener from holes.
5. Allow to dry **completely**.

embroidery stitches

STRAIGHT STITCH

Straight Stitch is just what the name implies, a single, straight stitch. Bring needle up at 1 and go down at 2 *(Fig. 39)*. Continue in same manner.

Fig. 39

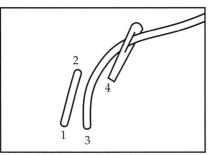

FRENCH KNOT

Bring needle up at 1. Wrap yarn desired number of times around needle and go down at 2, holding end of yarn with non-stitching fingers *(Fig. 40)*. Tighten knot; pull needle through, holding yarn until it must be released.

Fig. 40

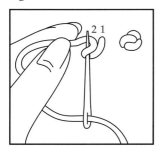

SATIN STITCH

Satin Stitch is a series of straight stitches worked side by side so they touch but do not overlap as shown in **Fig. 41a**, or entering and exiting the same hole as in **Fig. 41b**. Bring needle up at odd number(s) and go down at even number(s).

Fig. 41a

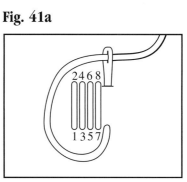

Fig. 41b

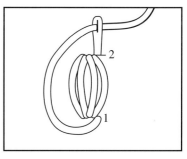

credits

We extend a warm *thank you* to the generous people who allowed us to photograph some of our projects at their homes: *Wrapped Up in Afghans* — Duncan and Nancy Porter and Bill and Susan Roehrenbeck. *All Through the House* — Duncan and Nancy Porter and Dr. Reed and Becky Thompson. *Rock-A-Bye Collection* — Duncan and Nancy Porter. *Fashion Corner* — Dr. Reed and Becky Thompson. *Hooked on Holidays* — Dr. Jerry and Gwen Holton and Duncan and Nancy Porter.

We thank The Empress of Little Rock Bed and Breakfast, Little Rock, Arkansas, for allowing us to photograph portions of our *Wrapped Up In Afghans* section at the inn. We also appreciate Dr. Dan and Sandra Cook for allowing us to use their antique coverlet as the inspiration for our *Thread Coverlet* shown on page 43, and for allowing us to photograph the project in their home.

To Magna IV Color Imaging of Little Rock, Arkansas, we say thank you for the superb color reproduction and excellent pre-press preparation. We want to especially thank photographers Larry Pennington, Ken West, Karen Shirey, and Mark Mathews of Peerless Photography, Little Rock, Arkansas, and Jerry R. Davis of Jerry Davis Photography, Little Rock, Arkansas, for their time, patience, and excellent work.

A special word of thanks goes to the talented designers who created the lovely projects in this book:

Dianne Bee: *Itty-Bitty Afghan*, page 52, and *Basket of Cheer*, page 54
Judy Bolin: *Diamond Cascade Layette*, page 76
Maureen Egan Emlet: *Handsome Cardigan*, page 96
Nancy Fuller: *Kingly Cover-up*, page 10; *Moroccan Tile Afghan*, page 28; *Moroccan Tile Coaster*, page 29; *Moroccan Tile Pillow*, page 29; and *Little Miss Magic*, page 119
Shobha Govindan: *Sentimental Sachets*, page 106
Ruby L. Graham: *Rose Lapel Pin*, page 100
Cindy Harris: *Charlie Cottontail*, page 112
Jean Holzman: *Watercolor Wrap*, page 79
Carol L. Jensen: *Ribbed Gloves*, page 99
Terry Kimbrough: *Snowglories*, page 8; *Diamonds for Him*, page 18; and *Delightful Doily Set*, page 50
Jennine Korejko: *Charming Carnations*, page 56, and *Round Dishcloth #3*, page 71
Patty Kowaleski: *Round Dishcloth #2*, page 70
Patricia Kristoffersen: *Radiant Mosaic*, page 22, and *Rainbow Swirls Afghan*, page 68
Melissa Leapman: *Argyle Afghan*, page 60
Kay Meadors: *Summer Sandals*, page 83

Helen Nissen: *Sweet Sewing Notions*, page 46
Margie Norris: *Dandy Diamonds*, page 14
Shirley Patterson: *Lingerie Hangers*, page 58
Sue Penrod: *Flower Basket Notekeeper*, page 72, and *Nesting Hen Candy Dish*, page 74
Carolyn Pfeifer: *Block Ornaments*, page 127
Lois Phillips: *Round Dishcloth #1*, page 70
Carole Prior: *Popcorn Ripple*, page 12, and *Easter Egg Afghan*, page 113
Cheryl Riley: *Crisscross Cover-up*, page 86
Katherine Satterfield Robert: *Hearts and Flowers Rug*, page 62
Martha Brooks Stein: *Granny's Granny*, page 16
C. Strohmeyer: *China Cabinet Edgings*, page 30
Mary Beth Thayer: *Suncatchers*, page 64
Beth Ann Webber: *Tiny Teddy*, page 66
Maggie Weldon: *Alluring Mile-A-Minute*, page 6; *Impressive Poppies*, page 20; *Apple Basket*, page 38; *Apple Coaster*, page 38; *Checkered Pot Holder*, page 40; *Apple Pot Holder*, page 40; and *Delightful Nursery Set tissue box cover*, page 80
Lorraine White: *Fancy Fingertip Towel*, page 49, and *Chic Evening Bag*, page 94

We extend a sincere *thank you* to the people who assisted in making and testing the projects for this book: Janet Akins, Anitta Armstrong, Belinda Baxter, Reba Beard, Jennie Black, Pam Bland, JoAnn Bowling, Mike Cates, Judy Crowder, Linda Graves, Naomi Greening, Raymelle Greening, Jean Hall, Kathleen Hardy, Chrys Harvey, Vicki Kellogg, Tammy Kreimeyer, Liz Lane, Carol McElroy, Kay Meadors, Dale Potter, Rondi Rowell, Donna Soellner, Carol Thompson, Sherry Williams, and Augustine Zajac.